ASPHALT JUSTICE

Recent Titles in
Praeger Series in Criminology and Crime Control Policy

ASPHALT JUSTICE

A Critique of the
Criminal Justice System in America

John Raymond Cook

Praeger Series in Criminology and Crime Control Policy
Steven A. Egger, Series Editor

Westport, Connecticut
London

Library of Congress Cataloging-in-Publication Data

Cook, John Raymond, 1962–
  Asphalt justice : a critique of the criminal justice system in America / by John
Raymond Cook.
    p.   cm.—(Praeger series in criminology and crime control policy, ISSN 1060–3212)
  Includes bibliographical references and index.
  ISBN 0–275–96827–8 (alk. paper)
    1. Criminal justice, Administration of—United States.   2. Criminals—
Rehabilitation—United States—Evaluation.   I. Title: Critique of the criminal
justice system in America.   II. Title.   III. Series.
  HV9950.C665   2001
  364.973—dc21   00–022345

British Library Cataloguing in Publication Data is available.

Library of Congress Catalog Card Number: 00–022345
ISBN: 0–275–96827–8
ISSN: 1060–3212

First published in 2001

Praeger Publishers, 88 Post Road West, Westport, CT 06881
An imprint of Greenwood Publishing Group, Inc.
www.praeger.com

Printed in the United States of America

The paper used in this book complies with the
Permanent Paper Standard issued by the National
Information Standards Organization (Z39.48–1984).

10 9 8 7 6 5 4 3 2

CONTENTS

ILLUSTRATIONS

FIGURES

TABLES

PREFACE

The genesis of this book lies in a time when I served as a psychologist working with adjudicated juvenile delinquents and gang members. The agency for which I was employed was officially responsible for the incarceration and rehabilitation of a large number of juveniles and young adults. It was during this time that I was able to witness first hand the utter lack of direction and the inappropriate efforts that are rife within the criminal justice system. At first I was under the impression that I had landed in a particularly inept system. However, subsequent discussion with other psychologists at various institutions across the nation and further examination of the system as a whole led me to conclude that there was little unique about the situation in which I found myself.

The degree of the problem became apparent with the filing of a class action suit on behalf of the individuals in custody. This lawsuit sought to address the numerous flaws in that system through legal remedies. Efforts taken during the course of these legal actions had the unintended effect of allowing a view into the culture that pervades both the juvenile and the adult criminal justice system. The insight into these systems led to the conclusion that there is an underlying systemic problem that prevents viable solutions to criminal behavior from getting a fair hearing. In fact, the problem is far deeper and serious, with the criminal justice system serving as a factor that exacerbates societal problems rather than alleviating them.

The culture that exists within the criminal justice system is one that works at cross-purposes to itself. The one-dimensional emphasis on punishment and the "get tough" approach that dominates current thinking in the daily operation of most facilities only serve to damage the individuals in custody, thereby creating a greater threat to society upon their release. The actions taken by those involved at every level of the system create a climate that only makes matters worse. From the politicians who make the laws, to police who enforce the laws and even to judges who interpret the law, the individuals in the system are parts of the problem. Even the prison workers and social services providers who turn a blind eye to what is going on, those working in the criminal justice system, directly contribute to, and often accept, a culture that leads to the detriment and endangerment of society. Instead of lessening the crime rate and changing the behaviors of those who commit crime, the criminal justice system engenders a disrespect for society and human rights all the while increasing the levels of violence in our society.

One may rightfully ask how these matters occur. While it would be convenient to be able to explain the issues in a one-sentence statement or a fifteen-second sound bite, the reality is that the problem is multidimensional and complex. Unfortunately, so is the solution. Throughout the criminal justice system, platitudes and simplistic solutions govern policy. Policy itself is often directed more towards addressing exceptions and sensational events than towards general cases and mundane issues. They serve no purpose but to give the public a false sense that something is being done. The illusion of safety is preferred to any real efforts to address the problems.

Thoughtful, comprehensive approaches that seek to address the core issues responsible for crime are embroiled in political haggling and bureaucratic red tape. Every election year brings countless politicians posturing that they will solve the "crime problem." The same tired simplistic solutions are then proposed with us continuing down the same path that has failed for thousands of years. Our policy towards crime has become "Lock up all the criminals and make sure that prison is such a bad place no one will ever want to go there." This idea is seen as the solution to crime. On the surface, the idea sounds good and is hard to argue with. Unfortunately, this time-honored approach is an abysmal failure leading to a most perilous situation. The lack of common civility and respect for one's fellow human beings is widespread and few people are optimistic about the future in this regard.

At present, the criminal justice system is ineffectual and barely holding its own in the best assessment. In the worst, it is a complete shambles. I mentioned earlier that I initially felt the system in which I worked was particularly inept. The sad fact is that it was no worse than many others and may actually have had some advantages due to the aforementioned class action suit. The class action suit, after several years of wrangling, led to the provision of some treatment. The culture of the agency and the organizational mindset actively hampered the provision of services (through such actions as demanding that treatment personnel work the second shift and other such actions), but nonetheless, there was some official acceptance of treatment as a fact of institutional life. A different scenario exists at most penal institutions in this country.

As I began to examine the state of criminal justice in the United States, the evidence became increasingly discouraging. I began to find that the entire system is not only ineffectual but is actually deleterious to the long-term welfare of society. The system is not just a failure in terms of changing felons for the better; it takes actions that compound problems that actually lead to an increase in the violence in our society. The current system goes against the tide of psychological research concerning punishment and is completely misdirected in terms of altering the behavior of criminals. Reliance on simplistic "get tough" approaches must be left behind in order to make progress. The text that follows seeks to document and illustrate the case for these assertions.

Whenever possible, I have endeavored to use crime statistics generated by government sources such as the FBI or the Department of Justice. When a political dispute in the interpretation of statistical information is present, I attempt to highlight or discuss information that would be preferred by those who would generally oppose the thesis of this text. This is done in order to avoid making this a discussion polemic concerning the interpretation of evidence. Also, this approach is based on the belief that no matter what spin is placed on the information, the facts speak for themselves. Matters are bad, if not desperate, regardless of the interpretation. For this reason, primary sources and government documents are the origins of most statistical information.

Certain examples, however, are taken from the most common of sources, the newspaper. Daily reading of any newspaper, especially with relation to crime, points to one inescapable conclusion: violent crime is sensationalized and made to appear normative. Yet, for every story discussing serious crime, there are usually two or three that relate to ridiculous outcomes or the effect of poorly considered legislation. Examples such as a man facing life for stealing a beer or another for stealing underwear are used to illustrate these points. Conversations and events that occurred while I was working in the system are also used to elaborate on these issues and to provide some insight into actual crime. Crime is not typically the stuff of movies like *Natural Born Killers* or even the well-made television show *Homicide*. Rather, typical crime involves the stories buried deep in the newspaper and not on the front page.

An additional factor related to the referencing of material in this book involves the Internet. Many of the sources noted include websites and can be accessed on-line through the directories provided in the bibliography. The reader can access these sites and follow links to gain a further picture of the state of criminal justice. Using this text as a starting point will serve to demonstrate that logic and common sense hold little sway in the daily operations of the criminal justice system.

I would like to thank two individuals who provided ideas that led to the title of *Asphalt Justice*. One, a coworker, Victor Churchill, a true light in the darkness of the criminal justice system, suggested part of the title in an off-hand comment. In attempting to explain the dysfunction of the system, he stated that we practiced the "rule of the asphalt." I thought this was going to be a commentary on society when he stated, "Around here, every time something goes wrong we're always looking to see whose ass is at fault rather than trying to fix it." This is the criminal justice system in a microcosm. Punishment and blame are emphasized instead of correction.

The other individual I would like to thank for suggesting the title is a gang member who will only be identified as "Big Red." In discussing his treatment by the court and prisons he stated, "the only place I get any justice is out on the pavement." In context he was referring to what he viewed as the illegitimacy of the police and the acceptance of death as a part of gang life. However, at some very real level, his statement is an apt appraisal of our correctional system. Reconciling his statement with that of Victor led to title *Asphalt Justice*.

In addition to Victor and Big Red, I would also like to thank several other coworkers for their efforts to bring something positive to the system and for their support in bleak times. DeLeon Fancher, whose day-to-day support was invaluable; Terri Brewer, who fought the good fight; Henry Caddell, who struggled through personal adversity to work with others; and Celeste Huntley, a true icon to us all. I would also like to thank all of those incarcerated and imprisoned who have provided so much insight into behavior and survival. I have left out many others who deserve praise for their efforts and some who likely should be chastised. The experience was profound and changed me in ways both positive and negative.

As I sit here now in the quiet life of academia watching my students take an exam while I write these words, I think back to the world I left behind. At times I would just as soon forget it but I know that I cannot. Nothing will improve just because I have quit thinking about it. Unless things change, matters will continue to worsen with only occasional recessions in the tide. Ultimately I write this with the aim of making a better world for my children. Only when we are all uplifted will any of us cease to be downtrodden.

Chapter 1

GET SMART ON CRIME

If you beat a man with a whip and he enjoys the whip, you're just making a fool of yourself.

—Charles Manson

Since the Code of Hammurabi there has existed the idea that punishment will alter the behavior of criminals. Yet, the fact that there are more people incarcerated than ever before seems good evidence that this approach does not work. In order to alter the behavior of anyone, one must examine their thoughts and the context in which the behavior occurs. However, in this country prison policy is guided by the simplistic notion that if you can just be hard enough on someone you can force them to change. This idea is not only overly simplistic in that it ignores the basic psychological facts of resistance and how people change, it also fails to take into account the unusual life circumstances of those who engage in criminal acts on a regular basis. In fact, if one were trying to develop a prison system geared towards ensuring an ever-growing supply of increasingly violent individuals, one should duplicate the criminal justice system of the United States.

In general, prison policy is made by those who have little understanding of the factors that motivate criminal behavior or the means by which human beings change. Those who make the laws generally rely on their ideas of what would be punishment to them if they were in prison. Granted, it may be a stretch to say that most politicians are noncriminal, but they have usually led lives that are very different than that of the average incarcerated individual. The vast majority of politicians in this country have led lives of privilege that provide them with little insight into the world of average citizens, much less professional criminals. Those with political capital force the debate from a viewpoint that has little, if any connection to the realities of crime. Because of their perspective, most politicians have little insight into the minds of criminals or what is aversive to them.

Without any real understanding of the nature of crime and driven by the need for reelection through constant campaigning, politicians have been forced to resort to fifteen-second sound bites to outline their approach to crime. Sadly, the sound bite nature of our electoral system forces the use of slogans that offer little in the way of thoughtful, sound approaches. "Get tough on crime" has become the rallying cry in political campaigns for the last couple of decades. This slogan is interesting in that it first sets up any opponent as "soft on crime." Further, it seems to imply that the only problem in the prison system is that we just aren't being tough enough. While this makes a good campaign slogan and an even better sound bite, it does nothing to address the problems of recidivism and the roots of criminal behavior. Yet, the current political climate in America is such that every politician is striving to be tougher and tougher and to outdo their opponents. Recent gubernatorial elections have featured candidates from both parties pledging to execute more prisoners faster than ever before. Shockingly, there seems to be a lack of a voice advocating a comprehensive and well-thought-out approach to addressing the problem of crime within our country. Until we are willing to move beyond platitudes and sound bites, we will never solve these problems. The peoples of the world have been trying to "get tough on crime" for the last 5000 years. It seems apparent that this approach has failed miserably. It is doubtful that there is any other area of human existence where the same basic approach has been tried for thousands of years, failed so utterly and completely, and yet continued to be the dominant approach to the problem. If there existed a business in private enterprise that functioned as the prison system does, it would no doubt be bankrupt. Consider any industry whose primary product was returned to be fixed 80 percent of the time. Further, each time the product was returned it cost just as much to repair it as it did the first time it was produced. In addition, this business has to continually throw out its first-line production before it is ready so it can have room for all the repair jobs being returned. It does not take a genius with a marketing degree to figure out that this business is in trouble. The outcome is a warehouse full of broken and damaged products that are being sent back out as quickly as possible just to keep the warehouse from overflowing. It would also be obvious that this business needs to get it right the first time and quit relying on the second and third repairs to get things right. While the state of affairs outlined here could in no way hold up in business for very long, the prison system works in just this manner. The prison system not only functions this way but with the initiation of "get tough" legislation it also does the equivalent of throwing the products of our imaginary business against the wall as hard as possible in order to fix them. To run a business this way is ludicrous, and I would argue that it is at least as ridiculous to run a prison system in this manner if the goal is to improve people.

Because the current system is so utterly ineffective, it appears that the need for a new approach is necessary. But before there can be an overhaul of the system we must have some idea of what we are trying to accomplish. At present we have a system that is totally focused on punishment as the method of social control and change. If such a system were even remotely effective, there would be little reason to reorder it. The reality of change and any effective system is that rarely does a one-dimensional, one-size-fits-all approach work. Part of the problem in our current system is that we have forgotten what the goals of the prison system should be. At present segregating prisoners from the rest of society seems to be our only goal. Given that there are many recognizable objectives of the criminal justice system, it seems unwise to make use of only a few of these purposes. It seems rather foolish to take any approach that does not fully utilize all the available methods. At present the criminal justice system utilizes only a few tools to meet only selected purposes. It's as if someone decided to build a house using only a saw and a hammer and then decided to eliminate the kitchen and bedroom from the floor plan.

Rather than taking the approach that if we're only tough enough it will solve all our problems, a comprehensive approach that works towards the goals of improving society by creating long-range and permanent decreases in the crime rate is needed. Prisons must stop being colleges of crime where individuals are locked away for a few years and then come out as better and more ruthless criminals. The most effective means of doing this is to change those who enter the prison system in such a way that the underlying motivations for their criminal behavior are removed. This can only be accomplished through an approach that recognizes that one size does not fit all. By this I mean that the idea of locking individuals up together who have committed very different crimes with very different life circumstances and expecting them to miraculously respond to the same type of approach must be abandoned. Further, this concept must extend well beyond the current classification of maximum, medium and minimum security. There must be a complete overhaul of the system if we are ever going to get it right the first time.

In working with gang members and run-of-the-mill criminals, a constant that one is confronted with is that the vast majority of people incarcerated in this country have led very harsh lives filled with violence, anger, and rage. The felon who has led a life of privilege and comfort is rare. Clearly, there are wealthy individuals who commit heinous crimes and when they do they are sensationalized and receive vast media coverage, but these individuals are rare in the prison system. This is not because the wealthy are any better than other people; it's that the crimes committed by this class tend not to be prosecuted (e.g., bank fraud) and that this group tends to have better legal representation that keeps them from prison. The typical convict, on the other hand, has led a life that is so harsh that the idea of "getting tough" with him/her is ludicrous. I recall once having a session with a group of gang members all under age eighteen and being the only one in the room who had not been shot! In fact, nearly half still had bullets in their bodies because to have received medical treatment would have involved the police. This incident made me realize that to most incarcerated individuals, prison is little different from their day-to-day existence. I have worked with incarcerated individuals who have shown me scars from cigarette burns inflicted by parents, cut marks made by being beaten with leather straps and, in one case, burn marks from where a father had attempted to scald his son to death. And these are just the wounds inflicted by parents. When one begins to talk of the gory scars inflicted by street life such as through having a knife pulled from the corner of the mouth to the ear cutting the jaw open along the way, one begins to realize that the life lived by many who are incarcerated is well outside the range of what most people can conceptualize or stomach. The whole idea of getting tough with people who live lives where such actions are commonplace is ludicrous. I will never forget an occasion when I heard a staff member tell an adolescent, "I'm going to be hard on you until you straighten up." The response from the adolescent was, "You think you can get tough on me. There ain't nothing you can do that ain't already been done."

Once a fourteen-year-old crack dealer put it to me this way, "My mother is a crack addict, my father is in prison, I have a blind, diabetic grandma that can't walk, a seven-year-old brother and a five-year-old sister. I'm too young to get a job and somebody has to pay the bills, you tell me what I'm supposed to do." This statement illustrates the realities of crime in that most individuals, contrary to popular belief, are not master criminals who have planned and plotted to live a life of crime but that life seems to have presented few other options. Let us face it, crime as a career is an exceedingly difficult way to make a living. What other occupation offers the threat of incarceration, being swindled by coworkers, and facing violence and murder as a normal aspect of the job? Remember, a drowning person will grasp at anything to save his/her life.

I am not trying to excuse criminal behavior by saying that people who engage in such acts are merely victims themselves and should not be held accountable for their behavior. Instead I am saying that the current setup of the prison system is ineffective because it fails to look at things from the point of view of the criminal. Furthermore, to the chagrin of those who advocate a "get tough" approach, the current system is not particularly punishing to a criminal mindset. That is the primary problem with the "get tough" approach and leads to it being ineffective. For that reason alone it should be abandoned. An example related to this that many people will likely remember are the recent news videos of serial killer Richard Speck sitting in prison bragging about the good times he was having with all the sex and drugs. While many were infuriated by these revelations, it should come as no surprise that such individuals thrive in the prison environment. Remember the Manson quote from the beginning of the chapter. This example points to one of the primary problems in our current system. Even if one buys into a "get tough" approach, our system fails to conceive of what is really tough for a criminal. Instead it looks at what would be harsh to an average law-abiding citizen. To most people living in an environment governed by violence and chaos would be hell. But to a person whose life on the street is little different, prison is an easy environment in which to determine what one needs to do to get by. It is no secret that the most ruthless and violent people have the easiest time in prison. In many large state prisons large populations of gang members band together and in essence control or run sections of the prison. For years, there have been sections of Riker's Island (the New York City holding area) where the prison staff will not even go. Some prisons, in an effort to minimize violence, determine prisoners' living assignments by gang affiliation. These examples are just a few of thousands that demonstrate that for the most wretched, violent offenders in our society, prison is little more than an alternative environment in which to continue living the same life as prior to incarceration. The only difference is that instead of the crime being inflicted on the community at large, it is now transferred to the weaker, unaffiliated, and less dangerous offenders. I am sure that some readers will say that is fine because it leads to even more punishment for some offenders. But it is to this group of offenders that the old adage of "go in a petty thief and come out a career criminal" applies. The long-range consequences of our current system are that the most reformable individuals within the prison system are preyed upon and forced to become more violent and criminal to survive. It is common for unaffiliated individuals to enter a prison and quickly discover that, unless they join a gang or some subgroup within the prison such as the skinheads, life is going to be very difficult and miserable. Since survival is such a primal need, most opt to do what it takes to get by. A brief review of Maslow's hierarchy (see Figure 1.1) reveals that people must meet survival needs first. Simply put, individuals must meet the basic lower-order needs before they can begin to address higher-level needs.

Our current system operates on the premise that people will make changes to meet higher-order needs without first dealing with survival. Yet most prisons force inmates to live in survival mode. As a result, few prisoners have any time to even consider their actions much less attempt to change core elements of their personality. When these individuals are released, the behaviors acquired to survive are then transferred to the

Figure 1.1
Maslow's Hierarchy of Needs

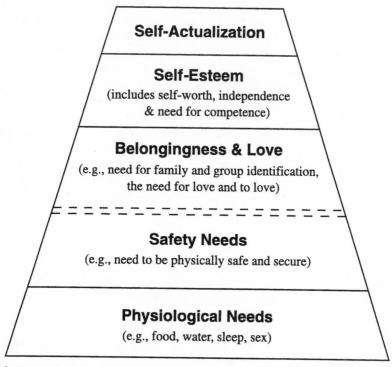

Needs are seen as progressing from lower-order needs to higher-order ones. Lower-order needs are primary and must be satisfied in order to move towards higher-order needs. If lower-order needs are frustrated, individuals must return to these levels until the needs are satisfied.

public at large. This leads to an ever-increasing cycle of more violent offenders being released. The most violent offenders, on the other hand, thrive in the prison environment and come to view prison as not all that threatening. What would be truly punishing to such a person might be something more akin to going to school than current prisons. Would that we could send all felons to college instead of prison as it is actually cheaper! According to the Bureau of Justice in 1988, the average cost per inmate in state prisons was $10,639 (Census of Local Jails, 1988 [1989]). Since that time prison expenditures have increased by enormous percentages. The National Criminal Justice Commission in its report *The Real War on Crime* (Donziger, 1996) put the figure at approximately $22,000 per inmate per year. Some states, such as Alaska, New York and California, spend well over that per inmate (Bureau of Justice, 1998). One could get a pretty fair education for this sort of money. Translating this money into educational dollars might give the impression that prisoners are receiving increased services and treatments. However, this would be a factual error as will be seen in later chapters.

The reason there is increased spending but no increase in services is that those making the laws (i.e., politicians) are afraid that programs such as literacy and job skills will make them appear soft on crime thereby causing an electoral defeat. This occurs even though such measures as job training and education might be viewed by criminals as truly punitive. This fact was driven home to me when I discovered shortly after beginning to work in a facility for incarcerated adolescent gang members that several of the roughest individuals were routinely removed from mandatory school early in the morning for being disruptive. When I visited the isolation area where they were sent, I discovered that the angry, disruptive troublemakers had instantaneously changed into jovial, agreeable fellows upon removal from the school. This incident made it clear to me that rules were being made with little understanding of how they actually affected the behavior of the inmates. By making a few simple changes, namely, that regardless of one's behavior school attendance is required, even to the point of creating several levels of removal to more supervisory intensive classrooms, the behavior changed. The particular group who had formerly managed to avoid school now attended with even more intensive schoolwork to do. This quickly altered the morning fights designed to get out of the school and was viewed by the inmates as horrible because they now had to remain in school throughout the day.

The capricious and arbitrary nature of the criminal justice system encourages convicted felons to see themselves as victims and leads to these individuals being more angry, more hostile, and more violent upon release than at initial incarceration. This acceptance of the victim mentality among prison inmates goes a long way in explaining why so few change. If they see themselves as victims of the system with the system acting upon them, one can expect little more than resistance to any efforts at rehabilitation. To solve this problem the burden must be placed on criminals to accept responsibility for their own life and to view change as something positive they are doing for themselves. To create such a view there must be incentives in place to encourage efforts to change and to place the criminal in a position where it is self-serving to change. The present system operates on the idea that being in prison is so bad that people will change to avoid it. This flies in the face of psychological principles regarding punishment and change. If the only incentive is to get away from the prison life, no real change other than of address has occurred. The emphasis on getting tough on crime loses sight of the real purpose of the justice system, which is to increase the safety and decrease the overall crime in society.

At present there is a much ballyhooed drop in the crime statistics. This is explained as resulting from new techniques of identifying crime patterns and the fine job the prisons are doing. But this an illusion. It would be shocking if we were not seeing such a drop in the crime rate at present. There are over one million incarcerated individuals in this country, juveniles are routinely being sent to adult prisons in state after state and jurisdiction after jurisdiction, and mandatory sentences have taken away all discretion in the sentencing of relatively minor offenders. In addition, several years of open gang warfare have left many dead. These factors serve to create an illusory drop in the level of crime and violence that can be expected to balloon again in the near future. Imagine what all of the fifteen- and sixteen-year-olds who have been sent to adult prisons are going to be like after serving up to twenty years when they are released at the ripe old age of thirty. Our current approach does nothing to confront the problems of violence. Rather, we have just postponed the problems for the next generation. When the next election cycle comes about, we will hear little discussion of these concerns. Instead, we will likely hear how the new crime bill has saved us all and how much safer society is today. Does that really match the experience to the average citizen? Very unlikely.

Rehabilitation has become a dirty word in modern day correctional facilities. Through the constant pounding of the "get tough" message, rehabilitation has come to be associated with being soft on crime. In other words, punishment is supposed to do the trick all by itself. The prevailing mindset is that if we just get tough enough, then even the worst criminal will see the error of his ways and change. But this attitude is what leads to the notion in the majority of inmates that they are being victimized by society. Beyond a certain point any type of punishment becomes abuse and this just leads to a sense of justification in viewing oneself as a victim. Further, when society is seen as the cause of the victimization, it leads to a greater sense of alienation and is counterproductive to the goals of changing criminal behavior. This is a point that we as a society once seemed to have understood but have now forgotten. In the popular culture, the movie *Cool Hand Luke* once reflected this idea. Excessive and unreasonable punishment of Paul Newman's character, who was initially imprisoned for vandalizing parking meters, led to an escalating cycle that created a martyr. Our current system is similar in that the punishment often does not fit the crime. The lesser offenders and less violent individuals are the persons upon whom the prison system reaps its worst toll. Being placed on a chain gang in Arizona or Alabama for being a petty thief is not so much likely to make one see the error of one's ways as to make one feel abused and justified in making society pay upon release. It is this lack of foresight that is causing the most deleterious long-range effects, all in the service of getting tough.

Nevertheless, I do not want to give the impression that punishment has no place in the criminal justice system. However, punishment for punishment's sake is just stupidity and meanness. It is likely that certain forms of punishment utilized in the past were far more effective than what we do today and if psychological principles were followed could still be of use today. Research has shown that in order for punishment to be effective it must meet three criteria: It must be consistent, quick and moderate (Bower & Hilgard, 1981). I would posit that our current system is none of these. I will address the need for quick and consistent punishment in other chapters. Here I will merely note that the overwhelming majority of research demonstrates that punishment is not effective if it does not meet these criteria. When punishment is not moderate, it has the effect of making the punished angry at the punisher. In effect the punishment must fit the crime. In this country people are horrified to hear of Islamic justice in the Middle East when someone has their hand cut off. We decry these actions as barbaric and inhumane and out of proportion to the crime. At the same time, however, it seems that subjecting individuals to anal rape for convictions for theft and minor drug offenses is considered acceptable in our society. Rape by fellow inmates seems to be widely accepted as a fact of prison life in this country and almost nothing is done to prevent it. Quite frankly, what happens to individuals in prison is at times far worse than any offense they may have committed. While the get-tough mentality might say this sounds good because it will make people think twice about committing crimes, it demonstrates a profound lack of understanding the ways people think and behave. This approach is also extremely shortsighted because it never considers the impact the prison experience has upon people and how they will inflict their newfound rage on society upon release.

But again, the get tough mentality dominates the debate in the area of criminal justice. Judge Harold Rothwax of the New York Supreme Court in his treatise, *Guilty: The Collapse of Criminal Justice* (1996), argues that the primary flaw in the justice system is that the laws are bad and that the solution is to reexamine the rights of criminals. Judge Rothwax seems to feel that the reason we have become a violent, crime-plagued society is that it is too easy to get away with crime. In his text he argues for such reforms as majority-rule jury trials (seemingly because he doesn't trust the jurors), weakening the fifth amendment, and other ideas that would have the effect of making it easier to get convictions. I would argue that with close to two million people incarcerated in this country there does not seem to be much of a problem getting convictions. Instead the problem seems to lie in the fact that the behavior of individuals involved in a criminal lifestyle are not changed by the current efforts of the justice system. The idea that weakening constitutional rights and applying stiffer penalties will reduce crime is akin to stating that abolishing labor unions and decreasing wages will strengthen the work ethic because people will work more. Surely people will work more out of necessity to survive but not because of a stronger work ethic. Likewise, reducing constitutional rights and increasing penalties will lead to more people in prison but that will likely have little to do with increasing respect for the law or changing the behavior of criminals. Realistically, some of the current efforts directed towards getting tough on crime have led to the exact opposite effect of their intent. An example of such efforts backfiring is the current trend towards "three strikes" legislation whereby anyone convicted of three felonies automatically receives life in prison This approach, while politically popular, demonstrates an amazing lack of forethought of its eventual consequences. Imagine the scenario of a twice-convicted felon who is about to be taken into custody on what would otherwise be a relatively minor offense for which a first-time offender might reasonably expect to get probation or a similar slap on the wrist. Being aware that he could now get life, this individual decides that given the options he should fight it out with police. One wonders how many police will have to get killed before the folly of this legislation is admitted.

In addition to shoot-outs with police, there will also occur events that no reasonable individual would think deserve jail time yet under "three strikes" get life in prison. The example that springs to mind is that of the man in California, Kendall Cook (no relation to the author, but the name certainly caught my attention), who received life in prison for stealing a beer from a convenience store (Moore, 1998). While law and order may have been preserved, it is hard to justify this action as serving the needs of society. The enormous costs involved in incarcerating this man (who likely needs substance abuse counseling) are ridiculous compared to what is hard to view as a serious crime. Yet the judge's discretion had been legislatively removed in this case so there was little chance to do the intelligent thing, which may have benefited everyone. Instead society gets to pay an enormous cost to clothe, house, and feed a man while forcing him to drink the prison-manufactured booze that can hasten his death from alcoholism. In this case, as in many others, getting tough on crime is more about being dogmatic and shortsighted. Removing judges' discretion in sentencing leads to a system where all defendants and inmates are viewed in a "rose is a rose is a rose" type way. This ignores the reality of crime and how it affects society. The vast majority of incarcerated individuals in this country are imprisoned for relatively minor offenses often related to drugs. Warehousing these individuals in our overcrowded system with no real efforts to intervene in their behavior and/or psychological difficulties only makes matters worse. In some ways the current emphasis on longer sentences and three strikes legislation is a surrender to the idea that prisons no longer reform but serve only to segregate offenders from the rest of society. This orientation ignores the basic reality that people get released and are often worse than when they were initially arrested because of the conditions in prison. To those who applaud increased sentences and intolerable conditions as a way to punish offenders, it should be pointed out how incredibly shortsighted this is, not to mention the burdensome toll placed on the rest of society. Imagine if the close to two million currently incarcerated could become productive members of society rather than a financial drain. Certainly it is unrealistic to expect any system to achieve a 100 percent success rate. But is 50, 60 or even 80 percent too much to expect? At best some facilities achieve a 30 percent success rate with success defined only as not being reincarcerated—forget any idea that people have actually been reformed and are productive citizens.

How then do we achieve these aims? Since the dawn of humans the approach seems to be that we take a harder and harder line to "get tough on crime." It would seem that after failing for millennia, it would be time to try another approach. I refer to this approach as *"get smart on crime."* Currently the criminal justice system and politicians running for office give the impression that everyone incarcerated is Charles Manson, Richard Speck, violent gang members, Mafioso, or some other type of career criminal. This is simply not the case. Most inmates fit none of these stereotypes. Such individuals comprise only a small percentage of the incarcerated and it is foolish to develop an approach to any problem that focuses on only a small percentage of the group of interest. In order to successfully alter the behavior of criminals, we must take an intelligent rather than a tough approach. Further, a comprehensive solution to the crime problem will necessarily involve a multidimensional approach that not only utilizes punishment and segregation from society but incorporates rehabilitation and the acquisition of skills that increase options upon release. In the following pages solutions will be proposed in addition to highlighting problems that impede the implementation of said solutions.

In order to truly alter the behavior of those convicted of criminal acts, a radical reorganization and conceptualization of the criminal justice system must occur. Prison must become a place where individuals are able to change their behavior. In addition, in order that behavior may be changed, prison must not be a place where individuals are damaged. In essence, we must prevent those who are incarcerated from becoming an even greater threat to society upon release or else what is the point? As a result, the criminal justice system will have to be redesigned with an eye to the psychological principles that govern behavior and change. One must also accept as a practical matter that most people do not change unless it is in their own interest. Only by making use of the self-serving nature of human beings will we be able to develop a system that reduces the number of people within the system as opposed to the current approach of building more prisons in a frenzy to keep up with our burgeoning prison population. In effect, if we "fix" people the first time, we will not need to keep fixing the product over and over, nor will we need to keep expanding our warehouse to have some place to keep our faulty product.

One essential element in addressing this problem is that individuals who are incarcerated must have some incentive to change their behavior. In effect, when one removes an objectionable behavior, there must be something to replace it. Many criminals engage in criminal behavior because they have no other options. When I was working with gang members within a juvenile correctional facility, I was shocked to discover that the average seventeen-year-old there read on approximately a fourth-grade level, had few social skills and few feelings of hopefulness concerning the future. Clearly, these were all areas that needed to be addressed. One might think that while incarcerated one would use all of one's spare time to address character weaknesses. If people could do that without any help, very few people would be in prison to begin with. In reality, there is little to facilitate change in a prison environment. Most inmates are aware that as a result of prison overcrowding, they will be released to make way for new inmates (Alleman & Gido, 1998). ABC News, in a recent broadcast, reported that the Los Angeles County jail, for example, releases 400 prisoners every day before they have served their time in order to make room for new inmates. Prison has become a place of limbo to wait out one's sentence. With this as the standard state of affairs, it is no wonder that most inmates spend little time on self-improvement. However, if there was some incentive to change, for example, work on improving oneself, perhaps prison could be more than warehousing.

Determinant sentencing, brought about by efforts on the part of victims rights groups and by politicians trying to prove they are tough enough, has contributed greatly to this warehousing problem. In determinant sentencing, judges have all discretion removed in the sentencing phase of trials so that people receive flat, predetermined sentences on the basis of their crimes. This leads to a mindset on the part of inmates that it does not matter what you do in prison, you get out when your time is up. When operating under this psychological reality, the purpose of prison becomes not to improve oneself but to survive the prison environment. Needless to say, the goal of doing what one needs to survive in prison and working to improve one's character are mutually exclusive. In order to change this state of affairs, one needs to ensure that release from prison is tied to positive actions that demonstrate one is attempting to leave behind criminal behavior. I am not just talking about time off for good behavior, which seems to be defined as not killing anyone today and is little more than a ploy to relieve overcrowding. Rather than this approach, inmates must truly have some incentive to participate in treatment and rehabilitation efforts.

The first step in such an approach is to disabuse ourselves of the notion that length of time spent in prison is in any way reflective of the amount of change that can occur in an individual and that the crime for which one is sentenced is in any way reflective of the amount of time rehabilitation should take to occur. While it is clear that individuals can change at different rates because of factors such as motivation and prior intervention, it may be somewhat unclear as to why the nature of the crime may have little to do with time for rehabilitation. While it may seem logical that those convicted of more serious crimes may have more serious problems, that may or may not follow in reality. It is here that the circumstances of crimes truly matter and determinant sentencing has taken away all discretion in judging these factors. The system being proposed herein is one in which release from prison would be predicated upon an individual demonstrating to the courts or parole boards that he/she has addressed the very circumstances that have led to criminal behavior. Then and only then would a person be eligible for release.

The above proposition requires several changes in the way business is conducted in the criminal justice system. First and foremost, every individual would require an extensive evaluation that seeks to pinpoint the causes that underlie the criminal behavior. Criteria would then be established to be able to demonstrate when the person has addressed these issues. In essence, this approach is similar to that of individualized service plans utilized in psychiatric hospitals and the individualized education plans used in schools. Obviously this would require a reformulation of the current setup in terms of personnel and staff training. It would also necessitate indeterminate sentencing so that when an inmate meets these criteria he/she is released. Should legislation concerning indeterminate sentencing be too difficult for people to swallow, then working towards such goals must at least reward achievement with time off for good behavior because without this incentive there will be no reason to participate in treatment. Before the uproar and cry that this will lead to people being released too soon, I point to statistics concerning those found not guilty by reason of insanity, who are usually in hospitals that use just such a service plan approach that I am advocating here. It will likely surprise the reader that persons who successfully use an insanity plea usually spend longer periods in psychiatric hospitals than they would have spent in prison if they had been convicted of the same offense (Slovenko, 1985). In fact, many people who are incarcerated in psychiatric hospitals for being "not guilty by reason of insanity" would serve little or no time if convicted for the same offense. When I was an intern I noticed on several occasions that individuals who had been in the hospital for years were charged with little more than low-level crimes, some of which would not even have risen to the level of criminal mischief or trespassing. The chapter on the insanity defense will present even more shocking and glaring examples of the abuse of the mentally ill within the criminal justice system. Yet, the mental health system does provide some direction in terms of a treatment model.

An important factor in the service plan approach is that it can also serve a punishment function. While the educated reader or member of Congress may not find going to school to be remotely punishing, imagine the mindset of the career criminal with no career skills (other than crime), poor educational attainment, and given to violent rages. Counseling and education are likely to be far more threatening and difficult for this person than spending time lifting weights in the prison yard. This approach further has the effect of making the individual responsible for his or her own life and actions. The service plan approach does this by making use of the common behavioral tendency of criminals to avoid responsibility for their own actions and to blame others for their state of affairs. Intervention occurs with the service plan approach because participation is voluntary. Those who choose not to participate are truly doing "dead time." The advantage under the indeterminate sentencing approach is that those who make no efforts to change their behavior remain in prison. At every opportunity it should be pointed out to those not participating that they are choosing to remain where they are and that it is their decision. This has the effect of instilling in a person that one has responsibility for one's choices and that these choices have consequences. This message alone would be a vast improvement over any current efforts going on in the prison setting with regard to accepting responsibility for one's actions.

In sum, this book concerns the pathetic state of the current criminal justice system, how it came to be this way, and what needs to be done to change it. It is time to stop deceiving ourselves that punishment alone is a panacea for the lawlessness of our society. While punishment may have its place in the criminal justice system, it is a useless and counterproductive method when used all alone. Attempting to "get tough" is a poorly considered, macho effort that plays the game on the criminals' home turf. Instead "getting smart on crime" begins to give society the home field advantage and forces those involved in crime to change their behavior in order to participate in the game. As I see it, America has two choices to address its crime problem: get tough and get bloodied or get smart and win.

Chapter 2

A HOUSE BUILT ON SAND

If you build it, they will come.

—*Field of Dreams* (movie)

The current emphasis on incarceration as the sole means of dealing with crime has gathered steam throughout the political and public arenas during the last twenty years. "Getting tough on crime" has led to an explosion of prison construction, longer sentences, and increasingly harsh approaches. The get-tough mentality that has come to dominate the system has been fueled by a public perception that crime is "out of control" and that our society is populated by large numbers of ruthless, vicious felons randomly committing heinous crimes, who are out to murder innocent people. Politicians, in an effort to grab onto a surefire, win-win campaign strategy have encouraged this point of view. Simplistic slogans and overly simplistic solutions (i.e., incarceration) have become the standard in today's criminal justice system.

Driving the engine of our current approach is a great deal of misinformation and disinformation disseminated and accepted as common knowledge. From popular movies to the focus of political campaigns, several erroneous ideas shape the direction of both debate and policy in the criminal justice system. This chapter will address and confront several of these misconceptions.

First and foremost among these ideas is the notion of the master criminal who is a ruthless murderer. Murder is often portrayed, especially by politicians, as the prototypical crime. The Willie Horton ads of the Bush candidacy, discussed in a later chapter, during the 1988 presidential campaign are a prime example of this approach. Efforts to increase penalties, institute mandatory sentences, and "three strike" policies were fueled by this image. The occurrence of shooting sprees in increasingly frequent numbers and the discovery of individuals like Jeffrey Dahmer and John Wayne Gacy raised the public consciousness to make these events appear to be the norm.

In psychological terms what is occurring is an illusory correlation. We, as a society, believe that these events are happening and as a result we notice those events that confirm our beliefs. This leads to all such events becoming more salient than they are in actuality. Additionally, sensationalistic events receive far more media coverage and increase the idea that these events are typical and occurring constantly, serving only to reinforce this perception.

Fortunately, this perception is an illusion. Even though seemingly common, murder is actually fairly static across time as a percentage of crimes committed and its proportion or per capita rate in the general population. For example, from 1996 to 1998, the FBI reported that murders accounted for only 0.1 percent of all crimes (*Uniform Crime Reports*, 1997, 1998). In other words, for every 1000 crimes cleared or every 1000 criminals convicted, only 1 was for murder. Surveys of prisons tend to obscure this fact because murderers, as opposed to other criminals, almost always get sent to prison and tend to serve longer sentences. As a result they tend to make up a larger percentage of the prison population than of actual numbers of crimes committed. However, the tendency when putting the spin on these numbers is to emphasize how severe crime is in our society, not to quell fears of random violence.

Beyond the realization that murder is exceedingly rare is also the fact that the murder rate is declining. According to the *Uniform Crime Reports* (*UCR*) published from FBI data, both the number of murders committed and the rate per capita declined steadily from 1993 to 1998 (*Uniform Crime Reports*, 1998). Likely those on both sides of the political fence could argue as to why this is so, but review of *UCR* for many years just points to the idea that crime is cyclical and varies with social climate and economic conditions.

Murder, based on crime statistics, is actually declining. Beyond this simple realization is the analysis of the circumstances related to murder. The notion of random or malicious murder for no reason is statistically unsupportable. To demonstrate this, the FBI crime reports for 1997 (*UCR*, 1998) will be examined. Of the total 15,289 murders committed, the relationship between the victim and the offender is known in approximately two-thirds of the cases. Of those in which the relationship can be determined, only about 20 percent of these murders were committed by a stranger (see Table 2.1).

As one can see, of the solved murders (the unknown relationships are mostly in unsolved murders), most individuals knew their assailants and were often even related to them. Even extrapolating from those where the

Table 2.1
Relationship Between Murder Victim and Offender, 1997

Relationship	Total	Arguments	Drugs	Gangs	Felonies
Family Member	1,932	989	40	1	128
Acquaintance	4,237	1,781	517	330	837
Work Related	16	8	0	0	6
Neighbor	154	67	7	1	42
Friend	432	353	54	3	54
Intimate Relationships	582	434	11	0	15
Strangers	2,067	532	154	213	783
Unknown	5,869	519	338	316	1,043
	15,289	**4,683**	**1,121**	**864**	**2,908**

Source: Federal Bureau of Investigation: *Uniform Crime Reports, 1998.*

relationship is known and adding in the unknown at the same percentage, we arrive at a number of 3355 persons killed by strangers in a country of over 250 million. That is mathematically 0.00001342, or only slightly over one thousandth of one percent. Subtract out the numbers for arguments, gangs and drugs (where one could make the argument that even if killed by a stranger, the victim was at least partially involved) and the numbers drop to 1896 out of 250 million or 0.00000758, or less than one thousandth of one percent. Taking into account the numbers of murders involving family members, acquaintances, friends, and intimates that occurred in the context of some other felony lowers this number even more.

The above numbers are not meant to diminish that murder is wrong or to suggest that the ideal figure would be anything other than zero. The point is that perception of crime and the policy based on that perception do not match the facts. The outcry and craze over gang-related crime has led to enormous numbers of young black men being incarcerated by the prison system, the perception and myth being that these crimes are the norm and account for the vast majority of killings. This is then used as justification for incarceration and the imprisonment of juveniles in the adult prison system. The reality is that there were only 864 gang-related killings (this includes street gangs, the Mafia, cartels, etc.) in all of 1997, or less than 6 percent (5.7 percent) of all murders committed. Even this number, which is substantially below what most people suppose, is likely to be an overestimate because if a gang member is killed, then it is considered a gang-related murder, no matter what the cause or circumstance. In essence, this hype over gang murders as a justification for arrests and incarceration is mere myth. At root, a policy that is based on almost completely inaccurate infor-

Table 2.2
Index Offenses as Defined by the FBI

Murder	Burglary
Manslaughter	Larceny-Theft
Rape	Motor Vehicle Theft
Robbery	Arson
Assault (aggravated)	

mation has been developed in such a way as to disproportionately incarcerate and punish young black men.

The lack of knowledge of actual murder rates and misperceptions about who is killing whom can be demonstrated to the average reader by quickly surveying one's own acquaintances. I had members of various classes that I teach estimate the number of murders in the U.S. prior to giving them the actual figures. Average guesses for different classes ranged from a low of approximately 50,000 to a high of over 250,000 for an introductory class. Even a survey of various faculty members estimating the percentage of crime attributable to street gangs drew responses as high as 50 percent and averaging around 30 percent. Actual figures show these perceptions to be far off the mark.

So if people are not being killed at random, what is behind most of the murders in the U.S.? Again, according to the *Uniform Crime Reports* (see Table 2.1), most people are killed by someone they know fairly well, usually in an argument. Even those killed by strangers are often involved in suspect circumstances. When one examines the numbers killed by a stranger and not involved in drug offenses, gang activities (one gang against another) or an argument, the number is exceedingly low. As previously noted, it is less than one thousandth of one percent. Yet, policy is based on the idea of random street violence.

Indeed, America is often portrayed abroad as a society of random street violence. Statistically, our levels of violence are anything but random. Most individuals are killed by people they know. By pointing this out, I am not trying to blame the victim or say that most people who get killed had it coming to them. However, to portray murder and crime as essentially random acts committed against completely innocent people is inaccurate and naïve.

If the perception of crime and the policies that flow from these perceptions do not match up with the realities of crime, a good approach might be to examine the realities. In other words, to form a coherent and appropriate policy, it is necessary to look at how crime is really committed.

First of all, the majority of crimes for which people are arrested are considered relatively minor and/or petty. This distinction is made by the FBI, which divides crime into two broad, major categories: index and non-index. Index crimes are those considered to be somewhat serious, while non-index crimes are generally viewed as less serious offenses. The crimes considered as being index offenses are listed in Table 2.2.

All other offenses are categorized as non-index crimes. These include crimes such as vandalism, trespassing, disorderly conduct, and the like. I think that general consensus would also agree with the FBI that the crimes listed above as index offenses are serious and are really those that are of the greatest concern to the average citizen and the general public when discussing crime.

NON-INDEX OFFENSES: THE MAJORITY OF CRIME

According to the FBI's own figures, fully 10 percent of all crimes for which arrests are made are for non-index drug offenses. If one adds in DUI and DWI charges, close to 20 percent of the total arrests in the U.S. are for substance abuse-related problems (*UCR*, 1997). Add in liquor law violations and public drunkenness and the total rises to close to 30 percent (*UCR*, 1997). These numbers may speak of a national substance abuse problem but really serve to show that much of the propaganda concerning crime rates is overstated.

Relating these statistics to incarceration rates begins to illustrate why incarceration rates have risen so dramatically. Since 1992 the percentage of federal prisoners sentenced for drug-related offenses has hovered around 60 percent (Federal Bureau of Prisons [FBOP], 1999). As a result, the vast majority of individuals incarcerated are imprisoned for non-index offenses. Yet, substance abuse programs and policy directed towards rehabilitation in prison are greatly underutilized (*Uniform Crime Reports*, 1987; Donziger, 1996).

With such large numbers being prosecuted and incarcerated for substance abuse, one needs to look at the rest of the picture to see what would be a reasonable approach to crime. Interestingly, what emerges is a picture far different from that generally perceived and/or believed (see Table 2.3). Index crimes account for less than 20 percent of all crimes committed (18.5 percent) (*UCR*, 1997, 1998). Of these, close to 75 percent are property crimes. Larceny and theft, the two major categories of property crimes, have remained fairly constant with close to 60 percent of those convicted (states tend to have lower percentages of drug offenders incarcerated than the federal government) for these offenses (*UCR*, 1996, 1997, 1998).

These numbers leave only about 5 percent (4.9%) of the total crimes for which people are charged as violent index crimes (*Uniform Crime Reports*, 1997, 1998). Making policy for the entire prison population and actually the

Table 2.3
Percent of Total Crimes Committed by Crime Category*

Crime	1988	1992	1997
Murder	0.16	0.17	0.12
Rape	0.28	0.28	0.21
Robbery	1.2	1.3	0.89
Aggravated Assault	3.0	3.6	3.6
Burglary	3.3	3.1	2.4
Larceny-Theft	11.3	11.1	9.8
Motor Vehicle Theft	1.6	1.5	1.1
Arson	0.14	0.14	0.13
Violent Crime (total)**	4.7	5.4	4.8
Property Crime (total)	16.4	15.8	13.4
Index Crimes (total)	21.0	21.1	18.2
Non-Index Crime (total)	79.0	78.9	81.8

*Figures based on arrests for each crime. May actually serve to overestimate the total percentage of index crimes as non-index crimes may be reported in lower frequency.

**Due to rounding, some figures may not add to 100 percent.

Source: Federal Bureau of Investigation, Uniform Crime Reports, 1993, 1998.

entire legal system based on 5 percent of inmates can only be seen as absurd. This is especially true when one realizes that most property crime (larceny, theft, motor vehicle theft) is committed to support drug habits. Again, substance abuse rehabilitation facilities would seem more appropriate to this segment of the prison population if we were serious about addressing the crime problem.

Incarceration, however, has become the buzzword of the day in the criminal justice system, so much so that we seem to have forgotten what we are trying to accomplish. Is the purpose only to incarcerate more and more people? If so, this would seem to be a particularly unusual aim of a free society. Yet, this is what we seem to be doing.

CURRENT OPERATION OF THE CRIMINAL JUSTICE SYSTEM

Willie Brown, mayor of San Francisco and former speaker of the California House, points out that penalties have tripled and quadrupled in the time frame from 1980–1995 while the inmate population went from 35,000 to 121,000 in California in that same time frame (Moore, 1998). In California, it is predicted that by the end of the year 2000, there will be over 242,000 inmates in the state prison system as compared to only 156,000 students in the universities and colleges of that same state (Moore, 1998). The Sentencing Project, a group that tracks inmate populations, using Bureau of Justice Statistics, has estimated that the total inmate population in jails, state, and federal prisons, will reach over 2 million by the end of 2000 (Sentencing Project, 1999). This figure is close to double that for incarceration rates at the beginning of 1990.

WHERE IS ALL THIS GETTING US?

Despite extreme incarceration rates, crime has remained relatively static as a percentage of the population since 1980 (*Uniform Crime Reports*, 1980–1998). Adding in the numbers on probation or parole a figure of between 3.5 and 4 million adults were involved with the criminal justice system by 1995 alone (*Los Angeles Times*, 1995). These figures suggest that America is a particularly lawless nation. Drops in crime statistics are relatively low and it would be exceedingly difficult not to experience some drop based simply on the proportion of the population incarcerated.

The rates of incarceration, probation, and parole point to the fact that our emphasis on incarceration and punishment as a means of addressing crime has been, and continues to be, ineffective and poorly directed. Beyond the ineffective nature of this approach, which leads to ever-increasing numbers, there are also related costs to society. If the prison system's lack of effectiveness existed within a closed system, it would be one thing, but its attendant costs lead to desperation in numerous other segments of society.

COSTS TO SOCIETY

As any lawyer will tell you—"follow the money." This truism is nowhere more apparent than when examining the costs of prisons' impact on society as a whole. The Justice Policy Institute notes that in 1995 the costs of prison construction surpassed the construction costs of colleges and universities (ACLU, 1999). The rise in prison construction was paralleled nearly dollar for dollar with a drop in construction spending for education, 954 million to 926 million, respectively (ACLU, 1999). With current projections of a continuing rise in the prison population, this trend is not likely to reverse in the foreseeable future.

Analysis of total government spending indicates that while total spending for education and libraries combined increased 236 percent from 1980 to 1993, the total increase for corrections was 411 percent (*Digest of Educational*, 1997). Going back to 1970 and analyzing the same data, provided by the U.S. Department of Commerce and the Census Bureau, we see an increase in education and library spending of 583 percent. This seems large until one recognizes that the increase in corrections spending during that time frame increased a whopping 1620 percent (*Digest of Educational Statistics*, 1997).

The rates mentioned above, even though astounding, are still somewhat misleading. In terms of sheer dollars spent, the factor by which education (serving at least 20 percent of the U.S. population) outspent corrections (serving less than 1 percent) has been steadily shrinking (see Table 2.4).

Per capita costs are even more alarming. Every state spends far more per capita on each inmate in its correctional system than on each child in its school system.

All states allocate far more dollars, generally at a ratio of greater than 5:1, for each inmate than for each child in the public school system. Yet the enormous complaints over the effectiveness of the public school system pale in comparison to recidivism rates.

Per capita prison costs vary from state to state as do education costs. However, one fact that is inescapable when looking at our prison industry in comparison with the education system is the number of dollars spent per individual within the system. Costs of incarceration average around $25,000 per year depending on the method used to calculate the figure. The National Criminal Justice Commission in its report, *The Real War on Crime*, set the figure at $22,000 (Donziger, 1996). Compare this with the figures for public schools, a paltry $5245 (U.S. Dept. of Education, 1994). As previously noted in Table 2.4, education is falling even further behind in terms of funding.

It speaks volumes about the priorities of a society when more is spent to simply detain and incarcerate a citizen than to educate one, especially when these same incarcerated people are arguably damaged by the system and the crime in society gets no better. If the education system performed as poorly as the prison system, there would be massive outcries to abandon

Table 2.4
Ratio of Education Spending Compared to Prison Expenditures in Absolute Dollars

1970–1971	32.4:1
1980–1981	20.2:1
1990–1991	11.4:1
1991–1992	11.6:1

Source: Digest of Educational Statistics, 1998.

the system and opt for other approaches. Poor educational performance in the past has led to increased efforts to ensure accountability and produce tangible results. With the prison system, poor performance has led to increased budgets.

By these statements I am not advocating that inmates be made to subsist on low-quality food and warehoused to an even greater degree. Rather, I am advocating that more be spent on education with an emphasis on proactive efforts to prevent the conditions that lead to crime. Preemptive approaches beginning in childhood would be far better directed towards addressing the crime problem than attempting to change five-time convicted felons at forty years of age. The ideal solution to the crime problem is a long-range, sustained approach geared towards preventing the development of criminal behavior not draconian measures to break the spirit of incarcerated individuals.

There is a vast bulk of literature, far too extensive to be reviewed here, that supports the notion that crime is caused by social and economic conditions. Poverty and dysfunction are the social underpinnings of crime (Lewis, 1985; Wolfgang, Thornberry and Figlio, 1987). Even Durkheim's classic formulation of crime as "social fact," which perceives of crime as a societal constant necessary to the functioning of the larger culture, recognizes the influence of poverty and disadvantage on crime (Durkheim, 1924/1974). While fascinating, the social underpinnings of crime are beyond the scope of this text. Herein the discussion will be confined primarily to the actual prison system.

Once in the system, the average inmate costs an average of $22,000 to $25,000, depending on the numbers accepted. This aggregate reporting of costs serves to obscure the true costs of the system and leads to the perception that each inmate receives a vast amount of resources each year. Were that the case, prisons would no doubt be very different places than they are.

Touring prisons, working in the environment, and talking to staff and inmates, makes one wonder where these expenses originate. Certainly it is not in the costs of food. Prisoners eat horribly. Food is prepared on a scale that makes the school lunch program seem luxurious. Some jurisdictions even brag about how cheaply they can feed people through "gleaning" programs (e.g., Phoenix, Arizona, and Sheriff Joe Arpaio, see Chapter 10). At an extreme, no more than $2000 is spent on food per inmate per year. Where then is all the money going?

PRISON COSTS

Expenditures related to prison costs are not uniform across the board. In fact, analysis of the increased expenditures in the corrections budget indicates that the dominant proportion of new dollars is going for construction. This boondoggle, dubbed the "Prison Industrial Complex" (Schlosser,

1998), is a runaway train bent on building more and more prisons in order to incarcerate more and more individuals. Schlosser argues that the primary motivation behind the current rates of incarceration has little to do with fighting crime and more to do with economic and political goals. Implicit in this argument is the understanding that such rates are unattainable under normal circumstances.

It is difficult to deny evidence that suggests the current rates of confinement are unsustainable. The U.S. already has the highest proportion of its populace incarcerated of any country in the world. In just the time this book was being written, we have overtaken Russia, our only close competitor (and using precollapse Soviet figures), and are rapidly surpassing them. In the process we have far outdistanced most other nations (see Figure 2.1).

Looking at the nations remotely close to us in incarceration rates is particularly revealing. Russia, as noted, using figures from the Soviet days that are deemed highly questionable (Donziger, 1996), is our only real competition. Even South Africa, in the midst of political revolution and turmoil for

Figure 2.1
Incarceration Rates for Various Nations

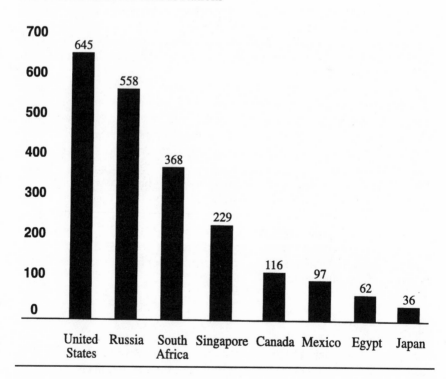

Sources: Mauer, M. 1994
    Reinarman, C. And Levine, H. C. 1998

the past half century or more (surely increasing incarceration rates), is well behind the U.S. in terms of incarceration rates. A particularly revealing statistic here is that an African-American man in the U.S. is four times more likely to be incarcerated than a black man in South Africa (Haney and Zimbardo, 1998), a nation that until recently was known for its oppressively racist form of government.

Canada, culturally similar to the U.S. even in its use of drugs and guns, falls far behind in terms of incarceration and crime rates. One reason for this could be that Canada emphasizes treatment and rehabilitation within its penal system to a far greater degree than in the U.S. Canadian prisons tend to have less overcrowding and a more collegial atmosphere. Punishment does not seem to be the be-all and end-all in the system, merely a tool. This point was driven home to me while watching a television documentary on an unidentified prison. I had begun watching the program halfway through and was unaware of its origin but quickly noted how unusual the approach, focused on rehabilitation, seemed to be. Continued viewing revealed that it was a Canadian prison and the documentary had originated with Canadian television.

As stated, little rehabilitation is going on in the U.S. system. Therein lies the heart of the problem. Instead of trying to address the problems that are at the root of crime, our approach has become incredibly one-dimensional and shortsighted. Removing offenders and locking them up has become our only solution. The result is that no one gets better, crime remains static, and recidivism is high.

California is a prime example of this approach. State expenditures increased by 30 percent from 1987 to 1995 during the same time that education spending decreased by close to 20 percent (National Association of State Budget Offices [NASBO], *State Expenditure Report, 1995*, 1996). During approximately this same time period, California built twenty-one new prisons but added only one new university (Ambrosio and Schiraldi, 1997).

The ten-year period from the mid-1980s to the mid-1990s witnessed California spend over 5 billion dollars on the building of new prisons (Jacobs, 1994). The costs of financing the debt on these has been predicted to double those costs (Africa2000, 1999). By the end of 1996, 5.2 billion more had already been allocated to build even more prisons (Lamb, 1996; Africa2000, 1999). The effect of a political change in that state should prove interesting to examine in this regard. At present, California is expected to have nearly 100,000 more inmates in its state system than in its university system by the end of 2000 (Moore, 1998).

The untold costs of the prison construction boom are incalculable. The proportion of the state budget allocated to prisons jumped from around 3 percent in the mid-1980s to over 7.5 percent by the mid-1990s with increases projected to continue for years to come (Africa2000, 1999; NASBO, 1996). This money has to come from somewhere. We have already noted the

loss of education funds, but also look to other measures in California denying funds to immigrants and their children for even emergency services
and education.

Proposition 13, a ballot initiative in California sponsored by the late
Howard Jarvis, strongly curtailed taxation and spending in that state. At
the time of its passage the state was allegedly on the verge of financial collapse and all services were slashed. As more budgetary dollars are freed up,
prisons are reaping a windfall. Unfortunately, nothing else is getting the
dollars needed. Nationwide our priorities can be seen with less than half as
much spent on welfare as on prisons (NASBO, 1997).

Even with the increases in the prison/corrections budget, little is going
to any type of treatment efforts. Little is left over after all the costs of construction and heightened security features are paid, but little emphasis is
given to treatment anyway. For example, in the federal system drug treatment is available for less that 10 percent of those needing it (Federal Bureau
of Prisons, Office of Public Affairs, 1997) and systemwide there are about
one thousand inmates for each psychologist (Clements, 1999). Treatment is
provided only at a bare bones level and usually only to satisfy court orders.
An example of this relates to a juvenile system in which I was once employed, which was under court orders to provide treatment and decrease
overcrowding. During the course of one fiscal year, the agency received a
special appropriation of 4 million dollars. The result of the appropriation
was that a new facility was purchased and sat dormant. Meanwhile the
treatment staff was given less than subtle directive to "provide faster, more
efficient treatment." In essence, we were asked to falsify treatment progress. This occurred despite protestations concerning the nature of treatment and the lack of resources granted to do this.

At the same time, the facilities in use were hopelessly overcrowded. At
one point, sixty juveniles were sleeping in an area designed for twenty-five
to thirty. In another living area an internal wall physically collapsed and the
climate control system in the educational unit became so dilapidated that
the area had to be temporarily closed. Certain living quarters were con-
demned even while people were living in them. Such conditions are not
unique to the juvenile system and are likely worse in adult facilities as a
whole.

Despite the above, no one was transferred to the new facility because
there was no money to hire staff for the institution. However, there was
enough money to build "escape-proof" fences around several facilities
(even though escape was a negligible problem), sell off valuable land assets
to members of the Board of Directors of one facility, and renovate the central
office where the administrators worked. Plans to construct a conference
center were finally squelched after employees threatened to go to newspa-
pers. This example is unfortunately fairly typical of the operation of prison
facilities. Dollars flow in due to new crime bills, the hype over security and

other such factors, but the real problem areas related to basic operation are often avoided.

FOLLOW THE MONEY A LITTLE FURTHER

The above example, of only one state system, serves to point to the larger issues within the system. The money flowing in is what is perpetuating prison construction and perhaps preventing treatment and rehabilitation. If treatment and rehabilitation were provided and inmates were actually changed in a positive sense by prison, the whole party might end. I once calculated the amount spent on rehabilitation at one facility where I was employed and had full access to operational costs, and determined that less than 5 percent of actual operating revenue could even reasonably be considered to go towards rehabilitation activities despite court-mandated treatment.

Interestingly, this same system often stated that it had no money to provide these services even though it seemed able to throw money away on matters of no relevance. An example of how money was thrown away out of the treatment budget was to test inmates caught smoking marijuana. Given that they were caught in the act, it seemed pretty obvious that they would test positive. Despite this, they were all tested at a fairly hefty fee. The primary reason seemed to be that the result of testing could be entered into their files and look more official than a simple notation. Legal implications of getting caught were nonexistent as no charges were filed and as a minor event would have little impact on parole hearings.

The phenomenon of private prisons illustrates the difficulties inherent in letting dollars drive social policy. Out of desperation due to overcrowding and projections concerning future incarceration rates, states have turned to the private sector for help in dealing with the numbers. Corporations, on the flip side, have recognized the enormous profit potential in the prison industry. Numerous corporations have established prisons for profit and inmates become a way to make money. In supply and demand economics, the demand for prison bed space is made valuable by the increasing supply of prisoners.

Given this setup, where high incarceration rates are actually good for business, can anyone expect private prisons to have any interest in lowering the crime rate through effective rehabilitation and treatment? Working yourself out of a job is not good for business, nor is providing for early release of easy-to-control prisoners. Ironically those who are most troublesome and by extension costly, as relates to issues like guard costs, restraint, vandalism, and so on, would likely be pushed from for-profit prisons faster than those more docile and easily controlled.

What is more likely to happen over time is that private corporations will realize that they have the states and federal governments over a barrel and will increasingly serve only the easy-to-manage and less difficult prisoners. The effect will be that the public sector will then serve only the difficult, high-risk and therefore more expensive prisoners leading to no actual savings. The folly of the approach to crime solely through incarceration will then reach mammoth proportions. The lack of oversight and controls inherent in the private prison industry will be considered in depth in later chapters.

BUILDING FOR THE COMMUNITY

Increased incarceration rates are not uniformly viewed as a negative feature. In fact, the boom in prison construction, although costly and a drain on other resources, is widely popular in many regions. Reasons are varied but are primarily economic. A large employer is added to the community with little social costs. The local construction business becomes involved at the beginning as do local politicians. Local businesses expect profits from retail purchases and even the hotel business recognizes the potential income from those visiting prisoners. The fact that prisons are generally isolated from the community adds to their attractiveness.

Prison work crews also are important, especially to many small municipalities, because they can be a source of cheap or even free labor. On my way to work on several mornings I have noticed individuals with "INMATE" emblazoned on their coveralls picking up trash, clearing underbrush, and other such actions. Labor such as this, which would prove costly to small towns, makes nearby prisons economically desirable. An example of how inmates can be transformed into laborers is the state of New Mexico, where inmates have staffed the phones at the tourism bureau for many years.

Even in the small community in which I now reside in western North Carolina, recent figures indicate that close to half a million dollars in savings were the result of inmate labor (Alexander, 1999). These savings were based on calculating labor at minimum wage and reflected close to 22,000 hours of labor in just a four-month period (Alexander, 1999). Such numbers in a relatively small county demonstrate the popularity of inmate labor for municipalities throughout the nation. Imagine the cost savings in a large metropolitan area if these figures are at all representative.

Contrast the widespread popularity of large monolithic prisons (Donziger, 1996) with the public reaction to smaller, more effective treatment centers and halfway houses. Communities, on the grounds of safety and crime, routinely oppose small facilities located in the middle of neighborhoods or small towns. This occurs despite the fact that those placed in these facilities have a great deal to lose by inappropriate actions and know they will be the first suspects if anything happens.

THE ILLUSION OF SAFETY

Of course, one factor that makes prisons, as opposed to group homes and halfway houses, more attractive to small towns is their apparent safety. Towns, neighborhoods, and municipalities all over the country routinely oppose the location of any type of transitional group home, halfway house, or drug rehab facility within their community on the grounds of safety. This occurs even though most individuals in these facilities are in some type of transition, heavily monitored, and have great incentive not to fail (i.e., return to prison). Further, officials wary of angering the public usually heavily screen the prisoners who qualify and get placed in the minute number of these facilities.

But a large prison facility, even one that holds maximum-security prisoners, is generally not opposed as much and may even be welcomed for reasons previously discussed. Primarily this is a matter of perception. Because inmates are locked behind bars, often several fences and a wall, the situation is viewed as safe. This perception of inmates locked away continues even though people may see the inmates on work crews performing different types of labor throughout the area and may even have contact with them on various out-of-prison trips.

This perception of safety may match reality but not for the reasons generally felt. The extreme overkill seen in most prisons with regard to security is what accounts for this illusion of safety. In reality, few prisoners ever attempt escape and few prisoners could actually escape from much of anything, even a locked door, without a tremendous amount of time and effort. Escape statistics, presented later in greater detail, indicate that an extremely small percentage of prisoners ever escape. Even those who get beyond the prison walls rarely remain free for very long. For those who might think that security measures are what keep people in, it should be noted that most prisoners cannot get out of their cells much less over walls and other such devices.

Escape attempts are not typically what is seen in movies and do not involve tunneling out through sewers as in the movie *Raising Arizona*. Nor do they involve takeovers and shootouts like in *Natural Born Killers* or other movies. Generally, and this is an opinion based on news reports, personal observation and anecdotal stories (if records are kept on such things, prisons are reluctant to release them, especially to people writing books critical of the system), escapes tend to be opportunistic. That is, prisoners tend to escape when the opportunity presents itself. This can be in the form of running from a work crew, fleeing during medical or dental visits outside the facility court hearings, and the like. Despite this, the walls around the prison provide a psychological protective barrier, or illusion of safety.

In real life, escapes have little to do with actual security measures and usually involve human error or even complacency on the part of guards or other personnel. Increased security measures and technology may even exacerbate this phenomenon because of the tendency to label every new advance as "escape proof." Realistically, figuring out who is going to attempt escape and segregating them under more watchful conditions would ultimately prove far cheaper and better directed. Actually evaluating prisoners and developing an individual approach, it will be noted in later sections, is not even considered an option in the prisons of today.

Prisons simply are not set up to work this way. Individuals are divided into the basic categories of maximum, medium and minimum security allegedly based on their perceived dangerousness. There is even the super-maximum designation recently developed in order to "contain" those prisoners considered especially "dangerous." In truth, these designations have little to do with any type of evaluation of dangerousness and are more likely to be administrative decisions. For example, Jack Kervorkian, the assisted suicide doctor, was placed in maximum security in Michigan when first convicted until he "adjusted" to prison life. While Kervorkian was convicted of murder, it is preposterous to consider him a dangerous prisoner or escape risk. Any knowledge of his case demonstrates that he dared the authorities to imprison him and that his motivations were highly political. To suggest that a physically frail, elderly man committing acts for political reasons should be placed in maximum security because he is a threat is ludicrous. Kervorkian's case also demonstrates how the removal of discretion and lack of consideration for circumstances negatively impact the distribution of justice in the name of preserving the law.

Kervorkian, however, is not atypical in his placement. Maximum security sounds as if it relates to some perceived escape ability and threat level of the prisoners. In actuality, the system has become so large and overburdened that little evaluation can occur and placement is more related to charges, prior convictions, and administrative concerns such as bed space. Poorly understood and misapplied behavioral management concepts also play a part. The idea that control of prisoners means providing as miserable an existence as possible is close to being the normative understanding of behavioral management that I have witnessed within the walls of prisons.

The super-maximum designation is a perfect example. Prisoners are generally placed there because they are difficult to deal with in other prisons, not because of their possibility of escape (Moore, 1998). Even when it comes to escape, there is little evidence that changes in security designations prevent escape. In fact, I know of no source that indicates that escape rates vary substantially from maximum to medium to minimum security. These distinctions refer more to a sense of internal oppressiveness than to any actual relation to security.

Unfortunately, in the world of prisons common sense and rational approaches are unusual. There is a drive towards increasing the number of maximum-security cells even though this substantially increases construction costs and costs of incarceration while doing little to lessen escape (a statistically rare event). Likely its most prominent effect is impeding rehabilitation and preventing any real change of behavior. Yet the focus in the prison industry has become increasingly harsh, leading to a greater emphasis on maximum and now "super-maximum" security.

To see the effects of increasing the numbers of maximum-security spaces (which makes an implicit assumption that not only are there more criminals but they are more dangerous and violent), one need only look at the numbers of dollars spent in construction. For example, the average cost of prison construction is around $54,000 per bed space (Edna McConnell Clark Foundation, 1993). The National Criminal Justice Commission goes a step further and points out that by the time the costs of financing bond debt and other features are calculated, the actual figure is closer to $100,000 (Donziger, 1996). These figures are aggregates for all new construction per bed space.

According to the Africa2000 project, the costs of cells and bed space increase significantly as security concerns are heightened and implemented. For example, the federal government averages $85,000 per bed space in its maximum-security cells compared to the $54,000 given above as an average (Edna McConnell Clark Foundation, 1993). California outspends even that amount with costs of $113,000 per maximum-security bed space unit as compared to $60,000 for its minimum security faculties (Africa2000, 1999). But in California, building at a pace that outstrips all other jurisdictions, Los Angeles County has broken all limits with a new lock-up facility costing $205,000 per bed. That's a cost of over $370 million *before* calculating bond debt.

The above figures suggest that the trend of ever-increasing incarceration rates leading to rampant construction is draining off enormous amounts of money that could be going to fund adequate rehabilitation and treatment efforts. This trend is made even worse by an overemphasis on security that is substantially raising the costs of construction. These two features have raised the cost of the entire prison system to enormous and unprecedented proportions. The misdirection of this money, away from treatment and rehab, suggests the abandonment of efforts to address the crime problem in a viable manner that reduces crime. Instead, policy seems directed only at incarceration and the fueling of an emergent growth industry.

PRISON AS A GROWTH INDUSTRY

Prison construction and the attendant focus on security have led to enormous outlays of capital expenditures (NASBO, 1995–1999). But this has gotten us almost nowhere. Significant increases in the incarcerated population have far outstripped the miniscule drop in the crime rate (*UCR*, 1995–1999). In fact, the increases in the incarceration rate alone might account for the small drops in crime simply because of the effects of decreasing the population.

Drops in crime attributable only to increased incarceration rates are only an artifact and thus no real drop at all. This contention is supported by the fact that dips in the rate of crime related only to incarceration obscure the realities of release. In effect, those incarcerated in a warehousing system are not becoming less criminal or reforming but are just not committing crime in a way that it is statistically recorded. Incarceration alone cannot do the trick unless no one is ever released. While that seems to be a stated goal of "three strikes" legislation, it can surely be the basis of no real policy. Such an approach would bankrupt us in the long run. Real and viable changes in the crime rate must be achieved through another means.

The means to achieve this actual lowering of the crime rate on a permanent and sustained basis are to change the criminals and address the problems that lead to crime. That can be accomplished only through sustained, directed and thoughtful approaches grounded in the principles of human behavior and therapeutic change.

To accomplish this feat, a rational approach examining the nature of the incarcerated population, the issues facing the criminal justice system, and the wheels that drive its engine must begin. Finally, we need to establish conditions that provide the proper environment and the necessary tools to create a medium of change. Incorporation of the nature of human behavioral management and the therapeutic process must become a component of this approach. Subsequent chapters will review the factors that sustain the current approach as well as the issues that are most salient to the discussion.

An understanding of the psychological underpinnings of criminal behavior is necessary to properly assess the situation. Further, it will be necessary to confront the current barrage of myths and misinformation that drive the public consciousness and psychology concerning this issue. Only a radical shift in our social policy to one that is focused on rehabilitation and change will produce the desired result in society at large. Without it, a downward spiral with ever-increasing corrections costs will continue until there is little left for any other government programs or services. Bleak, perhaps, but not unlikely.

Chapter 3

TWO SIDES OF THE SAME COIN

The police are not here to create disorder, they're here to preserve disorder.

—Richard J. Daley

When one looks at the people involved in the enterprise of crime and its counterpart, the criminal justice system, there is a tendency to see these groups as distinct and diametrically opposed. This apparent separateness is, however, an illusion. Rather than the good guy/bad guy dichotomy that seems clear in our minds and is encouraged by popular movies where one needs a protagonist and a villain, real life is far more complicated. The police and the criminals exist in a symbiotic relationship that leads not only to familiarity with and contempt for one another but to an underlying similarity that draws both groups to the playing field. It will be shown that this relationship is extensive and that there is little difference between the police and the criminal populace in terms of psychological makeup and respect for fellow human beings.

Our need for simplicity and the drive to avoid gray areas lead to a tendency to categorize and place things in nice, tidy packages. In our psychic consciousness, we are driven to see the police as the opposite of criminals because it is more comforting to us to believe that we are being protected and are therefore safe. It is as if we think that as long as we maintain this dichotomy we are secure and immune to harm. This dichotomy is false. Merely putting on a uniform does not make one above reproach, and engaging in crime does not take away one's desire to be treated as a human being. Because of the very nature of their lives, the police and the criminals are more like two sides of the same coin than two separate entities. Like the two sides of a coin, the police and the criminals are united in an unbreakable bond.

CULTURAL MILIEU

The police and those they chase, hunt, and arrest, operate and live in the same cultural milieu. In many ways those most aware of this fact are the two groups themselves. As a necessity of doing their jobs, both groups are constantly thrown into contact with each other. Part and parcel of being either a law enforcement officer or a career criminal is that one becomes very closely associated with the other group. As a result, these two groups rarely share the public perception of crime as a struggle between good and evil. Instead, matters become personal and an "us versus them" orientation emerges. The criminals see the police as harassing them unfairly. Meanwhile, the police feel justified in doing whatever it takes to "get" the criminals (Bouza, 1990; Cary, 1998; Dudley, 1991; Hosenball, 1999).

Despite the us versus them mentality that pervades the realities of the street, individuals on both sides see their actions as justified. Due to psychological factors related to the need to maintain a positive self-image, both sides rationalize their actions. The police, in order to "protect the public," justify cutting corners, "testilying," manufacturing evidence, and so on. Criminals, on the other hand, view the police as corrupt and illegitimate and feel equally justified in their actions towards law enforcement. These two points of view lead to the police existing as a large and powerful gang in the world of the street (Dudley, 1991; Sewell, 1999).

For those who may think this is a rather extreme point, let us examine the overt similarities between the criminals and the police. First and foremost, both of these occupations exist in worlds where everyone carries a gun on a constant basis. In few, if any, other areas of life is one involved in a lifestyle that necessitates the daily carrying of a handgun. The whole issue of gun use in this country has led to very unique challenges with regard to crime. The fact that guns are so readily accessible and easy to obtain directly leads to a heavily armed civilian populace. As a result, the police feel the need to carry guns to protect themselves or to be prepared for any eventuality. This creates a vicious circle where the criminals then feel the necessity to be armed, leading to the police needing larger guns and so on. It is this very action of carrying a gun and the very willingness to be involved in a setting that requires carrying a gun that solidifies the deep-seated similarity and connection between the two groups.

Other similarities between these groups involve the constant possibility of violence as an occupational hazard, the use of violence as a means of settling conflict, and the expectation of conflict with those outside the group. In addition, both occupations are exceedingly difficult ways to make a living that involve stress, low pay, and long hours. Thrills and excitement are features that likely attract people to both groups. The similarities are not so easily disguised by uniforms and clothing when one analyzes day-to-day activities. A deeper look at the psychological makeup of the two groups further elucidates the similarities.

THE MIND OF CRIME

Crime, contrary to popular belief, is not generally a well-thought-out career choice. From the popular literature to movies to congressional debate, crime is often presented as an occupation deliberately chosen and carried out by a class of career criminals, who are deliberately reeking havoc on society. The "master criminal" is in fact little more than a creation of Hollywood. The idea that there is a group of well-organized, well-trained, brilliant criminal masterminds at work challenging the civility of society is a myth. Yes, there are groups such as street gangs, motorcycle clubs or other groups that work together for illegal purposes, but by and large disorganized crime would be a more truthful description of the activities of this particular subset.

To say that there are no organized, intelligent criminals getting away with it is to commit a fallacy. However, to state that this is representative of the average felon is to commit an even greater error. If there really were so many people getting away with crime, our jails and prisons would not be so full. The average career criminal does get caught, and many get caught repeatedly. To some degree this is a self-selected group who have not figured out that they are no good at crime or have not figured out a better way to support themselves.

When working with incarcerated delinquents one fact that continually confronted me was the demographically unrepresentative group we received at our facility on a weekly basis. By this I am not referring to the well-documented trend of minorities to be overrepresented in an incarcerated population. This factor can well be attributed to racism and poverty. Other variables indicating a very skewed selection of inmates, however, were somewhat surprising and were noticed only because I had access to large pools of data on all inmates in the facility. These findings held regardless of the race or age of the individual tested and as such seem to indicate real factors influencing the commission of crime. Specifically, these variables related to scores achieved on intelligence tests and reading scores.

All individuals entering the facility were required by court order to be tested for intellectual ability and educational attainment. Tests were administered by seasoned professionals accustomed to working with a forensic population and therefore were felt to have administered valid tests. The average individual being incarcerated at the facility had a measured IQ of approximately one standard deviation below average and reading scores were between second and third grade (Cook and Brewer, 1992). I can recall on several occasions when large, violent gang members would break down and cry when asked to read during initial education screenings.

Intelligence tests are notoriously influenced by education, as obviously are reading levels. As a result it is likely prudent to interpret these findings more in light of poor education and lack of educational opportunities than as indicators of low intellectual functioning. These findings do point to a rather stark conclusion that those involved in crime are often poorly educated and without intellectual resources to find alternatives to a life of crime. As an aside, these findings also point out the futility of increasing penalties as a deterrent. In order for this to be effective, most criminals would have to have daily access to legal information and be able to read the criminal code. In conversations with incarcerated individuals I have occasionally asked them about their awareness of the law and penalties for various crimes. Few criminals have any conception of the penalties for most crimes.

The popular conception of most incarcerated people as master criminals is, as I have noted, a myth. Most people in prison are there because of poor judgment and an inability to learn from mistakes. It is a very typical scenario for someone to end up in prison because of a series of minor events that in and of themselves are not significant crimes.

What happens is that one impulsive or poorly considered action such as shoplifting gets an individual into the system. A few years later the person is caught doing something else. Likely they receive probation or some continued court supervision. After a while, perhaps while drinking, they get into a barroom brawl and are charged with assault. At this point the person may still be able to avoid jail or prison. But now a situation has developed where the individual has many priors, one of which (the assault) seems serious. What can now happen is that a minor event like missing a meeting with a probation officer or failing a drug screen results in a violation of probation (VOP) charge and the person can be sent to prison.

If the above scenario sounds unlikely, I assure you it is not. Violating probation is one of the easiest avenues to jail or prison in the current system (Uniform Crime Reports, 1989; Office of the Legislative Auditor, State of Minnesota, 1997). The noted impulsiveness and inability to learn from mistakes leads many individuals on probation to commit senseless and minor violations that result in imprisonment. These are not criminal masterminds but incompetent criminals. Rarely, if ever, are there efforts to intervene at the root of the problems that lead to incarceration such as substance abuse, poverty, illiteracy, or mental illness. The system is very good at jailing people but very poor at addressing the reasons behind the crime.

The preceding statements should not be taken as an attempt to excuse people for their actions or to state that most criminals are just victims of circumstance. Many people who end up in the court system display overt symptoms of an antisocial personality disorder and probably need to be incarcerated or at least provided with some type of intervention services. According to the *Diagnostic and Statistical Manual for Mental Disorders, Fourth Edition* (DSM-IV), it is estimated that about 3 percent of the male population and 1 percent of the female population meet the criteria for diagnosis as having antisocial personality disorder (DSM-IV, 1994). Estimates of those incarcerated who meet these criteria range from a minimum of 30 percent (DSM-IV, 1994) to a high of 94 percent (Lewis, 1985).

Antisocial personality disorder is the current label for what has been referred to in the past as psychopathic or sociopathic. Features of these individuals include a pattern of violation of the rights of others, deceitfulness, and manipulative behavior. These persons also display a noted tendency towards impulsive behavior and irresponsibility. They are often aggressive towards others and display a lack of conscience concerning their actions. Antisocial personalities also are able to rationalize and excuse their own behavior easily (DSM-IV, 1994).

A specific psychological instrument, the *Minnesota Multiphasic Personality Inventory* (MMPI), has been shown clinically to identify many individuals who fit this diagnosis. The MMPI is an objective assessment measure with three validity scales and ten clinical scales that are used to describe the individuals. According to Greene (1980), the code type 4–9 (indicates that the fourth and ninth scales are clinically elevated) is associated with individuals who are "overactive, impulsive, irresponsible and untrustworthy" (p. 134). Antisocial actions and a very high need for excitement are also seen in these persons. Further, they show poor judgment and a lack of conscience. These individuals have little ability to delay gratification and acting-out behavior and aggression are common (Greene, 1980; Gynther, Altman, and Sletter, 1973; Huesmann, Lefkowitz, and Eron, 1978).

In lay terms what one would see among these individuals is a pattern of reckless, impulsive behavior that is often marked by poor judgment and an inability to learn from mistakes. Persons who fit the diagnostic criteria for antisocial personality do pretty much whatever occurs to them at the moment and have little concern for the consequences of their actions. Only when they are caught are they likely to show remorse and then only in the sense that it is personally affecting them.

In essence, those who can be diagnosed as antisocial personalities are not nice people. Their manipulative nature may allow them to be socially facile and make a good impression, but underneath their concern is only for themselves. Only by viewing the legal system through their eyes is one likely to develop successful avenues of rehabilitation or even punishment.

A CRIMINAL'S VIEW OF THE COURT SYSTEM

An element of our current criminal justice system that is completely illogical from a psychological point of view is the idea that by making prisons tougher and sentences longer crime will be deterred and criminals will change. If most incarcerated people had this level of insight and judgment, they likely would be doing something else. Additionally, the educational and personality features of most felons render the notion of deterrence moot. For this reason alone, it is clear that efforts to change or rehabilitate those with the features of those commonly incarcerated will have to rely on more than simple imprisonment.

Most felons view the criminal justice system as something to be manipulated and twisted. The period that leads up to and precedes sentencing and trial is so disordered that it is difficult not to view it as a joke. It is here that many get the idea that nothing will happen to them because of the process itself. Yet, this is the time when one's lawyer and knowledge of the system actually matter. What most individuals who are involved in regular or even semi-regular contact with legal authorities understand, which the general public does not understand, is the barely controlled chaos that regulates the court system. The level of overload in the system is enormous. It has been estimated that 90–95 percent of cases never go to trial because of plea bargains and other procedural arrangements (American Bar Association, 1996). Passing familiarity with court proceedings and elementary logic suggest that if it were not for plea bargains, the entire system would grind to a halt. Imagine the backlog of court cases that would quickly develop if there were twenty times as many jury trials being conducted as there are currently. If everyone arrested requested a jury trial there would be no way the courts could function. Defense attorneys, prosecutors, and criminals are aware of this fact.

To get anything done, it's "let's make a deal" time in courts. So it's "cop a plea" to a minor charge, get several others dropped, do one third of the sentence because of overcrowding, and back to the streets. Savvy individuals make use of delays and procedural matters to drag out the process. By delays and procedural matters I am not referring to clever legal challenges to evidence or other such efforts to get the case dismissed. Instead, I am referring to making use of the necessary shifting of schedules and paperwork to accommodate the court. In the course of these delays, witnesses fail to appear, evidence is mishandled or lost, paperwork is misplaced, defendants miss court dates, and a host of other such eventualities occur.

The inevitable outcome of this process is that those in the system come to view it as a game to be manipulated and toyed with. Sanctions are so far removed from actions that little connection is made between behavior and consequences. On numerous occasions while reading background information on individuals with whom I worked, I would notice arrest dates as compared to eventual incarceration dates. It was not unusual, and in fact may have been more the norm than the exception, for over a year to pass between arrest and sentencing. For some individuals so much time had passed that they were unaware of why they were incarcerated. It is exceedingly difficult to feel sorry for your actions if you are not even aware of why you are in jail.

Increased penalties only lead to more desperate efforts to subvert the system. The mindset that evolves in many felons concerning the system is that it is an arbitrary and unfair system that is an impediment to living as one chooses. Legitimate or not, this opinion demonstrates the necessity of any rehabilitation efforts being aimed at the attitudes and inner motivations that accompany criminal behavior.

At a very core level, the involvement of judges, police, and courts is seen as illegitimate by most felons. Many individuals in the system are frankly antisocial or at least unbound by the conventions of society. The term being a "citizen" is often contemptuously used in crime circles. As a result, the actions of the whole criminal justice system are viewed as interfering where one does not belong.

The reverse of this is that many criminals are surprisingly open to the idea that retaliation is to be expected from victims. I recall hearing two incarcerated rival gang members express that they had no hard feelings about efforts to kill each other because "that's just the way it is on the outside, it's business." They even felt the other had gotten a raw deal from the police because it was "none of their business." This attitude is common. Most criminals feel that they get more justice from the streets and even other criminals than they do from the legal system.

Such attitudes are extremely difficult to change and are likely made worse by draconian punishment measures. It is this very idea that violence is acceptable and that efforts to adapt to societal demands and accept responsibility for one's action are useless that needs to be confronted in the criminal mindset. Only when people are in agreement with the goals of change and feel that it is in their best interests do they cooperate. Our current system plays right into the criminal mindset and inadvertently encourages individuals to see themselves as victims. Reactance, as earlier noted, also causes individuals to struggle against any efforts to force them to do anything against their will. The current heavy-handed measures employed by our system lead directly to efforts to resist change. In turn, this drives those involved in the legal system outside the mainstream and further to the fringes of society.

THE GOOD GUYS ?

The Thin Blue Line: The Culture of the Police

The police, like any clearly identifiable group, have evolved their own culture. This culture is intricately linked to the culture of crime and criminals due to their constant contact. But this constant contact between the two groups leads to a siege mentality. Despite the similarities between the two groups, each side, particularly the police, defines itself according to the other group. Thus, it quickly becomes "us versus them." The metaphor "thin blue line" used to show the police holding back the tide of crime clearly illustrates this phenomenon. This mentality is then used to justify any actions taken by the police that are illegal or unethical. Consider the following:

- In Los Angeles, Rodney King is beaten senseless by several policemen caught on videotape in a scene that shocked America and has entered our national consciousness.

- Abner Louima, a Haitian immigrant, is tortured by uniformed officers in a police station house.

- Amadou Diallo, an unarmed twenty-two-year-old street vendor has forty-one shots fired at him by an "elite" crime unit in New York City. He dies instantly. In protests that follow, over 1600 individuals are arrested.

Listed above are just a few of the more dramatic and extreme abuses of power committed by the police in the past few years. The reaction of law enforcement is to portray these actions as aberrant and rare events committed by rogue cops. While such events may be rare (although I doubt as rare as one might believe), they serve to illustrate a very disconcerting fact: The systematized and institutionalized acceptance of the abuse of power within our nation's law enforcement agencies has become commonplace.

It is my contention that a systematic dehumanization of the general public has occurred in the police mindset and allows for the rationalization of abuse and outright criminal behavior in the name of justice and law and order. In fact, I can recall at least one public official making an attempt to justify, excuse, or minimize every single one of the cases of police brutality listed above because of the circumstances. In the Rodney King case, this scenario played out for days with the police and numerous Los Angeles officials stating that the police were afraid of King and suspected him of using PCP and other such excuses. Such actions are only the tip of the iceberg and point to a much broader abuse of power than the relatively extreme and severe events listed here. It will be shown that this systematic abuse of power has led to an erosion of respect for and trust in law enforcement.

Fortunately for society, events such as the Rodney King beating and the Diallo killing are not the typical avenues of police abuse in this country. Unfortunately, these events are symptomatic of a much larger and more systemic problem throughout the criminal justice system. In many ways, these problems, while not as extreme as assault or murder, have become integral parts of the system, rationalized away as necessary to maintain law and order. Several broad categories of this behavior will be examined in turn, including the personality of the police, the lack of concern for civil rights, the lack of professionalism, political pressures, and the "code of silence." For the purposes of this chapter, please note that the term "police" is used collectively to refer to police officers, sheriffs, highway patrol, and various other such personnel.

The Police Personality

As with all occupations, certain personalities are drawn to police work. It likely will come as no surprise to the reader that the personality of the police officer parallels that of the authoritarian personality. The work on the authoritarian personality, originally conducted by Adorno et al. (1950) demonstrates that those who are identified as authoritarian see the maintenance of the status quo and adherence to authority as paramount social goals. Individuals with this bent to their personality see law and order as more important than any vague notion of justice and express a rather rigid and conventional moral system. The essential element of the authoritarian personality is that those in authority are "right" simply because they are in authority and those who are opposed are "wrong." This feature goes a long way towards explaining how one gets individuals to carry out such historical travesties as the clubbing of civil rights demonstrators, the attack upon students at Kent State, the firebombing of MOVE headquarters in Philadelphia, and others. All of these groups were questioning authority for moral purposes, yet I am unaware of any police officers questioning or refusing their orders in any of these situations. In the minds of the police, the people involved were wrong because they opposed those in authority. It is not that these groups were overtly breaking any laws, rather they opposed the status quo, which made them guilty.

In the late '80s there arose the "offender profile" developed by various law enforcement agencies, which suggested that criminals could be identified on the basis of features such as minority status, hairstyles, bumper stickers, and so on. None of the features of the "profile" relate to any type of criminal behavior but rather seem to fall into a stereotyping of groups out of the mainstream. Before the ACLU successfully challenged such means to identify suspects, this country was on the verge of making nonconformity a crime. It is interesting to note that despite court rulings against this action, the state of New Jersey was found to be doing this as late as 1999 despite claims to the contrary (Hosenball, 1999). One wonders how many law enforcement agencies are still doing this without "officially" acting in this way.

Even despite rulings against offender profiles, there continues to be blatant discrimination against minorities by the system. The practice has become so widespread that there is a term used in minority communities to describe these actions. The term, "driving while black or brown" or DWB, refers to the tendency of police to disproportionately stop minority motorists (Harris, 1997; Roberts, 1999; Susskind, 1999). One study found that over 50 percent of those stopped by a field interrogation unit were members of minority groups even though they comprised only about 4.8 percent of the population in the area (Walker, Spohn, and DeLone, 1996). Even the control group in this study found that roughly 50 percent of those stopped were minorities in a community of 17.5 percent minority composition (Walker, Spohn, and DeLone, 1996).

The above indicates relatively serious implications concerning the nature of police and minority relations. Deputy Attorney General Eric Holder admitted that many African-Americans believe they are treated differently from whites by police ("Public satisfaction with local police varies by race,"1999). Apparently this tendency is more than mere perception. Weitzer (1996) found that 79 percent of white officers and 28 percent of minority officers expressed racial prejudice in front of researchers examining the idea. If the numbers are that high for individuals who know they are being observed, what are the numbers when opinions occur only behind closed doors or out of sight?

Aaron Campbell, an African-American motorist, found out the depth of police racism when he was stopped in Orange County, Florida, in April of 1997. Campbell was stopped for an alleged traffic violation and requested a police supervisor come to the scene at the time of the initial stop. Officers refused and proceeded to pull guns on him, pepper-sprayed him, and finally at least three officers tackled him and took him down. The officers then searched his person and his vehicle against his will. In a final insult Campbell was arrested and tried for battery and resisting arrest even though he was the one who was beaten.

Minority persons all over the country would likely not be surprised with this scenario. The judge at the trial, A. Thomas Mihok, not only ruled on the basis of the videotape from the camera in the police car that there was no traffic violation, but also ruled that there was no evidence of the battery or resisting arrest charges. What made this case unique is that the victim, Aaron Campbell, is also a police officer, a deputy sheriff with the rank of major in Dade County, Florida. The footage from the arresting officer's car shown during his trial on Court TV clearly demonstrates that Campbell not only identified himself as an officer, but went out of his way to be cooperative. Viewing the tape of the incident leaves one with a feeling that Campbell was lucky to escape with his life.

Numerous such events have routinely occurred (ACLU, 1999) to the degree that it would be impossible to list them here. In New York City alone police searched close to 50,000 people in a two-year period with only 5000 arrests. The vast majority of all these stops involved minority persons (Glasser, personal communiqué, 1999). The conclusion can only be drawn that the police have little respect for the common citizen and easily rationalize rights abuses as necessary to maintain order.

To various law enforcement agencies legal challenges concerning stop and seizure, profiling, and any other rights violations prevent them from doing their job. This attitude illustrates a major problem with law enforcement: Few have little understanding of their job beyond some vague notion of preserving law and order (Bouza, 1990; Skolnick, 1994). Only a small percentage of the police can recite the Bill of Rights, and most view these as a hindrance in carrying out their duties (Bouza, 1990; Ellis, 1991; Sewell, 1999). A Louisiana state patrolman once stated to the author that anyone talking about their rights must be guilty and should be viewed with suspicion. Unfortunately, this attitude is not reserved for police from backwoods jurisdictions. Instead, the attitude is pervasive and demonstrates that to the average police officer it is not justice that must be served but order and conformity.

Clearly, the job of the police is a difficult one. Long hours, poor pay, little respect, and the possibility of life-threatening circumstances as a routine part of the job make one wonder why anyone would want such a job. Certainly there are police officers who are motivated by higher ideals and have genuine prosocial motives for entering this line of work. My experience has been that these are few and far between. The typical police officer is motivated more by internal need than by any sense of community service.

Internal need, especially for power and authority, is prominent in police officers. Power strivings can be met and internal self-worth is bolstered. As a result, authoritarians are strongly attracted to police work. Once an authoritarian becomes a police officer, then he or she becomes the authority and is in the position of "might makes right." The officer is the authority and anyone expressing opposition or questioning his/her actions is aligned with the criminal element in society. The identification of the authoritarian nature of many police may go a long way towards explaining the seeming lack of interest most law enforcement systems seem to have in detecting and prosecuting white-collar crime. Analysis of *Uniform Crime Reports* over the past twenty years indicates that fewer than 3 percent of all arrests relate to white-collar crime even when applying the most liberal and inclusive definition of white-collar crime. In many ways white-collar criminals fit police ideas of proper behavior and may even be seen as representing authority!

A disturbing element of the personality of the police is that in many ways the police are similar to career criminals. Many individuals attracted to police work demonstrate elements of the antisocial personality that one finds in chronic, habitual offenders. This writer has firsthand knowledge of a university psychology department that lost its contract to screen prospective police officers for a city because they were rejecting too many applicants as psychologically unfit. The vast majority of those rejected were obtaining MMPI profiles with a 4–9 pattern. Please note this is the same pattern listed earlier for career criminals and also note the features of this profile. These are alarming characteristics in anyone, particularly someone who carries a gun and has the weight of the law behind him/her.

The combination of the authoritarian personality with antisocial features is frightening. This combination leads to an individual who feels justified in almost any action they take. Clubbing suspects into submission, searching individuals without cause, even framing someone can all be rationalized away as doing one's job. I once had the occasion to interrupt the interrogation of a fifteen-year-old, mentally retarded individual by State Bureau of Investigation (SBI) agents, who were attempting to get him to confess to murder by telling him they had the evidence on him. This was obviously a blatant lie because if they had the evidence, there would have been no need for a confession. Leaving that aside, the fact that a mentally retarded child (who happened to function at such a low level that I doubt he would have been competent to stand trial in most jurisdictions) has being questioned by legal authorities without his parents present should be alarming to anyone. My interceding on behalf of a client I felt I had an obligation to protect made the agents extremely angry to the point that they began threatening me over the incident.

The use of coercion and even overt force has become pervasive in law enforcement. The use of police dogs, tear gas, batons, pepper spray, and the like is routine and rationalized as "just doing the job." In early 1999 the Clinton administration even acknowledged the problem and dedicated $40 million dollars to improving police training. Citing questionable police shootings throughout the country, the president noted the lack of trust between citizens and the police who are supposed to be protecting them. In response, the Justice Department allocated funds to address civil rights abuses by the police (Galvin, 1999).

These problems with police aggression, however, may not be solely attributable to poor training. It has long been noted that extreme antisocial aggression is engaged in primarily by those who are either undercontrolled or overcontrolled (Megargee, 1966). In essence, those who are undercontrolled tend to act out in a routine fashion in their day-to-day lives and appear to most people as obviously dangerous. It is the overcontrolled group, which seems to blend into the general populace, that can be so incredibly dangerous. This can be seen in the rash of shootings in the workplace and throughout the country where people comment that the person was so quiet and withdrawn and that they never would have expected it. These individuals are psychologically conceptualized as being extremely repressed and dealing ineffectively with stress. In short, they are something of a ticking time bomb. The personality attributes of repression and overcontrol are common among police (Schmalleger, 1997).

Another example of the pervasiveness of questionable behavior in the name of law and order is the act of "testilying." This is a term used by police to describe the process of distorting testimony in court in such a way that the defendant's guilt is "proven" or made to appear more obvious. Use of this "technique" can range from subtle omission of police misconduct to blatant falsifications concerning the commission of the crime. The fact that this action has a name that is used jokingly in police departments nationwide indicates the pervasiveness of this behavior.

I invite the reader to verify the above statements by attending a trial or even watching one on Court TV. One will note that the quality of the testimony presented by police officers is markedly different from that of other witnesses. The testimony of the police invariably seems rehearsed and designed more to support their claims than honest recollections. In the O. J. Simpson case, reasonable doubt was likely created by the parade of highly incredible testimony from several of the police officers involved. To some degree the lack of credibility of the police in Los Angeles had more to do with Simpson's acquittal than evaluation of the evidence.

Leaving O. J. behind, as it is far more plausible that wealth more than any other factor contributed to his acquittal, consider any time you have been to court as an observer, juror, defendant (even in traffic court), or other capacity and ask how you felt about the testimony of the police. I recall once observing in traffic court six people in a row who had been given tickets for going 54 in a 45 mph zone on the same day of the month on the same road. It strains reason and certainly probability to believe that every single individual given a ticket was going the exact same speed. Yet, on the stand, the officer dutifully stated in each separate case that the person was traveling the exact same speed. It is interesting to note that the officer was unable to note from what direction he was traveling when he stopped the vehicle but was able to state with certainty how fast they were going.

It is common for law enforcement to lament the lack of respect they receive and complain that citizens do not support them. As long as police work continues to attract individuals who enter the field to meet their own needs for power and control, no one should be surprised to witness a decline in trust and respect for the police. At present, there exists nationwide a large number of authoritarian police with antisocial features. Given this set of circumstances, it is not surprising that abuses of power occur; it is only surprising that they are ever brought to light.

One wonders what would have happened that night in Los Angeles when Rodney King was beaten if someone had not been testing a video camera or if Abner Louima had not been so severely beaten that he nearly died. In the Louima case, one officer, Justin Volpe, plead guilty and another was found guilty primarily because other police under fire testified against them. Officials held this as positive because other police had actually violated the "blue wall of silence" whereby police cover for each other. It should be noted, however, that these police did so to save themselves. In essence, the code of silence was violated in response to a setup very similar to the prisoner's dilemma game in which "selling out" one's codefendants leads to more lenient treatment. What is disturbing is the unknown number of individuals who have experienced such abuses but who have had no recourse because the actions were shielded behind the thin blue line.

In sum, the primary parties involved in the criminal justice system at the street level, the police and the criminals, can be seen as similar. It is unlikely that the criminals of the world will adopt a code of ethics and rapidly change their behavior. However, unless the police begin to behave in a manner more respectful of people and their civil rights, there can be no expectation of advancement in society. The police must adopt a higher standard of behavior or their support will be completely eroded in the communities they serve. More training, better screening, and careful attention to ethics and civil rights are the only means by which the police can avoid being viewed as just another well-armed street gang that dresses in blue.

Chapter 4

POLITICIANS AND BUREAUCRATS: GARBAGE IN, GARBAGE OUT

Congress shall have power to make all laws. . . .
—U.S. Constitution
Article 1, Section 8.18

A major problem with the criminal justice system stems not from the fact that the Congress of the United States and the various state houses make the laws of the land. Rather, the problem stems from the politicians who comprise the Congress and the professional bureaucrats who have far too much influence on policy. The nature of the political process has led to a class of politicians who are constantly campaigning and permanently indebted to their contributors. In our current political climate, every single vote or sponsored bill is fair game for the next election cycle. Spin control and posturing have emerged as far more important than the development of reasoned, comprehensive and coherent policy. As a result, little attention is given to the consequences or effects of new legislation with the primary focus instead being on how it will be perceived when the next election rolls around.

The effects of having a class of career politicians indebted to financial contributors and driven only by the need to get reelected severely impairs our ability to address significant problems in our society. While it is beyond the scope of this text to elaborate fully upon this idea, several factors related to this issue lead to very poor decision making and policy development as it pertains to crime in our society. This is especially true given the emotional nature of the debate concerning crime and the ability of political analysts to manipulate public opinion.

The area of crime lends itself to political mishandling. Being against crime is an easy way to stake out a position that is sure to be popular. Running on an anticrime platform is about as safe a political move as one can make. It also serves a double purpose of setting up any challenger as out of step with the public. After all, who will vote for the "pro-crime" candidate? This state of affairs has led to a situation where candidates of both major parties have adopted the tough-on-crime agenda to the point that many races seem to be contests of who is tougher.

It is just such twisting of events, depicting anyone advocating a different approach as wrong, that is hampering our ability to address the issue of crime. The use of advertising strategies and the ability to manipulate the electorate has seemingly become more important than ideas in our electoral process. It is this very need to pander in order to get elected that prevents those who hold office from putting forth thoughtful long-range plans. Further, those who make any attempt to address complex issues and not be guided by polls have come to have little chance of election. It is a chicken-and-egg type question to ask whether this low level of debate results from or causes our typically low election turnouts.

The small percentage voting leads to situations where entire elections can be swung by duping the uninformed on emotional issues. In the 1996 presidential election, for example, less than two-thirds of the registered voters bothered to go to the polls. Further, the numbers of people who are not even registered to vote led to a circumstance where less than half (49 percent) of the voting-age population cast ballots (Wright, 1998). This trend is of long standing in American politics with fewer than 60 percent of the voting-age population casting ballots in every presidential election since 1968 (Wright, 1998). In off-year and non-presidential elections this trend only worsens. Compared to other countries where voting is seen as something akin to a sacred duty, many Americans see participation in the system as illegitimate. I used to chastise people for not voting until it became apparent to me that this was not merely an extension of apathy but an active decision based on alienation and principle. The low turnout itself does suggest that there is a large audience that has become very disillusioned. Perhaps this is the market that is ready for complex and thoughtful solutions. If not, we will continue to be governed by slogans and superficialities.

THE FIFTEEN-SECOND SOUND BITE

The need to reach a mass audience in a timely and cost-efficient manner makes television a natural choice among political candidates. In a time-pressured society where many, if not most, live at a harried pace, information is at a premium. Although I lambaste the lack of complexity put forth by many politicians in their solutions to problems, there is another contributory element to this issue. This element is the awareness that most individuals do not have the time, energy, and/or interest to investigate sufficiently their elected officials' positions on most issues. For many people, merely making a living and dealing with the demands of everyday life leaves no time or energy to become fully informed. Therefore, slogans and samples of information become the focus of campaigns.

Crime, and particularly the rallying cry of "get tough," is tailor-made for this game. The electorate is clearly opposed to crime and making it an easy choice for politicians searching for a popular strategy. The use of television and radio spots serves the purpose of putting forth a message without seriously having to define the program. In a sense, one gets to avoid indepth reflection and frank discussion of the issue and instead put forth a message with pollster-proven appeal. Further, when one is the "get tough" candidate, this serves the dual purpose of suggesting that one's opponent is soft on crime.

In the 1988 presidential election, George Bush brought out the infamous Willie Horton ads, which suggested that his opponent, Michael Dukakis, had paroled this felon, unconcerned that he would commit more crimes. These ads, when paired with debate questions concerning what Dukakis' actions would be if his wife were attacked, led to a perception that he was soft on crime and that he did not have the fortitude to be president. These ads seemed to signal a major shift in the way Dukakis was viewed and may have been the turning point that decided the election.

For those too young to remember the 1988 presidential campaign, these ads featured the mug shot of a scruffy African-American convict with a voice-over indicating that Dukakis had paroled this individual so he could commit murder. The facts aside, including that the parole board, not the governor, paroled this individual, the purpose was to make Bush's opponent appear pro-crime and push the "three strikes" agenda. This advertising campaign was at heart an appeal to fear and racism playing into hysteria concerning crime. In reality, unless we parole no one, it is impossible to ensure that no paroled individual will ever commit another crime.

Paroling no one is a choice loudly championed by some. Pete Wilson, former governor of California, advocated on at least one campaign stop that "three strikes" was too many and that he wanted "one strike" legislation. This is a prime example of the way in which the very nature of the political process drives politicians towards grandstanding and catering to media sound bites rather than making reasonable policy. With prisons already packed to the gills and new sentencing guidelines keeping individuals incarcerated for longer periods of time, there is an inability to deal with those already in the system. One-strike policies would completely break the system, not to mention what it would do to the fabric of society. But as a sound bite, this gathered a lot of applause at the time it was stated.

The fifteen-second sound bite lends itself easily to the issue of crime. One reason is that with practically every aspect of the criminal justice system in poor shape, it is easy to come up with a solution that sounds good in the length of the standard commercial. "Get tough," "three strikes," and "truth-in-sentencing" all sound good when presented without any substantive information. In the long run, simplistic platitudes described as solutions are about as useful as the "Whip Inflation Now" (WIN) campaign of the Ford administration was in dealing with the economy. The "Whip Inflation Now" campaign was a proposal by Gerald Ford that if everyone wore buttons saying "WIN," we would somehow pull ourselves out of bad economic times through increasing our participation in the economy. We learned the lesson that such slogans, without substance, do little for the economy and now it is time to apply the same to the crime problem. Complex problems can rarely be solved with simplistic, one-size-fits-all solutions, especially those that can be summarized in a commercial.

Before blaming the political process completely for what has ensued in the debate on crime, acknowledgment must be given that politicians have little choice but to participate in this war of slogans and platitudes if they seriously hope to be elected. In order to get elected most need to pander to the lowest common denominator. Trotting out a few crime victims or their families makes for good media appeal. So in that sense, the situation is unlikely to change in the foreseeable future. However, the nature of the process is one thing, the nature of politicians is another.

Rudy Giuliani, the mayor of New York as the century closed, successfully used a get-tough policy to gain election. Claiming that he would clean up New York and make the city more civil and safe, Giuliani was swept into office on the basis of these promises. After his inauguration in 1994, Guiliani replaced the head of the police department and proceeded to install a quasi-police state encouraging officers to stop citizens who "might" be dangerous or carrying weapons (Giuliani, 1994, 1997). Numerous abuses occurred, culminating in the shooting of Amadou Diallo by an "elite" crime force. Mr. Diallo did nothing and was shot forty-one times, apparently because he was the same race as the suspect. The protests and lawsuits that ensued did little to get Guiliani to change his position.

While the political right wing has been seen as a major abuser of the sound bite approach to criminal justice policy, it is not alone. Dianne Feinstein, D-CA, a purported liberal, has sponsored and pushed legislation making it easier to try children as adults and to kick children out of schools (Gun Free Schools Act of 1994). Approaches such as the Gun Free Schools Act, which originated out of shootings at several schools, sound good on the face until one looks at the long-range consequences. Certainly, the Gun Free Schools Act allowed for denying many students a right to an education, but it did nothing to address the problem of children carrying guns. Poorly considered, knee-jerk reactions to sensational events make for good media coverage, great letters to the electorate, and nice, safe positions for future office-seeking, but do little to address real issues.

In many states and localities, so many people have bought into the get-tough approach that both sides of the political aisle sing its praises. The far reach of the "get tough" umbrella can be seen when one recognizes that individuals as disparate in orientation as Feinstein and Jesse Helms are using the same political maneuvers. In some areas, politicians must identify with this position to have any hope of election. In the gubernatorial election of 1994 in Alabama each candidate bragged that he had caused more people to be executed than his opponent. Fob James, the winner, later went on to repeatedly defend the position that the United States Constitution did not apply to Alabama when a dispute arose over prayer in schools.

THE LIVES OF POLITICIANS

When it comes to politicians, few have any experience with the realities of life, such as working two jobs just to provide the necessities of life, much less a life of crime. As a general rule, few politicians have had little contact with the day-to-day life of street criminals. Most of our elected officials have led lives of privilege that are well outside the experience of most Americans. This split between the governed and the governing leads to policy disconnected from reality as the rule. Politicians are likely the only individuals outside of Hollywood who believe in the concept of master criminals. Unfortunately, politicians make policy and laws while Hollywood only makes movies.

Ruben "Hurricane" Carter, the former middleweight boxer who was convicted of a triple murder in the 1960s and spent many years on death row until his conviction was overturned in 1985, stated that he could count on the fingers of one hand the number of individuals of privilege and power he had met in prison (Carter, 1999). He then placed his thumb and forefinger together making a zero. This statement illustrates a very important fact concerning the criminal justice system. Namely, those who make the laws, hold political power, and develop the plans to solve the crime problem have little understanding of the realities of crime. Even when such individuals do go to prison, such as in the Nixon administration or those caught in the Iran-Contra affair, the facilities to which they are sent tend to be that most unusual of all facilities, the federal minimum-security prison, which houses less than 2 percent of the total U.S. inmate population (Federal Bureau of Prisons, Weekly Population Report, 1999).

When one thinks of various names associated with the wealthy in this country and then compares those with any list of politicians, a few very startling conclusions become apparent. It seems dubious that the family names of Rockefeller, Kennedy, Bush, du Pont, and so on, carry any magical ability to govern. Yet, our political system seems to be filled with career politicians from wealthy families. When someone like Steve Forbes, Donald Trump, or Ross Perot can immediately become a viable contender in a political race, what does that say of the political process? A sense of entitlement leads to these individuals feeling justified in putting forth "solutions" to crime and holding forth on the way to affect the behavior of those living in abject poverty.

Pierre du Pont, former governor of Delaware and scion of the du Pont family, provides a perfect example of this tendency. In an article published not coincidentally in a publication for which he is the editor, du Pont advocated draconian measures as the solution to the crime problem. Using unrelated correctional research he drew the conclusion that increasing punishment leads to less crime (du Pont, 1997). The idea that a man from one of the wealthiest families in the world, who has led a life of privilege, believes he can affect the behavior of street-level criminals through legislation is to strain credulity.

Du Pont is not alone in his belief. Politicians, who seem more governed by polls than any particular ideas, push their solutions without thought as to the long-term outcomes or consequences to society. In the wake of the Columbine High School shootings in Littleton, Colorado, politicians were coming out of the woodwork to grandstand on the issue of gun control. Conservatives who had never expressed a single gun control idea were suddenly big supporters and liberals were all of a sudden demanding we get tougher on those who brought guns to schools. Interestingly, even though polls had for many years routinely showed the public to favor some form of gun control, few politicians would touch the idea because of the fear it would politically decimate them by making them appear "soft on crime." Contributions from groups like the National Rifle Association also make it difficult for many politicians to vote for legislation that is truly in the interests of the electorate.

BUREAUCRATS AND CORRECTIONS "PROFESSIONALS"

Politicians are not alone when it comes to the need to manage public perception. The administrators and corrections professionals who comprise the bureaucracy of the criminal justice system are also in a position where the public perception of their performance is important. In order to continue to receive funding and public support these administrators and bureaucrats at all levels of the system must demonstrate a need for their services. This places them in a somewhat conflicted position when it comes to policy. On the one hand, prison officials need to demonstrate that their efforts are effective in the removal of criminals from the street and in the subsequent reformation of these same felons. For example, in late 1998 it was discovered that several major police departments, including Philadelphia,

New York, and Atlanta, had been falsifying crime statistics to demonstrate the effectiveness of their crime control efforts (Butterfield, 1998). The city of Philadelphia engaged in such serious underreporting of crimes that the FBI removed their statistics from the nationwide database. It was noted at the time that "because of Philadelphia's size . . . removal of its numbers could skew the crime rate for the nation" (Butterfield, 1998). Despite these irregularities, when crime statistics were released for 1998, there was a much-touted drop in the national crime statistics (Burrell, 1999). Never was there mention of the irregularities in reporting.

On the other hand, these same individuals have a stake in increasing their budgets, expanding their agencies, and increasing their domain of control. In order to do so, there must be some idea that crime is out of control and society is at risk. That is, prisoners must be demonized and viewed as subhuman to justify increasing prison budgets while all the veneer of effectiveness is maintained. It is difficult to have it both ways.

Difficult, but apparently not impossible. Prison officials have it both ways by playing on the vast hysteria surrounding crime and the attendant media hype. By paying lip service to the idea that criminals are increasingly violent and beyond control, they stress the need for more resources. However, as already mentioned, little money goes into actually dealing with those already incarcerated. The extra flow of cash goes to construction. Reform is devalued because the population served is seen as unsalvageable. Prison officials are constantly touting their new security measures, police their new crime-fighting technology, and both groups have "zero tolerance" for wrongdoing. If any of these measures were truly effective, we should see a sustained, long-range drop in crime and a decreasing supply of felons.

Instead, rehabilitation has become shunned in the prison industry and punishment has become the focus. The excuse usually given is that the political climate dictates this approach. The truth is that rehabilitation is not just currently out of favor, it has always been out of favor. Prison officials generally pay little more than lip service to the idea of rehabilitation. Inmates are routinely viewed as subhuman and without compassion. Most prison administrators and officials concern themselves not so much with the rehabilitation of prisoners as with the orderly operation of the facility. An example of the true nature of the thoughts of most prison officials can be found in the words of Phillip Parker, warden of the Kentucky state prison, "I could care less whether inmates get rehabilitated" (Schernberger, 1999).

The smooth operation of the institution dominates the mindset of corrections officials. Rather than workers being evaluated on the basis of interactions with inmates or any efforts to aid rehabilitation, job security and advancement is attained by having a record unblemished by conflict. State workers are taught that being responsible means you get blamed when something goes wrong. In fact, one part of the title of this book was suggested by a fellow worker who jokingly stated that the agency practiced "the rule of the asphalt," and went on to say "whenever anything goes wrong, we look to see whose ass is at fault" (Victor Churchill, personal communiqué, 1992). Compounding this problem is that in any large group there exists diffusion of responsibility, which leads to letting others do the work or handle crises (Darley and Latane, 1968; Sheppard, 1993). As a result, no one wants to be in charge of anything.

I once suggested that we start a small garden at a facility in which I was employed. I thought that working in the garden could be used as a reward for inmates and that it would also be therapeutic. I further felt that the experience could be beneficial to the physical health and nutrition of the inmates. The plan was immediately squashed by superiors whose rationale was "the ACLU will sue us for working inmates." I was stunned by this reply since I am a card-carrying ACLU member and could not figure out the objections on any grounds. Beyond this bizarre explanation was the fact that the institution already worked inmates without pay by having them mow the grounds, work in maintenance, and clean the facility. Besides, work is an established and encouraged part of rehabilitation as set forth by the United Nations at its Congress on the Prevention of Crime and the Treatment of Offenders (1955). At root, the answer was that this was another program someone would have to oversee. Laziness drives a large segment of the prison work force among administrators. It seems to be part of the mentality of administrators, especially those who rise through the ranks in a state agency, that promotion to administrative capacity means that one does as little as possible. It is as if the job is viewed as a reward for all those years of working hard in order to get promoted. The old adage concerning "not making waves" also seems to play some role in the inactivity of prison administrators.

In fairness to some administrators, they work with very little in the way of resources. Although prison expenditures are up greatly, most of the funds are tied up in prison construction and security. At the level of running the prisons that hold inmates, few funds are available to do so. Many prisons operate on shoestring budgets because of demands on administrators to cut costs. Usually this happens by cutting staff and personnel.

I recall once working for an agency that received a $4 million special appropriation in the middle of the year. The agency proceeded to buy a new facility that sat unused for over two years. Meanwhile, students continued to live in older buildings which were actually falling apart. This is not hyperbole, we actually had a wall fall on students in a youth facility. When staff ratios were mandated by the courts by a federal monitor, the facility administrators encouraged the falsification of forms rather than hire staff. Only constant complaints to federal court monitors and numerous contempt of court citations of the agency's director led to new personnel being hired.

The effects of understaffing can be dramatic in a correctional facility. The difficulties that arise as a result of inadequate staff numbers include increased danger to both staff and inmates, increased rights abuses due to staff who feel under siege, and increased warehousing. When funds for staff become an issue, the treatment staff, who usually earn more because they are professionals, are the first to go in order to save costs. This is another factor contributing to the lack of rehabilitation services provided. The prison industry, when compared to other governmental expenditures, is unique in that funds are allocated readily. Unfortunately, these funds are rarely used for long-range, substantive treatment programs, but are primarily spent on warehousing and bed space (see Chapter 2). The emphasis on providing space for all the people incarcerated has created a new industry, previously unheard of, that of private prisons. Part of the privatization craze of the 1980s, private prisons signaled the entrance of private, for-profit organizations into the criminal justice system.

PRIVATE PRISONS

Since the emergence of the political state, prisons have typically been under governmental control. The basis for this is the notion that society has judged its citizens and has a responsibility to punish and rehabilitate them. In the 1980s, subsequent to the domination of the political structure by the conservative right, a new point of view emerged. This philosophy, based on extreme capitalism and free-market ideals, suggested that all services could be more efficiently delivered by the private sector. As a result, there were efforts to privatize all sorts of services, such as education, infrastructure development, and so on, that had previously been considered the sole domain of the government. Prisons became one of these areas.

As previously noted, an enormous amount of money has been flowing into the criminal justice system in recent years. It is only natural that entrepreneurs and capitalists would want a piece of the pie. As of July 1999, there were over 120,000 prisoners held in private facilities according to the Private Corrections Project (Thomas and Bolinger, 1999). California had over 10,000 private bed spaces while Texas had over 30,000 (Thomas and Bolinger, 1999). Even juveniles have been placed in for-profit private facilities ("Neb., W.Va. pull youths," 1998).

The social experiment leading to the development of for-profit, privately managed prisons has opened the door for widespread abuse and mistreatment of prisoners. Corrections, like education and health care, is an area where the drive to make profits can only lead to poor quality of services. When profit enters the picture, all sorts of reasonable practices are scuttled. Efficiency, the primary justification for private prisons, has become defined in terms of keeping costs low. Every corner that can be cut leads to increased short-term quarterly profits. Cutting back or eliminating rehabilitation efforts and engaging only in warehousing leads to maximum profits. Remember, the duty of a corporation is its fiduciary responsibility to its stockholders, not to society. It has been suggested that it is not beyond reason to expect that private prisons could attempt to increase alarm over crime (Smith, 1993) or even encourage criminal acts (Wideman, 1995) in order to increase profits. Beyond all these factors, private prison corporations do not have to concern themselves with failure of their efforts.

The lack of accountability of private prisons has been noted in several investigative reports (Smith, 1993; Wideman, 1995). Evidence of the degree to which private prisons subjugate everything else to profits can be seen in the tremendous number of rights abuses brought to light in these facilities. For example, West Virginia and Nebraska removed youth from a facility in Colorado after a thirteen-year-old hanged himself. An audit of the facility found twelve cases of child abuse during the short time the facility was open. These numbers were found to be equivalent to the totals for the ten state-operated facilities in the same region during the same time period and led to the license of the facility being suspended ("Neb., W.Va. pull youths," 1998). In addition to Colorado, Texas and South Carolina pulled operating licenses for facilities after concerns over poorly trained staff and overcrowding (Wood, 1998). Louisiana even raided and shut down a private juvenile facility after allegations of brutality and documentation of over thirty serious injuries in one month (Stewart, 1998).

The previous examples illustrate a noteworthy feature of private prisons. Namely, private prisons serve as a means to deal with overcrowding. As a result, bed space is the primary consideration in placement. Individuals are often incarcerated tremendous distances from their home and isolated from governing agencies. Not only does placing people in prisons far from their home sabotage efforts to maintain family connection, it can also create a system where redress of grievances is nearly impossible. Private prisons can compound this problem because they are exempt from some rules governing publicly operated facilities (Smith, 1993; "State grapples with private prison problems," 1999).

Rights abuses seem to be common in private prisons. At a private prison in Hobbs, New Mexico, that housed over 1100 inmates, there were two inmate deaths and at least two coverups of incidents involving excessive use of force (Fecteau, 1999) prior to a riot a few months later arising out of inmate complaints (Taugher and Fecteau, 1999). A state representative, Max Coll (D–Santa Fe), noted that the corporation running the prison "cut corners to save money." Costs were estimated to be more than 40 percent below that for publicly run facilities (Taugher and Fecteau, 1999).

A private facility in Ohio, operating at a capacity of 2000, had twenty stabbing incidents in the first ten months it was open. Two fatal stabbings occurred in a three-week period. After a lawsuit was filed alleging the mixing of medium- and maximum-security inmates, U.S. District Judge Sam Bell issued an injunction against the facility accepting new prisoners (Thompson, 1998). After escapes involving sexual predators, the governor advocated shutting down the facility ("State grapples with private prison problems," 1999).

The list of abuses detailed herein is by no means exhaustive. Severe abuses occur in prisons, both private and state run. However, private prisons seem to create even more avenues for abuse due to their focus on profit. Inmates receive few services not mandated by the contracts with the state and prisoners are warehoused even more than in the public sector. With little accountability for their actions and immune to laws governing the public sector, these institutions are primed to create more abuse and more dangerous felons.

THE LAWYERS

Shakespeare once wrote "The first thing we do, let's kill all the lawyers" (*Henry IV*, Part 2). Since Shakespeare's day the reputation of lawyers has only gotten worse. The vast array of lawyer jokes attest to the fact that attorneys are viewed with suspicion and distrust. Surely, fees and billing procedures have something to do with this lack of respect. Popular stereotypes of lawyers as money-grubbing ambulance chasers also play into this image. In addition, the adversarial nature of the courtroom may serve to contribute to the negative image of attorneys by the public.

The intent of this text, however, is not to examine why lawyers have a negative image but to examine the criminal justice system. The role of lawyers is great in the fiasco our system has become. Lawyers deserve a special share of the blame in the big picture, because unlike the public or even politicians (granted a large percentage are attorneys) lawyers interface with the criminal justice system daily and have knowledge of the process. To determine the manner in which lawyers adversely affect the criminal justice system, let us more clearly define the parameters of the discussion. Civil cases, probate court, and the like will be excluded so that the focus may be more clearly on the criminal justice side of the equation.

Attorneys, both prosecutors and defense, are officers of the court. While defense attorneys have a clear allegiance to their clients, prosecutors also have the duty and burden to see that justice is served. The legal system is founded upon the adversarial nature of the process, presenting both sides of the case and letting the case be impartially judged by a jury. The idea is that through presentation of both sides of the issue, justice will prevail.

Rarely do cases proceed in this manner, however. The American Bar Association (1996) estimates that over 90 percent of all cases are routinely plea bargained. It has been estimated that, if every defendant in the U.S. requested a jury trial, the entire system would grind to a halt in a matter of weeks. In the service of keeping the system running, therefore, felons are offered plea bargains to various offenses as a matter of course. Often, the charge for which an individual pleads guilty has little connection to the offense he committed.

At face value the degree of plea bargaining that occurs appears to be a necessity that has emerged from desperate attempts to handle the volume of cases in most courts. But this is a naïve position that fails to consider the operation of the business of an attorney. Defense attorneys make money by either (a) getting their client off the hook or (b) obtaining a lesser sentence than the defendant expects from trial. No lawyer gets rich by engaging in a long jury trial where their client gets life. Only in high-profile cases where one gets a lot of free publicity or has a wealthy client does it make economic sense to take a case to trial. Those willing to represent an indigent in a protracted trial without media exposure are rare.

Court-appointed attorneys operate even more under this strain. The wages paid to public defenders for defending indigents do not amount to a large cash cow for them but rather a means to an end. Many states even have limits on the amounts they will pay for defense in these cases. Alabama, for example, limits even capital cases to $2000 (Herringer, 1999). As those aware of attorney billing procedures can attest, most funds utilized for public defenders are used up even in a plea bargain. It is then in the financial interest of public defenders to settle the case as soon as possible.

Prosecutors are likewise encouraged to attempt plea bargains as a matter of course. One does not move up in the district attorney's office by taking twelve cases a year to court and convicting twelve of the most desperate felons in the city. Instead, getting ahead politically in the prosecutor's office is more a matter of clearance rates and volume of cases handled. Recent court trials have demonstrated that it can be politically and professionally damaging to try a case and lose, especially if it is high-profile and politically sensitive. Witness the damage done to Marcia Clark and Christopher Darden's careers as a result of losing the Simpson verdict. Both eventually left the Los Angeles County prosecutor's office and appear to have begun new careers as television analysts. Note that the prosecutor who went after Kervorkian came to be seen as more and more fanatical as he persisted in trying someone with wide popular support. Although he eventually won conviction against Kervorkian, future political aspirations were diminished by his actions.

The argument could be made that attorneys are merely doing the best they can under trying circumstances. But is this really the case? An alternative view is that both prosecutors and defense attorneys shirk their duties through the practice of plea bargaining. District attorneys often use their office as a stepping stone to political office. During elections, former D.A.'s trot out statistics concerning their conviction rates and the number of felons they have put behind bars. I cannot recall a single campaign ad that stated the candidate plea bargained the majority of their cases, even though this is how one is able to put large numbers behind bars.

If the courts are truly "getting tough," should this be the case? After all, if someone has committed premeditated murder, should they be allowed to plead guilty to a lesser charge in order to keep the court calendar running smoothly? Should drug dealers be allowed to plead guilty to possession to avoid trial and sentence? At present our system not only says yes but rewards defendants for cooperating. Justice has become a game that both sides play, colluding to avoid trial.

The presence of plea bargaining has become an accepted part of the system. Plea bargaining is so ubiquitous that it has become a tool of sorts in keeping the court system flowing smoothly. The nature of the plea bargaining process was made clear to me through reading arrest reports, initial charges filed, and then seeing the actual charge for which an individual would be sentenced. It is so heavily used that defendants are routinely overcharged, that is, charged with a crime more serious than they committed or that there is evidence to support, in order to force the issue of a plea bargain. This process creates a situation where those facing trial are made to feel that they are getting a deal too good to refuse by plea bargaining to lesser charges. Only the occasional felon will risk a jury trial even on trumped-up charges because of the nature of the process, which is stacked heavily in favor of the prosecution.

One factor has begun to alter the practice of plea bargains. The emphasis on determinate sentencing and the possibility of life in prison under "three strikes" has forced many people into jury trials. Twice-convicted felons have no choice but to request jury trials under three strikes. Sentencing guidelines are so strict that plea bargains do little to reduce jail time in these cases. As a consequence, anyone facing sentencing under this legislation should request a jury trial. At least a trial might lead to some possibility of getting off, even if guilty. Defense attorneys plea bargaining in such cases are likely bordering on malpractice.

In sum, a court system that relies on plea arrangements between the prosecutor and the defense attorney does little to further the cause of justice. It exists for expediency and is viewed by most criminals as a game to be manipulated. Attorneys should be held culpable for their participation in this charade because they are aware of the consequences. At present, both sides, prosecution and defense, exist in a duplicitous contract to further their own ends and cover up the disservice being done to society at large.

Chapter 5

BALL FOUR: "SOLUTIONS" THAT MISS THE PLATE

This isn't a court of justice son, this is a court of law.

—Billy Bragg

As noted in the previous chapter, the drive to get reelected on the part of politicians has led to criminal justice policy being shaped by the fifteen-second sound bite and complete pandering to the lowest common denominator. Such efforts to put forth simplistic, one-size-fits-all solutions to extremely complex and multiply determined problems such as crime has led to a plethora of nice-sounding but ill-fated "solutions."

These various solutions have invariably made matters worse with regard to issues of overcrowding, violence, fairness in sentencing, and the attendant costs of prison and justice efforts (Alleman and Gido, 1998; Johnston, 1999; "Senate OKs tighter drug penalties," 1999). Moreover, these efforts have hampered what little attempts there are towards rehabilitation. Some of the major culprits that have issued forth from get-tough, feel-good legislation include determinate sentencing, mandatory minimums, truth-in-sentencing, "three strikes," pay-for-stay, and the resurgence of popularity of the death penalty. These efforts, which are little more than attempts to lengthen sentences and make prison even worse, are detrimental in the long run to the goals of rehabilitation and to lowering crime.

DETERMINATE SENTENCING, MANDATORY MINIMUMS
AND TRUTH-IN-SENTENCING

Determinate sentencing is a new trend in the criminal justice system that seeks to remove judges' discretion in the handling of cases. Previously, sentences for various crimes were wide ranging with penalties stretching from no time to many years. In some circumstances this may have led to arbitrary and capricious sentences being handed down. But it allowed for the judge to consider the circumstances of the case, the nature of the individual charged, and many other factors. Determinate sentencing takes this discretion away from the judge and dictates for how long certain crimes require incarceration.

No longer are judges allowed to consider whether someone was stealing to feed their family or any other circumstance, the sentence is determined by the charge. California alone has over 1200 different determinate sentencing laws (Moore, 1998). By this practice, judges become little more than rubber stamps. The exact point at which the experience and expertise of the judge can help ensure that justice is served most properly is the moment at which all power is taken away. It is as if some decision has been made on the part of the politicians making the laws that judges cannot be trusted to do their jobs.

Related to determinate sentencing, and at times synonymous or nearly indistinguishable, are the approaches referred to as "mandatory minimums" and "truth-in-sentencing." Mandatory minimums come from the idea that for certain crimes, mandatory sentences of at least a certain minimum length are required. In the case of crimes covered by these laws, individuals must serve a certain amount of time no matter what their behavior in prison, no matter their actual involvement in the crime or even past criminal history.

Interestingly, but likely not coincidentally, mandatory minimums seem to be applied primarily to areas that disproportionately affect minorities the most. An example is in the penalties formerly applied to crack versus powder cocaine. Chemically identical, the two substances are essentially just two different forms of cocaine. However, the use of crack is heavily associated with African-Americans, while powder is associated with whites. The federal penalties for the two substances have long been drastically different, with crack having a mandatory minimum sentence of five years for five grams while powder cocaine can be zero time for the same amount. There exists no logical basis for this disparity. Congress recently attempted to address this disparity, but instead of lightening penalties for crack only engaged in more "get tough" legal policy by increasing the penalties for powder cocaine. Despite pleas that this action would further increase prison overcrowding, the measure was easily ratified ("Senate OKs tighter drug penalties," 1999).

Mandatory minimums are quickly becoming a growing and significant segment of the prison population (Moore, 1998). Meanwhile, as a result of overcrowding, large numbers are being released who were incarcerated prior to this legislation. As mandatory minimums apply primarily to drug offenders, a situation has been created where violent felons are being released to make room for drug offenders. Ironically, this legislation is having the effect of releasing the very people who should be incarcerated, while holding for excessive periods of time those who should likely be in rehab or the mental health system. I envision that in the very near future those doing mandatory sentences will overwhelm the system to such a degree that parole dates will be set at sentencing so that inmates can be released to make room for others as soon as possible.

Truth-in-sentencing, another of the efforts to lengthen sentences and remove any efforts from judges to exercise discretion, is similar to the other approaches. The origins are slightly different, with truth-in-sentencing arising out of the victims' rights movement. As such, its focus is on ensuring longer periods of incarceration and the abolition of "good time" in prison. This approach basically turns a blind eye to the idea that people can change or rehabilitate by seeking assurances that those convicted will do their full time and not be released early.

All of these approaches, which at base seek to lengthen sentences, fail to consider their long-term effects on the system and within the walls of prison. Such efforts have a deleterious effect on the ability to control successfully the prison population. When time served is predetermined, there is little left to modulate the actions of those who are incarcerated. As a result prison becomes a very dangerous place for both inmates and staff. Effects on staff is an issue rarely considered in most prison proposals. When prison becomes dangerous and harsh to inmates, it does so to staff as well. By creating a miserable work environment, a revolving door of prison personnel soon results in an overworked, stressed-out staff that struggles just to survive their shifts.

The ultimate detrimental effect of efforts to increase sentences is the increase in prison populations and the resultant overcrowding. It is already a burden in terms of resources and economic costs to incarcerate the numbers we have in prison as figures throughout this text will support. By ensuring that parole is more difficult and sentences are longer, the situation can only get worse. Prisons will become more violent because behavior has nothing to do with release. Costs will rise as the need for greater security and the massive construction of infrastructure becomes apparent. In fact, both the building of infrastructure and heightened security have already been necessitated, but this phenomenon is only beginning. This is particularly tragic in light of the fact that if prisons were remotely successful, the prison population and costs would actually be going down. At times it seems as if we are trying to make matters worse.

THREE STRIKES

"Three strikes" legislation on the surface sounds good. This approach is grounded in the concept that "enough is enough" and after a certain point society needs to remove career criminals from our midst. "Three strikes" adopts the solution that after three felonies a person should receive life in prison, basically to be removed from society. As I stated, this sounds good initially, but as one begins to look at the policy in practice and its psychological impact, a wide variety of problems become apparent.

"Three strikes" legislation was first proposed in California by Mike Reynolds, the father of a murdered teenager. Originally the legislation appeared to have no chance of winning. However, during the campaign the Polly Klaas kidnapping and murder occurred. The arrest of Richard Allen Davis for these crimes served to catapult three strikes into the limelight. Davis was a multiple felon, who made the perfect "poster boy" for three strikes (Moore, 1998).

Ironically, Davis would likely never have been paroled had it not been for determinate sentencing laws. He is exactly the kind of individual who would never be released under the more indeterminate sentencing structures that existed before California legislators got tough and began to "fix" the system. Interestingly, the entire Klaas family eventually opposed three strikes because of their concerns about the legislation and its effect on nonviolent offenders (Meet the Press, 1994).

First and foremost, "three strikes" policies are the pinnacle in the surrender of the rehabilitation approach. The approach that after three felony convictions one is completely beyond efforts to produce change sends the implied message that our system can do nothing. As our current approach makes only a minimal effort at rehabilitation, this assessment is probably accurate. "Three strikes" seems to further concede that our current approach is a failure or we would not be producing three-time felons. The admission that our policies are an utter failure is likely the most valuable contribution of "three strikes" legislation to future productive policy.

A tricky assumption lies at the heart of the problems for "three strikes" legislation. This assumption is another variation of the one-size-fits-all approach and views all felonies as the same. In application, "three strikes" legislation views theft of a candy bar as equivalent to armed robbery and violent assaults. In the four years following the passage of "three strikes" legislation, one in five inmates in California were sentenced under three strikes. Ninety percent had only one strike and up to 80 percent were nonviolent (Moore, 1998).

Consider the case of Gregory Taylor in California. Taylor was convicted of burglary in 1997 and given twenty-five years to life for breaking into a church kitchen. Even though the church's minister testified on his behalf that he had given him food in the past and had even allowed him to sleep in the church, this sentence was upheld by appellate courts in 1999. Making the case even more egregious is the fact that his previous convictions had occurred in the 1980s with his most recent brush with the law being for a parole violation in 1988 ("Life sentence upheld," 1999).

It is a strain on credulity that the intent of "three strikes" legislation is to incarcerate for life a homeless man stealing food. Further, when ten years have elapsed between crimes it is difficult to imagine that this man was a serious threat to society. Likely he is a victim of a collapsing social service net that is becoming weakened from dealing with the increasing numbers of marginalized people in our society.

Then there is the case of Kendall Cook, who was given a life sentence for stealing a beer from a convenience store (Moore, 1998). Here again, an individual who in all probability needs substance abuse treatment is going to receive life in prison. As a taxpayer, I cannot believe the lack of foresight that suggests it is better to pay $25,000 a year to incarcerate a man than to place him in treatment. This case clearly illustrates that focusing on punishment for the crime while excluding the motivation for the crime can create a complete miscarriage of justice.

The case of Phillip Sanders of Florida is perhaps the most shocking in this tragic parade. Arrested for stealing a roll of toilet paper from Wal-Mart, he now faces life. Although a shoplifter, Sanders was prosecuted as a violent offender because he had a pocketknife during the theft ("Underwear thief gets life," 1998). It is not clear that he used the pocketknife in any way in commission of the theft but merely that he had it in his possession. Such cases serve to demonstrate the poorly considered consequences of such policies as "three strikes." Surely, such outcomes could not have been the original intent of the legislation, yet without judicial discretion all checks and balances on this sort of travesty have been removed.

When Gregory Taylor was sentenced, the dissenting judge on the appellate bench commented that he viewed the individual as some pitiful version of a modernday Jean Valjean ("Life sentence upheld," 1999). This character in Victor Hugo's *Les Misérables* is often thought of as an example of how draconian punishment was under less enlightened governments in harsher times. It seems to register with few people that under three strikes legislation, Jean Valjean got off easier than Gregory Taylor.

Cases such as the above are by no means rare. To list all the individuals convicted of petty or trivial offenses and given life would likely consume this entire volume. But the effects of "three strikes" can be even more extreme. Consider the result when an individual who has been to prison, been gang raped, and subjected to all the other features that go along with the miserable prison experience is about to be apprehended by the police for a third felony. It is not a stretch of the imagination to suppose that such a person would want to avoid capture. Rather than surrendering and dealing with a short sentence, a person might flee to avoid arrest. If armed, shooting it out with police might be seen as a viable alternative.

It is impossible to say exactly what percentage of those attempting to flee crimes in high speed chases or who shoot at the police to get away are facing life for a third felony. However, CBS News reported as early as 1997 that there was a noticeable increase in high speed chases and attempts to flee capture as a result of three strikes laws. It is highly probable that a certain percentage of those committing such acts are acting out of fear of life in prison. One wonders how many police and innocent bystanders will have to be killed by felons who may otherwise have surrendered before we see the folly of this approach.

Earlier I implied that "three strikes" is unfair because it treats all crimes the same. Beyond this issue is the fact that in application three strikes has racist overtones. This results from the interaction of several factors. Primary among these is that minorities are disproportionately stopped, detained, and searched. As a focus of police attention, it is far more likely that minorities will be caught, and this may account to some degree for the numbers of minorities arrested.

Whether or not the above explanation is accurate, "three strikes" legislation disproportionately affects minorities. Forty percent of those incarcerated under three strikes legislation in California are African-American, even though African-Americans comprise only about 3 percent of the population of that state (Moore, 1998). With one in every three young African-American males in California under some type of supervision by the criminal justice system (*Uniform Crime Reports*, 1998), it is hard to believe the system is color blind. The disproportionate application of the law to minorities can be seen in the statistics showing that although African-Americans constitute only 13 percent of drug users (also proportion in the general population), they constitute 35 percent of arrests for drug offenses, 55 percent of those convicted of possession, and 74 percent of those serving time for drug offenses (Wideman, 1995).

Finally, the unavoidable effect of "three strikes" is that it produces even more overcrowded and violent prisons. By having so many unpardonable inmates, prison populations will necessarily rise, necessitating the construction of even more prison space. Moreover, lifers tend to have few constraints on their actions. As a result, prison becomes even more dangerous not only for inmates but for correctional employees as well. Even those doing mandatory minimums are likely to be at risk from "three strikes" lifers. As I stated, the approach initially sounds good and that is why it made such a nice sound bite. In practice, however, it is a horrible approach with numerous unforeseen consequences.

PAY-FOR-STAY

In addition to the above efforts to strengthen penalties and lengthen sentences, a corresponding approach seeks to make the prison experience even more miserable. This approach is grounded in some mistaken notion that life in prison is easy. The argument usually put forth is that prisoners are costing society too much for us to be content for inmates to sit around all day lifting weights and eating for free.

The above argument seems to suggest that prison is a place where inmates do nothing but enjoy themselves all day. The image that springs to mind is film footage of Richard Speck, a mass murderer, who bragged on camera that he was having a great time in prison. I guess if being a homosexual prostitute in prison in order to feed one's drug habit is great, then he was having a good time. His statement is more a comment on the need for individuals in prison to act tough for the outside world than any real comment on the prison experience. In reality, prison is a vicious, miserable experience. Few inmates or parolees are honest with people on the outside concerning the realities of prison life because they are shamed and embarrassed by their lives. If any reader truly believes prison is a good and easy life, I invite you to visit a prison. If you can arrange it, maybe you can even spend the night to see how much fun it is.

Let us look at some of the recent efforts to make prison more miserable. Numerous politicians and law enforcement officials have decried the fact that weight rooms and exercise yards are leading to prisoners becoming physically fit and strong. The assumption is that this is "fun" and, therefore, prisoners should be deprived of this activity. Among inmates, there is a different motivation for this activity. Namely, if one is going to survive in prison, becoming physically strong is a necessity. This is not in order to fight with guards but to deal with the other prisoners. Without weights inmates resort to calisthenics and other forms of exercise in their cells to remain healthy.

Excruciating boredom is a secondary factor that motivates exercise. A fact of prison life that is often overlooked is that there is nothing to do. In order to remain sane, one must do something. With few rehabilitation efforts and little to keep one occupied, prisoners rely on what they have access to. To maintain order in prison, more activities are needed day to day, not fewer. It is in this area that policymakers demonstrate a complete lack of awareness. Bureaucrats, administrators, and the general population often view efforts to provide prisoners with any type of activity as coddling them rather than assisting in the orderly operation of the institution. If prisoners were kept busy, prison officials would not have to spend all of their energy ensuring that the prison operates smoothly.

Depriving prisoners of exercise is not only mean-spirited and likely unconstitutional, it is also senseless and almost guaranteed to create problems. The concept that links boredom and frustration to aggression is not new. Numerous social psychologists over the years have maintained that aggression is the result of frustration (Allport, 1954; Dollard, Doob, Miller, Mowrer and Sears, 1939; Pettigrew, 1971). The frustration-aggression hypothesis of violence clearly predicts that the efforts to make prison harsher and more punitive would only lead to increased violence. By depriving inmates of exercise, physical activity, and even mental activity is to increase the restlessness, stress, and aggression that exist within the prison. This can only lead to more violence and less acceptance of prosocial values.

Of particular note in poorly conceptualized measures designed to be more punishing is the idea of pay-for-stay. This idea, which derives from the notion that using taxpayer money to house and feed inmates is a burden, can only be called stupidity at its height. This approach, especially popular in county jails, attempts to bill inmates for their stay. By charging inmates, the rationale goes, they are truly paying for their time.

Albuquerque, New Mexico, is a municipality that attempted such a program. Inmates were billed $40 a day for their time in the Bernalillo County jail. After eighteen months the program was abandoned as an absolute failure after administrative costs had led to a $141,636 deficit. The deficit occurred as a result of costs of staffing the program and attempts at collection. The final reason was, not surprisingly, that 93 percent of those incarcerated refused to pay for their jail time (TV7–KOAT, New Mexico).

Therein lies the bottom line in all pay-to-stay programs: They fail because people refuse to pay. By expecting people to pay for jail time as if it is a service, logic and human nature are completely disregarded. Few people, and even fewer criminals, are going to pay for something that is forced upon them and that they do not want. There is really no way to make people pay for such an offense as we no longer have debtors' prisons. Will we begin to look at refusal to pay for jail time as a theft of services charge similar to leaving a hotel without paying? If so, will this count in three strikes legislation?

ONE SPECIAL CASE

Maricopa County, Arizona, under the direction of its sheriff, Joe Arpaio, deserves special mention with regard to unusual and draconian measures. Professing a "zero tolerance for the criminal element," Arpaio has instituted a variety of measures to address crime in the Phoenix area. According to the web site for the sheriff's department, the jail houses 1600 inmates in tents and has banned tobacco, coffee, movies, unrestricted television viewing and hot lunches. Further, the department brags that its "gleaning" program, which utilizes substandard and nonfood items in meal preparation, has cut the cost of meals to 40 cents per inmate per meal. The web site (Maricopa County Sheriff's Office, 1999) also states that Maricopa was the first jurisdiction to place women on chain gangs and in tents.

The department refers to itself as on the leading edge and reports an 85 percent approval rating from the public. Further, over 2500 local citizens have been involved in a volunteer "posse" to help eradicate crime. This "posse" has participated in actions against both prostitutes and cigarette distributors.

Arpaio's background is as a DEA agent who served in Turkey in the 1960s. Apparently it was here that he also developed his understanding of human rights. While many of Arpaio's programs enjoy wide support and many other jurisdictions are interested in adapting these programs, there is no evidence that these measures lower crime. The real motivation for these actions can be seen in the information left off the web site in that one of the "features" of the county jail is the introduction of pink jumpsuits for inmates. Clearly, this action is designed to humiliate and degrade inmates.

This case is enlightening in that it demonstrates the level to which the criminal justice system has descended. In the name of get tough and zero tolerance we are moving steadily towards an abusive system that tramples on human rights and dignity. Programs that are harsh and overly punitive are favored even though there is no indication that they actually reduce crime. Meanwhile, efforts to increase rehabilitation are scoffed at as "soft on crime."

THE DEATH PENALTY

Since Gary Gilmore requested that the state of Utah execute him in 1977, the various states of U.S. have executed a total of over 580 people as of November 1999 (Death Penalty Information Center [DPIC], 1999). Southern states as a whole execute the majority of all people. According to the Death Penalty Information Center (1999), southern states have executed over 80 percent of the total number of people receiving the death penalty in the United States. Two states in particular, Texas and Virginia, seem to be in a contest with each other executing 192 and 71, respectively, since 1977 (as of November 1, 1999). Texas leads in actual numbers, while Virginia leads in per capita executions (DPIC, 1999). At present there are over 3500 individuals on death row throughout the country including over seventy juveniles, according to the Death Penalty Information Center (Streib, 1998). At present the death penalty seems to have wide governmental support and mass public appeal.

Despite the above support and frequency of use, the case can be made that the United States is greatly out of step in its use of this measure being the only western industrialized nation to have the death penalty and one of only a few countries in the world that executes juveniles. In fact, when we examine the countries in the world that still utilize the death penalty, the United States finds itself in some pretty terrible company. According to the Death Penalty Information Center, 104 countries have completely abolished the death penalty. Further, of the twenty countries that utilize the death penalty the most frequently, most tend to be countries that are dictatorships or have miserable human rights records (see Table 5.1).

Table 5.1
Ten Countries Executing the Most People*

Country	Number Executed
China	1,876
Iran	143
Saudi Arabia	122
United States	74
Kazakstan	35
Sierre Leone	35
Nigeria	33
Belarus	30
Taiwan	29
Kyrgystan	26

*Figures given are for 1997, the most recent year available.

Source: Death Penalty Information Center (DPIC) website, http://www.essential.org/dpic/dpicintl.html.

Nevertheless, there seems to be almost fanatical devotion to the death penalty as a means of punishment in our country. Deterrence is often given as one of the primary justifications for continuation of the death penalty as a sanction. Were this true, then there would be less crime in states that pursue the death penalty. Texas and Virginia, as noted, execute more people than any other states. Yet, according to *Uniform Crime Reports* (1998), neither of these states has murder rates lower than the nation at large. In fact, the six states with the lowest murder rates have no death penalty (Uniform Crime Reports, 1998). These statistics leave only two possible conclusions: Either Texas and Virginia are particularly lawless or the death penalty is not a significant deterrent.

Deterrence is relevant only to those who plan to get caught or think there is a good chance they will be caught. Most crimes that warrant the death penalty involve either premeditation or a particularly gory and grisly set of circumstances. When people commit crimes, especially premeditated murder, they almost always attempt to get away with it. Those who commit the crime and then get caught are certainly not deterred. Conversely, if one commits murder and plans to get caught, one's mental capacities are in question and an insanity defense is a likelihood. Deterrence, therefore, is not a viable rationale for the continuation of this sanction.

Cost is the other rationale often given to support the death penalty. Unfortunately for those who put forth this argument, they are on the wrong side. It has long been established that it costs more to execute an individual than to imprison him/her for life (DPIC, 1999). The factors that contribute to this situation are myriad and include heightened security measures on death row, additional staff, and suicide watches. The most costly factor is the nature of appeals and legal efforts to ensure this is the appropriate measure.

The knee-jerk reaction to the actual costs of executing someone has been to limit appeals and court processes. But this is not a solution and serves only to undermine our entire legal system. The U.S. system of jurisprudence is founded on the belief that it is better for 1000 guilty people to go free than for one innocent person be wrongfully convicted . Arguments to limit appeals are essentially arguments to abandon the cornerstone of our entire legal system.

Limiting appeals is particularly egregious in death penalty cases because once the sentence is carried out, there can be no further reversals or presentation of new evidence. This is the reason why it is necessary to exhaust every means of appeal and every avenue of legal action before the sentence is applied. The state of Illinois provides a perfect example of the problems with the death penalty in this regard. Since 1977, when the Supreme Court reversed itself and began allowing death sentences to be carried out, Illinois has executed eleven individuals. However, during this same time period they released ten people who were on death row after they had been exonerated (CBS News, February 3, 1999). Three more individuals were later exonerated that year leading to the governor of Illinois imposing a moratorium on further executions.

Note that the ten did not have their sentences commuted. They were exonerated. In at least one case the officers were later charged with manufacturing evidence (Moran, 1999). To make matters worse, the police and prosecutor who went along with this faced less time upon conviction than the wrongfully convicted man, Rolando Cruz. But Illinois is not alone. Since 1977, as of June 1, 1999, seventy-seven prisoners nationwide have been freed from death row after being found not guilty of the crimes for which they were originally convicted (DPIC, 1999).

Logic would suggest that in order to gain a conviction in a capital punishment case there should be an overwhelming preponderance of evidence to support the conviction. But as the statistics from Illinois suggest, this is not always the case. Psychological reasons likely are at least partially responsible. In order for capital punishment even to be raised as an issue, the crime generally is either exceptionally gory, emotionally touching, or involves some other factor that takes it out of the mainstream. The infusion of emotions into matters leads to poor decision making. The outrage over the crime, coupled with prosecutors' "someone must pay" declarations, leads to poor legal decisions. It is these very factors, emotionality and the possibility of being wrong, that demonstrate the importance of the appeals process in capital punishment cases. Remember, the purpose of the legal system is not to uphold every verdict and ensure everything functions smoothly, but that justice be served.

When one looks at the arguments against the death penalty there are basically two major ones. The first is that the death penalty is unequally applied and the second is that it is a barbaric practice. The idea that the death penalty is inequitably applied and thus in violation of the Constitution seems to have sound support. The Government Accounting Office conducted an empirical study of the death penalty and concluded there is "a pattern of evidence indicating racial disparities in the charging, sentencing and imposition of the death penalty" (Herringer, 1999). The race of the victim has been found to have a strong influence on the imposition of the death penalty. An individual charged with killing a white person is 4.3 times more likely to receive the sanction than someone who killed a black person. Factoring in the race of the accused makes the results even more startling. A black person who kills a white person is nineteen times more likely to draw the death penalty than a white person killing a black person (United States General Accounting Office, 1990). Gender inequity is even greater, with men receiving almost all death row placements.

The case of Dawud Abdullah Muhammad in North Carolina indicates the extreme effects racism can have upon the judicial process. Muhammad was convicted of a double murder that occurred in 1980. Even though the prosecutor, Carroll Lowder, was chastised by District Court Judge James McMillan for "a pattern of prosecutorial abuse" for withholding evidence and the fact that there were at least three other possible suspects, Muhammad was convicted by an all-white jury and sentenced to death (Bates, 1998). The U.S. Supreme Court denied final federal appeal and the execution occurred on November 19, 1999. Although there is evidence that points to Muhammad in the case, there is also the presence of many other factors, including a blond hair at the crime scene and a witness who saw a blond man jump from the victim's balcony around the time of the murder, which suggests he may be innocent (Bates, 1998).

The idea that the death penalty is cruel and unusual punishment is another issue in this hotly contested battle. Psychologically, it is likely that the waiting period prior to the execution is in some ways worse than the punishment. In fact, the lag between sentence and execution seems more closely attuned to torture than the actual sentence. The average length of time on death row prior to execution is over ten years (DPIC, 1999; Steib, 1998). To almost anyone, spending ten years contemplating the possibility of death around the corner is taxing.

Despite efforts to make the punishment more "humane," as if killing someone can be done in a humane way, things occasionally go awry. Consider the case of David Lawson. Diagnosed while in prison as being chronically and clinically depressed, he was executed by the state of North Carolina. Of course, execution of the mentally ill is not unique. In Harper v. Washington, the defendant was forcibly treated against his will for "his own good" so that he could become sane enough to be executed. But in the Lawson case, his mental state was not the most cruel nor unusual element of his execution. Unique to his case was that it took him over eighteen minutes to die in the gas chamber in 1994. After gasping and flailing for nine minutes, he was still alive and took another nine minutes to die. Botched executions are not especially rare. The Death Penalty Information Center has posted an article attributed to Michael Radelet (1999) on its website (http://www.essential.org/dpic/botched.html) of at least twenty-five executions where things went awry including "blood pouring" from the head of the executed and the electric chair catching fire. The presentation of the death penalty as something that can be carried out in a humane manner is one of the factors that makes it more palatable to the vast majority of people. The often grisly nature of real executions is an issue few people choose to think about.

Retribution is another, and perhaps most honest, reason for support of the death penalty based on the rationale that this is the ultimate punishment and prevents the person from killing again. This approach seems to ignore the alternative sentence of life without possibility of parole. It is reasonable to suggest that for most people on death row, the actual sentence is something of a relief. Gary Gilmore began the current trend towards capital punishment when he requested that he be executed. His point of view was that life in prison was intolerable. Many inmates on death row view the wait as the difficult part. Life in prison is no great bonus. Those serving life are in some ways being punished more than those executed.

What then is wrong with life without the possibility of parole? It meets all the requirements for punishment, retribution, and even cost given for the death penalty. It just doesn't satisfy our bloodlust. To illustrate the role this plays in our psyche, note that Texas even has a law that allows relatives of the victim to witness executions. It may be that the psychological need for capital punishment is just another symptom of the violence inherent in our society.

Chapter 6

GANGS, MILITIAS, AND ORGANIZED CRIME

When you live in the shadow of insanity, the appearance of another mind that thinks and talks as yours does is something close to a blessed event.

—Robert Pirsig

Since at least the 1920s with the advent of prohibition and the resulting profits that flowed from it, criminals have organized themselves to work towards certain goals. This activity is not limited to the U.S., as can be seen from the *yakuza* in Japan, La Cosa Nostra, both here and in Italy, triads in Asia, drug cartels in South America, and many other such groups. The fact that these and similar organizations exist across time and geographical regions indicates this phenomenon is neither unique nor in danger of extinction.

Throughout other sections of this text I have argued that by and large crime is committed in a poorly thought out, opportunistic fashion by individuals. On the whole, this is true. However, it is with the presence of organized groups that there is some truth to the idea that a small group can have enormous and widespread effects. It can be demonstrated, however, that this effect is radically different from the public perception and that many of the most challenging aspects of organized crime could be best addressed though social policy. Unlikely as that is, the onus is on the justice system to develop a more successful approach to dealing with this subset of the prison population. The development of a successful approach to this group will require understanding of the social conditions in which these groups exist and the acceptance of certain unpleasant and stark realities of gang life.

The old-style Mafia, made famous in so many movies, is at present a crumbling, faded empire. The advent of RICO (Racketeer Influenced and Corrupt Organization) laws, which circumvent actual evidence and use association and intent as proof of wrongdoing, have severely disrupted the primary families of the Mafia. The "Teflon Don," John Gotti, is in prison along with many other leaders. The unheard of, testifying against fellow "goodfellows," occurs with frequency and things are not what they once were when Al Capone ruled Chicago and Bugsy Siegel created Las Vegas. Despite all this, the Mafia does serve as a viable starting point for examining the nature of organized crime.

The Mafia, in a way, established the pattern for the successful organization of a criminal enterprise. First and foremost, they were a close-knit, closed society. One could not join merely by asking. There had to be an invitation to join based on factors such as friendship, kinship and prior actions. To show up and try to infiltrate such a group was to risk one's life.

Basing inclusion on kinship, family ties, friendship and even allegiances going back to the "old country" led to bonds being formed that made this more than a criminal enterprise—a social and cultural phenomenon. Outsiders who did not fully fit the mold had to prove themselves through the commission of serious illegal acts before being allowed any privilege within the group. In this manner, bonds are also formed and strengthened because everyone has something on someone else.

These factors led to an ability to avoid infiltration by police, especially at a time when police were stereotypically Irish and Mafioso were Italian. Those apprehended never talked because to do so meant death for oneself and one's family. Taking the rap conversely led to increased status and protection of one's family. Also, the ensuing social and cultural ties that developed led to a sense of a higher purpose in one's actions and even imprisonment.

When incarcerated, membership had a somewhat protective effect and at times status within the system. The ruthless reputation that proceeded led to better treatment by other prisoners and likely by prison officials as well. It also had the effect of establishing a support network in prison by association with others with similar ties. Although the Mafia is not what it once was, many of the patterns established by it are prominent among other organized groups today and present a major challenge for justice officials.

STREET GANGS AND MOTORCYCLE CLUBS: WHERE OGs MEET MCs

The rise of street gangs in the 1980s such as the Crips, Bloods, Vice-Lords, Disciples, Latin Kings, and so on, was largely fueled by the enormous profits of the crack trade. The violence that ensued was mainly caused by investing a percentage of these profits into the purchase of firearms. If one believes the popular media or most politicians, one would think that drugs and guns are the only reason such groups exist. In reality this is nothing but a myth. Perpetuation of the myth serves to push an agenda aimed at undermining these groups through legal methods such as RICO laws and questionable search and seizures.

As someone who has worked closely with gang members in a therapeutic capacity, my view of the gang world is shaped by real-life experience. Gang members to me are not an abstraction that I read about in the newspaper or see on television. Rather, gang members are real people with real lives, shaped by the world that is so terrified of them. Gangs exist for a variety of reasons, but it is overly simplistic and simply wrong to insist that drugs and weapons are the only reasons. At best, guns and drugs are secondary to the overall purposes and goals of most gangs. Making guns and drugs go away will not curb the prominence of gangs unless underlying social conditions are also addressed.

Gangs, in the form of motorcycle clubs and street gangs, have existed in this country since at least the 1940s. The first motorcycle clubs were formed by pilots and soldiers returning from World War II, who could not find the thrills they had become accustomed to during the war. Many found something missing related to freedom and excitement. Often these clubs remained nothing more than groups that rode motorcycles together. Others mutated and became groups such as the Hell's Angels and Pagans, which are now the stereotypical image of motorcycle clubs.

In the 1950s gangs were ubiquitous, being little more than social clubs in many senses. The popular television show about this era, "Happy Days," even features a former gang leader as a main character. Yet despite the comedic spin later put on this period, gangs were widely viewed with fear and suspicion. In many ways, the underground or counterculture association of gangs has led to their being viewed with distrust.

Today the rise of the numerous national and local gangs, coupled with their association with drugs and violence, has led to heightened fear of anyone remotely resembling a gang member. This can reach the point of absurdity, especially in areas that have many different gangs, when the police and the general public begin to act upon these stereotypes. One example is the identification of gangs by type and color of clothing. In large cities, hardly a color can be worn that is not associated with some gang or the other. Further, youth style and culture have come to be associated with so-called gang attire to the point that any young person, especially of color, would be considered a gang suspect by the police. But it is this identification of gangs with superficialities that ultimately defeats any efforts to intervene in the gang world. Clothes, colors, and so on, are only surface issues and do not define gangs or their members. Rather, the social organization and context are the defining features and ultimately the glue that binds the groups together.

Social Context of Street Gangs

Like any other social organization, gangs tend to exist to serve purposes for their members that often have little to do with the public image of the group. Further, it is the social organization of the gang that is its primary reason for existence, not the other overt activities engaged in by the group. In this sense, gangs are similar to fraternal organizations that engage in philanthropic and/or quasi-religious activities such as the Rotarians or the Freemasons (interestingly, at least one national gang claims to have been started by the Freemasons).

To put the social nature of gangs in perspective, let us examine the reasons individuals join gangs. To understand the phenomenon of gang life, one must look to where gangs flourish. Generally speaking, gangs do not form in intact traditional societies nor in zones of economic wealth. Instead, gangs thrive in areas of economic depression and social disintegration. The void gangs fill in these respects partly explains their popularity.

Those attracted to association with or membership in a gang are usually searching for something to replace that which is missing in their life. Positive features bestowed by gang membership include:

- sense of family
- sense of belonging
- life direction
- protection
- economic security or benefit
- rites of passage/ indoctrination

To those who did a double-take at the phrase "positive features bestowed by gangs," let me reiterate that I am making the case that gangs have positive benefits to their members. If people did not get something out of belonging to a gang they would not join.

The sense of belonging and the sense of family bestowed by many gangs is likely their ultimate attraction. These functions, whereby one can adopt a group that is explicitly loyal and cohesive, providing protection and power to its members within a society where they would have none of these, are its primary reasons for existence. In this sense, gangs serve to provide positive emotional and social support for their members.

One feature of many gangs for which I developed admiration while working with their members was their ability to be inclusive. Individuals who were ostracized by the larger community, given up on by schools, and so on, were able to find a place in the gang. Gangs tend to be accepting of those who are poor, unusual-looking, disadvantaged, or otherwise disenfranchised. Some gangs seem to be masters of organizational prowess in terms of matching individuals with their skills. Those good with numbers handle and count the money; those who are paranoid make good lookouts; the mean and ruthless are good enforcers. If someone can't read, gangs will find a place for them so that they don't need to read.

Belonging also goes hand in hand with a sense of family. Many gang members come from disintegrated and dysfunctional families. The gang often fills this void and becomes the de facto family. To many, this may be the only family they will ever know. As a result, fierce loyalties develop to the gang, which becomes the dominant social group in the lives of members.

This sense of belonging can even be seen in the protection of "turf." Among many gangs it is common to claim a well-defined area. Those from rival gangs are not permitted to enter its boundaries and to do so is an affront of the highest order. It may seem odd to defend a project or decaying portion of the inner city from rivals, but the larger purpose of this serves to build a sense of belonging and group identification.

Gangs, like all social organizations, exist with a shared set of values. It is ironic that gangs are one of the few elements of our society that attempt to instill a sense of values in its members. Certainly, some of these values are antisocial in nature, but other values such as loyalty, dedication, and commitment to the group would likely be seen as positive by most people. By these statements I am not implying that most street gangs are benevolent societies but that the underlying social structure serves valuable and important functions.

In many areas of numerous inner cities and even in certain prisons, gang membership serves a protective function. To be an independent operator may be exceptionally dangerous. One may need to join a certain group in order to be safe in one's own living space. In certain projects, for example, many kids join gangs just so that walking home is less dangerous. In prison, membership may be a matter of survival.

Finally, gang membership and initiation provide a rites-of-passage experience. In modern society, we no longer have rites of passage for youth to mark their transition to different stages of life. This factor contributes to a sense of directionlessness, malaise, and angst experienced by many youth. By addressing this and other needs, many gangs have become enormously popular with adolescents and young adults. This extends from the inner city to rural areas of reservations.

These rites of passage as marked by gang initiation also serve the purpose of strengthening group identification. Initiation usually involves some form of violence like being "beaten in" where the new initiate is attacked and beaten, sometimes brutally, by every member of the gang. This serves to produce a type of cognitive dissonance that further strengthens ties to the group. Further, membership usually involves adopting a new name or a "street name" that increases identification with the group. Like the old-style Mafia, joining becomes more than just signing up, and the group becomes the dominant social structure of the individual's life.

Organizational Structure

When I began working with gang members, one factor that surprised me was the organizational structure of most of the larger national gangs such as the Disciples, headquartered in Chicago, or the Crips or Bloods from Los Angeles. Basically, these groups are organized along a principle similar to a blending of Amway franchises with pyramid schemes or multilevel marketing concepts. This organizational feature serves to encourage the recruitment of new members and expand the resource base.

The organization of most gangs is decidedly hierarchical and as a result is well suited to utilize a multilevel marketing approach. In fact, one moves up the hierarchy in the same way. When one joins a gang one starts at the bottom and takes orders from the person above. To gain status, one can bring in new members to further the distribution process. To expand, one member moves elsewhere and sets up shop, just like starting a new franchise. This feature is visibly noticeable from within the system when gang members incarcerated in Atlanta or Birmingham are listing Los Angeles and Chicago as residences.

Beyond this organizational overlay there is an intraorganizational structure that is fascinating. Gangs are essentially hierarchical brotherhoods with extremely rigid social structures. While to outsiders some of the following material may seem humorous, even ridiculous, it is taken as seriously as life and death. It can even mean life and death.

One national gang, the Gangster Disciples, allege in their gang mythology that they were started by the Freemasons (*Book of Knowledge*, date unknown). This idea is extended all the way to gang symbolism and "knowledge." Gang "knowledge" is essentially a mythological story of the gang that serves an intricate and intimate function in the gang world. Knowledge is revealed to members only as they rise in rank (similar to the Masons) and serves the function of guarding position in the organization and preventing infiltration. Knowledge is tested among all new or strange/unknown members. Basic knowledge, which is fiercely guarded, is used to determine if one is a genuine member. Knowledge is tested by a series of questions and answers called "spitting." How far one can spit (i.e., answer questions) determines one's rank or place in the pecking order.

Another method of gang identification involves the utilization of hand signs and symbols. Most gangs have a sign that can be made to signify to other members what gang they belong to. Showing this hand signal is known as "flashing a sign." Turning another gang's sign backwards or up-

side down is the ultimate show of disrespect and can be grounds for immediate retaliation and violence. Crossing out another gang's graffiti is a
similar offense.

Between members of the same gang or even rival gangs there is another
process called "stacking" that is more or less a display of rank within one's
own gang. This involves moving one's hands in a complex series of movements that have agreed-upon meanings in order to signify rank. This is a
quick pecking-order display that serves the function of establishing social
rules between near strangers as in cases when two chapters of the same
gang meet. In this sense, the establishment of rank is similar to many
quasi-secret societies. A side-feature of "stacking" is that it also serves the
purpose of filtering out those faking membership, the so called "perpetrators," in the gang world.

A final word on gangs: Contrary to popular belief and to the actions of
law enforcement officials, membership in a gang is not illegal. RICO statutes notwithstanding, in this country individuals have a right to freely associate with anyone they choose. To allege that gangs are solely a criminal
enterprise is to engage in a factual error and to miss the big picture. Gangs
serve a multitude of purposes, particularly for those alienated from mainstream society. If crime were to completely disappear and guns were completely off the street, gangs would continue to exist. Only by examining the
social context that supports these organizations can realistic efforts be
made to address the accompanying social ills. Attempts to cut crime by focusing on organizations, demonstrates a poor understanding of the causes
of crime and the context in which it occurs.

CHALLENGES TO THE CRIMINAL JUSTICE SYSTEM

The ascendance of street gangs in the late 1980s and early 1990s created
challenges for the criminal justice system that few jurisdictions have been
able to address. As noted, there has long been the existence of organized
crime in our society and this will likely continue. Unfortunately, given the
long history of organized crime there has been little substantive effort put
forward to address this issue. Approaches have centered around laws to
make prosecution easier (e.g., RICO statutes), police actions to break up
gangs, and prison efforts that give up any attempts to control the larger and
more organized groups.

All of the above efforts fail to address or even comprehend the real issues. By focusing on the group itself, be they gangs, motorcycle clubs or the
Mafia, instead of behavior (read "criminal activity") as the problem, individual perpetrators are let off the hook to some degree for taking responsibility for their actions. Further, to attempt to break up these associations,
which have been noted to be the only positive feature in many members'
lives, is guaranteed to engender resistance on the part of the groups mem-

bers. This also leads to a sense on the part of prisoners/gang members that they are being persecuted for trying to hold onto the only positive aspect of their life.

These efforts to break or weaken group ties lead to a situation where there is little possibility for change. Instead, the individual is forced even deeper into the us versus them mentality. By concentrating on the trappings of membership such as clothing, beads, hand signs, and so forth, the focus is taken off behavior. It is not the fact that someone is wearing the colors of a certain gang that leads to crimes. And while street gangs or their old-style counterpart, motorcycle clubs, are often the hub around which criminal activity occurs, gangs themselves are not criminal.

A side issue, rarely considered by prison officials, is the fact that most criminals are very content with the current approach, which focuses on irrelevancies. When prison officials and law enforcement focus on membership and association as the problem, the actual criminal behavior tends to take a back seat. As a result, focusing on the trappings of gang membership ultimately lets individuals avoid responsibility for their criminal behavior. What occurs is that gang membership becomes the issue rather than the crime committed by the person. To see the hysteria surrounding this issue by local police one need only enter the phrase "street gangs" into any search engine for the Internet. One will find an enormous number of sites established by police agencies seeking to provide information on gangs and how to identify their members.

But it is not the presence of gangs that is the problem. Instead, it is how to deal with extremely large numbers of inmates who are aligned in one way or another with each other. The presence of many individuals with a common bond leads to the creation of social dominance groups within the walls of prison, which in turn creates large numbers who have the ability to work in concert with each other. These groups can then control and manipulate less powerful prisoners or even groups of prisoners. As dominance and control are major factors of prison life, this leads to even more problems. Large cohesive groups become increasingly difficult for guards or staff to manage. Further, prisoners without any affiliation or peer group often become targets or worse. This is the reason why many individuals join gangs while in prison, it is the only way to function and have any security and peace.

In efforts to address the "gang problem" within prisons, two radically distinct approaches have been tried. Both have their positive and negative features but both ultimately fail for the same reason. Namely, they make membership in the gang the focus rather than the actual behavior that led to incarceration.

The first approach is to try to suppress the gangs. As noted above, this may actually strengthen ties and lead to even greater dedication to the group. An example is when prisons try to ban things associated with group membership. For example, prisoners may be forbidden to wear bandannas associated with their gang. What I have observed happen in this scenario was that members develop clandestine means of identification. This creates a scenario where all the inmates know who belongs to a particular gang but prison staff are clueless. This actually increases the danger to staff during disturbances because it is then impossible to identify who is fighting whom.

Law enforcement and the court system also make this blunder by efforts to suppress and control gangs. An example of such an action is the case of Luis Felipe or "King Blood," the leader of the Latin Kings. Sentenced to life in solitary for allegedly ordering murders from inside prison, the action likely served the interest of the gang itself. By placing him in solitary without any contact with the outside world, he is for all purposes dead to the gang. But no criminal activity will cease. Instead, someone else just becomes the leader. Remember from the organizational structure of gangs that they are rigidly hierarchical. This creates a case where cutting off the head does not kill the beast, it just grows a new head.

In a realistic sense it is advantageous to let the leader operate from behind bars no matter what he may be doing if the purpose is to weaken the gang. Leaders who are incarcerated become notoriously out of touch with what is happening on the street. As a result they are subject to manipulation by their lieutenants and make poor decisions. The nature of life on the streets requires contact in order to know what is going on. A further manner in which letting a leader rule from inside is ultimately detrimental to the gang is that by getting their orders out they eventually involve those outside in conspiracies that are prosecutable as well.

The other approach is to accept gangs as a part of prison life. The only way to do this realistically is to devote certain areas to a particular gang. Some prisons, such as Joliet, have attempted this with, for example, the Bloods getting one cell block and the Crips another. While this solution may minimize the violence within the prison to a minor degree, it does little to address criminal behavior. In fact, this approach likely encourages even more negative behavior within prison by letting group members constantly reinforce each other for their actions. In total, neither suppression nor complete acceptance works. In order to effectively address the behavior of those in gangs the whole issue of gang membership must become a nonissue and not the focus of intervention efforts. In the treatment section, a proposed approach will be advocated.

SPECIAL OFFENDERS

In a sense, gangs are not the only challenge for the criminal justice system that has emerged in recent times. In addition to street gangs, motorcycle clubs, and other organized groups associated with criminal activity, several unique groups present challenges to the criminal justice system by their very nature. For these groups, both organized and not, it is extremely difficult to develop a coherent approach simply by virtue of their crimes.

The groups exist for various purposes, usually to push certain agendas or political philosophies. Among these are militias, hate groups, and what can only be referred to as "politically motivated offenders." The philosophical positions held by these groups make their members psychologically resistant to any consideration that they have acted in a way that is illegal, immoral, or unacceptable. As a result incarceration and treatment of these individuals present a unique challenge to the criminal justice system.

Militias and Hate Groups

According to the Southern Poverty Law Center (1998), there were 523 militias/ "patriot" groups and 474 hate groups in the United States as of 1998. The number of these groups is expected to grow and to have an even greater impact on the criminal justice system. While militias and hate groups are not necessarily the same, there is a great deal of overlap and contact between these various entities.

Hate groups are those whose primary reason for existence is the disparagement of others based on skin color, religion, sexual orientation, or other factors. These groups may express belief in some particular philosophy or set of beliefs, but in general are marked by intolerance and violence. To call these groups politically motivated is to extend far too much credit to actions motivated by hatred.

Militias and the "patriot" groups, in a strict sense, are based on a distrust of and repudiation of the legitimacy of the federal government. Espousing a doctrine based on the Magna Carta, the Articles of Confederation, and other tenuously connected materials (Zeskind, 1998), these groups generally see themselves as consisting of politically persecuted individuals who are fighting a noble and selfless battle against a monolithic entity set on controlling their existence.

Beyond the stated philosophy, however, there often lurks a more sinister background that drives the militia movement. The majority of militia groups are associated with white supremacist organizations and ideology to such a degree that they are at times indistinguishable (Zeskind, 1998). Many of the leaders of the organizations first gained prominence in the "Christian Identity" movement such as Richard Butler of the Aryan Nations and John Trochman of the Militia of Montana. The prominence of such documents as The Protocols of the Elders of Zion (widely regarded as a forgery, but attributed to Nilus [1919]) or the Turner Diaries (Pierce, 1978) muddies the waters when trying to conceptualize these groups. It is this overlap that makes it difficult at times to tell whether they are committing political crimes or are just using this as a front for the commission of hate crimes.

The mix of political and criminal activities is a noteworthy feature of militia groups. In the political sense almost all militias are vociferously opposed to the federal government and view it as illegitimate. Many of their criminal activities are rationalized as the only way to fight against their oppressors. However, in contrast to most political prisoners designated in the following section, their motivations often stem from reasons not necessarily political but driven by hatred, racism, and intolerance.

Political Prisoners

Although Amnesty International recognizes political prisoners in the United States (e.g., Mumia Abu-Jamal and Leonard Peltier), the government officially does not. As that argument is well beyond the scope of this book, discussion here will be limited to a class of individuals who can reasonably be seen as having committed crimes for political reasons. This group of individuals must logically be considered separately, as the motivations behind their actions are paramount to any efforts to change their behavior. Their stated motivations often suggest strong moral or ethical beliefs that make them immune to the majority of treatment efforts that could be utilized with other types of offenders.

Those who commit crimes for political reasons run the gamut of the political spectrum from far left to far right. Usually those who commit these crimes are the most fervent believers in the particular philosophy espoused by their group. Examples of groups or individuals that represent this category of offenders range from the Chicago 8 (often erroneously referred to as the Chicago 7) and Black Panthers of the past up to militia members, anti-abortion protesters, EarthFirst!ers, Ted Kaczynski, Jack Kervorkian, and even animal rights activists of the present. Whether one agrees or disagrees with their viewpoint is not relevant to this discussion. What is important are the motivations behind their actions.

The very commission of crimes by these persons often demonstrates a strong, if not rigid, adherence to a belief system. Their dedication to their beliefs makes them unique in that their crimes are not generally motivated by the typical factors related to crime. Even when apprehended, these individuals rarely feel as if they have done anything morally wrong. Incarceration often makes them martyrs to their causes. Therefore, in many cases, incarceration likely adds some fuel to their movement and may actually strengthen their cause.

When individuals commit politically motivated acts, these are generally well-thought-out and well-planned attacks. Many commit acts that by their very nature tend to draw long prison sentences upon first offense. The acts are often violent and arouse strong feelings in those who want them prosecuted. However, for these particular crimes, no matter how violent or extreme, those who agree with their philosophy often do not think they should be prosecuted at all. Interestingly, this is a good benchmark to determine if a crime is politically motivated. For crimes such as armed robbery or burglary, rarely does any proponent suggest prosecution is immoral.

An example in contrast demonstrates the difficulty in addressing politically motivated actions. Jack Kervorkian, the right-to-die advocate, and Paul Hill, an anti-abortion activist who killed physician John Britton, can be seen as very similar in their adherence to their belief systems. Although clearly on different ends of the political spectrum, their dedication to their beliefs, no matter the outcome, indicates a strong similarity. Also, both serve as prime illustrations of the futility of attempting to change those motivated by political ideology.

In many ways, efforts to change or rehabilitate such individuals go against the grain of American society. Our country is founded upon the belief that one has the right to dissent and to hold unpopular ideas. To attempt to change those motivated by political philosophy violates this concept. Beyond this is the practical concern of what approach is appropriate given that these individuals come from all over the political spectrum. What would be the approach? Make leftists become rightists, make rightists leftists, turn anti-abortionists into pro-choice advocates, ecodefenders into developers? When stated in this manner, efforts to change seem pretty strange and unsettling. Unless we are willing to undertake some type of Khmer Rouge-like reeducation camps, it is nonsensical to suggest these individuals can be changed.

What then can the criminal justice system do to respond to the challenge of political prisoners? Treatment efforts as outlined elsewhere would likely be ineffective. Many of the individuals who commit acts along these lines are extremely different from the general prison population in that they are more educated, have careers, and possess a deeply rooted sense of morality and a willingness to go to prison for their beliefs.

The presence of politically motivated prisoners is a challenge for the criminal justice system. There are no easy, sure remedies for this dilemma. It is safe to say that the reader can identify these unique challenges simply by reflecting on his or her own reactions to one group or the other mentioned herein. It is likely that one's political orientation affects the very conceptualization of what is criminal or not.

One solution is to focus on actions, not motivations. However, this goes against the central premise of this work in that motives do matter. Further, as previously noted, there are enormous practical and philosophical problems with this approach. It may be that the best we can do is to segregate these prisoners into different settings away from the general prison population. Providing a separate facility would at least prevent the expenditure of resources on individuals highly unlikely to change.

It must be recognized that this is an extremely small percentage of the total inmate population. Since most are serving very long sentences or even life, parole is a distant possibility or nonconsideration. Because of these two factors, low numbers and long sentences, making any policy related to other inmates based on this group is misdirected. At present, mere recognition of a class of prisoners who act for political reasons would be a giant step forward.

Chapter 7

JUVENILE CRIME

> Children have never been very good at listening to their elders, but they have never failed to imitate them.
>
> —James Baldwin

Jonesboro, Arkansas. Eleven- and thirteen-year-old open fire on school shooting from the woods. Five are killed and 11 wounded.

West Paducah, Kentucky. Fourteen-year-old opens fire on prayer group at high school. Three killed, 5 wounded.

Springfield, Oregon. Fifteen-year-old kills four at school.

Stamps, Arkansas. Fourteen-year-old wounds two while shooting from the woods.

Pearl, Mississippi. Sixteen-year-old kills two, wounds seven. Six others later charged in connection as part of satanic group.

Littleton, Colorado. Seventeen- and eighteen-year-old juniors assault their high school killing fifteen and wounding over thirty. More than sixty bombs were later found planted in the school.

Englewood, Illinois. Seven- and eight-year-old confess to the murder of an eleven-year-old.

There is perhaps no area of the criminal justice system where public perception so completely overshadows facts, research, and common sense as in the area of juvenile crime. For many reasons, the fear generated among the general public as a reaction to juvenile crime seems to raise more concern than in any other area. Much of this fear arises from the shock value imparted by actions as seemingly discordant as children committing murder. Such actions pull at the fears of a complete breakdown of society and herald a much darker and more frightening future. This is nothing more than letting our hearts get the better of our minds.

The public perception of juvenile crime is wrong. There is no trend towards juveniles committing more crimes today than in the past (see Table 7.1). Rather, our perception and awareness are different. In the distant past when young outlaws like Billy the Kid or John Wesley Harding (who killed his first man at age twelve) were committing crimes, there was no outcry over juvenile crime. General awareness was lower due to poor communications. In the information age the constant barrage of sensational media stories about "natural born" killers with utter disregard for life sells and that is why we are now so sensitized to this issue. According to the American Bar Association, murder coverage quadrupled in the media during the years 1990 to 1995 (ABA, 1996). The real trend is not that there is more juvenile crime. The real trend is that increasingly younger people are being treated as adults by the legal system. This not only ignores the realities of child development but fails to offer society any hope for positive change.

As with many aspects of the criminal justice system, the public perception and subsequent outcry have led to vast changes in public policy that are leading to disastrous decisions. The spate of children shooting children in 1997–1998 has led to increasing cries of "lock 'em up" and "try them as

Table 7.1
Juvenile Arrest Trends, 1990–1996

Crime/Offense	1990	1992	1996	percent change 1990–1996
Murder/Manslaughter	2,169	2,541	2,074	−4.4
Forcible Rape	4,088	4,036	3,768	−7.9
Arson	5,946	6,350	6,783	+13.7
Aggravated Assault	44,613	51,861	52,766	+18.3
Robbery/Burglary	125,629	132,543	128,608	+2.4
Larceny/Theft	336,631	315,942	343,316	+1.4
Motor Vehicle Theft	63,957	64,029	50,925	−20.4
Violent Crimes (Total)	73,756	93,441	96,022	+30.2
Property Crimes (Total)	509,295	483,861	492,218	−3.4
Index Crimes (Total)	583,051	577,302	588,240	+0.01
% Index Crimes/Total	37.9	35.8	30.0	−7.9

Sources: Federal Bureau of Investigation, *Uniform Crime Reports 1996* and Federal Bureau of Investigation, *Uniform Crime Reports 1990.*

adults." The idea that "adult crimes" should get adult time is ubiquitous (Funk, 1997). Again, the slogans are useless and the approach is completely backwards. We do not need to treat children as adults on the grounds that children claim to be adults. Just because kids are acting like adults and telling us vociferously that they are adults, it does not make them adults. There has long been recognition in society that children are different than adults. That is why we have a juvenile justice system, schools, and child labor laws. Children *are* different.

The current trend in the legal system to treat children as adults has vast historical roots of which few seem to be aware. Not so long ago (less than 100 years) children were primarily viewed as domestic commodities necessary for farm work. It was not uncommon even fifty years ago in rural communities for children to leave school with minimal literacy because they were needed on the farm. Further, the movement to end child labor is a relatively recent advance. All of these, schools, child labor laws, and so on, are viewed as positive steps in the advance of society by most people.

The present approach by the legal system would seem to suggest that the pendulum is swinging the other way. Although most states have laws allowing children to be tried as adults as young as fourteen (National Center for Juvenile Justice, 1989), there was a massive uproar in one of the cases listed at the beginning of the chapter because one of the suspects was eleven and therefore could not be tried as an adult. Senators John Chaffee and Oren Hatch advocated lowering the age for the death penalty to eleven as a response. Federal legislation proposed in 1998 (and defeated) would have required states to prosecute juveniles thirteen or older as adults for a wide variety of offenses. Children are already being certified to stand trial as adults at younger ages and in many states certain crimes require prosecution as an adult (National Center for Juvenile Justice, 1998). Where does such thinking end? The U.S. is currently one of only eight countries that execute juveniles (Death Penalty Information Center, 1999). Will it take a nine-year-old being sent to the gas chamber or the electric chair before there is a sense we have gone too far?

Following such thinking to its logical conclusion presents a very unsettling picture. The extension of treating children as adults for legal purposes could provide greater impetus for pushing the entire conceptualization of children more towards that of miniature adults. When this occurs, that will be the end of schools and child labor laws. Particularly troubling in this scenario is that the public debate is driven more by erroneous information and illusions than by facts. It has already been noted that the perception of increasing juvenile crime is based on media sensationalism and heightened awareness as opposed to reality. Further, there has come to be an identification of juvenile crime as gang-related and therefore violent. This combination of variables has led to a perception that the youth of today are engaged in serious crimes and violent felonies. Nothing could be further from accurate. The vast majority of juveniles involved in the legal system are prosecuted for status offenses, which if committed by an adult would not be considered a crime (U.S. Department of Justice, 1996). When one adds in drug offenders and those charged with non-index crimes (i.e., very low-level offenses like trespassing), one quickly realizes that only a small percentage of juveniles arrested are actually charged with violent and/or serious offenses. According to the Bureau of the Census, juveniles account for about 26 percent of the U.S. population but only 13 percent of violent offenses. Murder has the lowest rate of juvenile involvement with only 8 percent committed by juveniles (U.S. Department of Justice, 1996). The only real trend concerning juveniles and crime is that juveniles are increasingly becoming the target of violent crimes with most murders being committed by adults (U.S. Department of Justice, 1997). In fact, the most lethal event in the history of school violence was perpetrated by an adult in 1927, who killed 45 people, mostly children (Woodruff, 1999).

Despite the facts concerning youth crime and violence, the public debate focuses on a statistically unrepresentative sample of youth. Due to the nature of the public debate, we have a system dedicated to addressing the most serious and violent offenders while those truly "in need of supervision" are left by the wayside. This problem has already reached mammoth proportions in many areas. Those who are the most reachable and most salvageable are left without services and little in the way of intervention. This problem is so ubiquitous that this group has been dubbed "crack kids," because of the recognition that they fall through the cracks in the system (this term is fading from use as the rise of the drug crack made the term confusing). However, once this group commits a crime, everyone in the world is there to make sure that incarceration occurs. The rates of incarceration for juveniles have become so extreme that Amnesty International has called on the United States to stop punishing juveniles as adults (BBC, 1998).

LEGAL ADULTS, EMOTIONAL CHILDREN

Our legal conceptualization of children seems out of step with other actions in our society. While the age of marriage and supposed "full adulthood" (marked by living independently) are increasingly put off until later and later ages, the level at which individuals are given "junior" adult status is younger and younger. In social areas, we have become more restrictive with the drinking age rising to twenty-one, driver's licenses requiring a more gradual and controlled entry to full driving privileges, curfews in many cities, and other such reactions. All of these point to the idea that the young are different and generally less responsible. On the other hand, we also hold them legally accountable at the age of eighteen for entering contracts, going in the military, and being able to vote. This leads to a very large and uncomfortable age group of individuals, generally between fifteen and twenty-four, that are neither children nor adults in a sense of social reality. At some point, it must be noted that society has adopted an odd and nonsensical approach to this matter when it is deemed necessary for one to be older to drink than to vote. While the legal trend appears to be firmly entrenched at present, it is likely that what we are seeing is the dying gasp of the idea of children as miniature adults. The present trend of applying adult sanctions to children may be an aberrant action of a supposedly advanced culture in the future.

We need to reevaluate our position. Blaming children for the ills of society is like blaming the horses when the barn burns down. Children did not make this world; they inherited it. But it is often easier to find a scapegoat than to seriously address problems. The real responsibility for the actions of children lies with the adults. In nearly every case of children shooting children mentioned at the beginning of this chapter, there were many warning signs that all was not right. Yet little had been done to intervene with any of these children. In the Littleton, Colorado, episode one of the slayers even had a web page where he discussed the events beforehand. The adults in the community had apparently done little, and nationwide we continue to do little.

We all pay lip service to the saying "It takes a village to raise a child," but raising children is more than talk. People in American society need to quit blaming children, stop looking for easy answers (e.g., lock them up or censor their access to information), and put their actions where their mouths are. One positive element that has likely come out of the various school shootings is that attention has been focused on youth. Only a long-term, consistent approach dedicated to reconnecting with youth will begin to solve our problems. But no matter what we do, events such as those listed at the beginning of the chapter will continue to happen. As a nation we have become an increasingly violent society of which children are only a reflection. Beyond reconnecting with our children, American society needs to seriously reflect upon the violent course our nation has taken. Until this occurs, all efforts at addressing crime will be hampered.

Before we can make progress on the issue of juvenile crime, a very obvious and simple fact must be realized. Children are children and need to be treated as such. A child without guidance is not an adult. Even if a child is an emancipated minor, emotionally he/she is still a child. Children have an innate understanding of their capabilities and limitations. They look to adults for guidance. When that guidance is lacking, children often attempt to act like adults with tragic results. As a psychologist who works with children, people sometimes ask me what is wrong with the youth of today. My answer is always the same—"They're practicing to be adults." While many may take this as a flippant answer, it is not. Instead it merely points out that children are the product of their environment and do what is modeled for them. The answer to the juvenile crime problem lies in the actions of adults.

As a society we need to look at the way we are handling ourselves and our children and the messages of our actions. Forcing children to live in adult jails and prisons will almost assuredly not improve the future of our society.

WHAT MESSAGE ARE WE SENDING?

In our muddled approach to children in this society, adults often attempt to force children into proper behavior. The tendency to rely on institutions, government officials, and the police to solve problems has had many of the reverse effects we would hope for if the village were truly raising the child. A few examples will more clearly illustrate the nature of the problem.

- A girl brings her mother's lunch to school and is suspended because there was a sandwich knife in the bag. The expulsion/suspension occurred even though the student turned in the knife as soon as she discovered it.
- Several children in kindergarten and first grade are charged with sexual abuse for kissing other children.
- A high school student was suspended for wearing a Pepsi t-shirt to school because the school was hoping to receive money from Coca-Cola.
- A high school reinstates corporal punishment because the school board feels there is a discipline problem.

Do the above examples teach children any values? Likely not. Instead, children begin to see adults as petty tyrants more interested in enforcing rules than in trying to help them. Given the reactions in the examples above, imagine the reaction of school officials to students viewed as committing serious offenses. Indeed, many schools operate more based on maintaining order than on teaching children. Certainly the students who are most in trouble are the ones who most need to be in school. Instead we get a rash of laws aimed at kicking "troublemakers" out of school. The Gun Free Schools Act of 1994 proposed a minimum one-year suspension for any child caught bringing a gun to school. Dianne Feinstein (D-CA), who supported the Gun Free Schools Act, also proposed legislation that would require the expulsion of children for a variety of offenses. For the sake of order, children are sacrificed. Beyond any progressive ideas on child rearing, let us face the simple fact that the last place a teenager needs to be between 8 am and 3 pm is out of school. A study in San Diego found that 44 percent of violent juvenile crime is committed between 8:30 am and 1:30 pm while a Florida study indicated that 71 percent of those prosecuted had been truant at the time they committed their crime (Patania, 1999). And what of those teens caught bringing a gun to school? Throwing them out of school addresses neither the problem of a teenager carrying a gun nor of this youth's lack of education.

Educators, along with most adults, feel pressure to maintain their image as good adults and do what they feel will make them team players. This leads to an ever faster pace of out of school, out of society, into Youth Corrections, into prison. When the need to control events becomes more important than building up children, it does not speak well of a society. In fact, even referring to youth in trouble as "troublemakers" bespeaks of an already skewed orientation. The justification that these students are disrupting the learning of others is nothing but a copout to pass the problem along. Expulsion just tells children they are being given up on.

The example concerning the reinstatement of corporal punishment occurred in my local community. The stated reasons for the policy, according to the president of the school board, Roger Phelps, was that "it's more for humiliation and the mental aspect" (Bell, 1998, A8). Apparently the rationale is that if no visible scars are left, the person has not been abused. A vast literature on shame and humiliation indicates this is not the case. Dysfunctional systems, whether they be families or large organizations like school districts, fail to address the cause of problems because it is easier on the system to find a scapegoat. No doubt the school board feels it is "getting tough" to solve its problems. However, no one ever learned to respect authority by being beaten. Martin Luther King Jr. once commented that "an eye for an eye leaves the whole world blind." Humiliating children and teaching them to fear adults is no way to improve society. It will only lead to more violence. Reinstating corporal punishment across the country would have the effect of decreasing the number of children shot in school because angry, disgruntled children with access to weapons would likely start firing on school officials instead. However, I don't think this is the intended result.

It is educators who must take the steps to stop relying on punishment, expulsion, and disciplinary actions to solve problems in the school environment. I am not advocating that teachers become social workers and psychologists but I am advocating that there needs to be a realization that unless problems are addressed they will not go away. Hiring a few social workers and psychologists whose job it is to work with children (rather than fill out paperwork to feed the bureaucracy) would likely have far better long-term effects for society than expulsion of the same children. Recent evidence demonstrates that it is worthwhile to make intervention efforts very early. Donald Lyman has shown that it is possible to identify the small percentage of offenders at an early age who commit most crimes and to successfully intervene with them (Lyman, 1996). It is important to recognize that individuals do not just suddenly begin committing violent crimes, there are almost always antecedents. Several of the students who committed the shootings outlined at the beginning later made comments to the effect that they were tired of being bullied and picked on. While this in no way excuses their actions, it does point to the need for adults to be more involved in the life of children. Many of the youth who committed these acts were complete outcasts without any ability to impact their own situations. Many were alarmed when the Pearl, Mississippi, group were alleged to have been involved in a satanic cult. Yet, at the same time many seemed almost relieved that they had this to fall back on as an alternative to believing that these children were a product of their town. This belief, creating a false sense of security, that these actions are completely without reason and due to outside forces beyond our control is doomed to lead to even more such actions. To solve the problem of youth violence and crime the adults must not look for easy answers but must attempt to deal with the complexities of adolescence.

IDENTITY VERSUS ROLE CONFUSION

The central developmental task of adolescence is identity versus role confusion (Erikson, 1963). It is at this period in life that individuals develop their core identity. If this is not done, there is a sense of confusion concerning one's identity and self-image. This is why adolescents can be so changing. They are trying on new identities. This is also why adolescents change their hair styles, friends, peer groups, and so forth, on a constant basis. It is this need to figure out who they are and how they are going to be that is the at the core of adolescent development. If teenagers are left to their own devices they will usually make fairly successful transitions at this stage. However, if at this stage, rejection, impoverishment, abuse, and so on, occur, the normal process is disrupted and children can quickly come to identify with a very negative set of values.

At this point, I would like to briefly mention the compensatory facade. This is a process whereby those who feel they are lacking in something attempt to present an image that suggests it is present. Examples are very poor children wanting to have items that suggest economic wealth or those who feel powerless adopting a self-presentation of a very dangerous and strong individual. In some sense it is the very things they do not have that can most shape and alter their actions. In children this can even effect personality development.

This developmental stage is further complicated for the adults who are around adolescents by the other hallmark of this stage, rebellion. With a little thought one can easily see how conflict with authority while attempting to develop one's identity can lead to antisocial behaviors. Those who work with adolescents often notice that the adults who are the most effective are often somewhat odd and unusual. By unusual I am referring to their manner of interacting with youth and even such mundane factors as mode of dress or speech. Because adolescents can't quite figure these adults out and since they seem a little out of the loop themselves, they are more readily trusted by youths. Also, by creating a gray area concerning how adults are supposed to be, these individuals encourage a more complete identity development that is not tied to rebellion against adults. By trying to stifle rebellion at this stage one is swimming upstream. Rebellion at this stage is developmentally appropriate. Trying to force a child in the teen years to behave in a certain way is almost guaranteed to fail. Therefore, to be successful one must make use of these tendencies.

Unfortunately, this is not the approach encouraged by most institutions. At the developmental stage when the very word "rules" is likely to be met with resistance, most adults work the hardest to establish rule compliance. An example involves a facility where I formerly worked that utilized a point system. The purpose of such a system is to encourage students to work for the points and the subsequent reward. Staff, in an effort to show other staff that they were good employees, severely penalized students for any possible infraction and took away points. By 8 am when school started many students had already lost the possibility of gaining any points for the day. As a result, this became a free day to act as one wanted. It also had the effect of making the students see staff members as unconcerned about them and as bullies who enjoyed being punitive. A further effect of this action was that it just encouraged even more acceptance of the role of delinquent.

Zero tolerance for misbehavior leads to a society that abolishes gray areas. All is either black or white. Either a child is considered good or bad. Either people are peaceful or they react violently. This approach inevitably leads to explosive situations where people believe that if they are going to offend at all they must go all out. I recall a student with whom I previously worked who had taken his teacher and entire class hostage so that his father would not see his bad report card. While it may seem illogical to commit such an act, this story illustrates the danger in interpreting the actions of children by adult standards. A further message here is that dichotomous thinking about good and evil ultimately leads to adolescents developing incomplete identities that are either all good or all bad. Since no one can be all good, it seems the tendency would be to see oneself as bad. Compound all of this with the poor self-image of many adolescents and one sees the problem of our approach to juvenile crime.

Shockingly, for all the lip service paid to solving the crime problem, we do very little when it comes to the actions that would most have a positive effect. That is, to work with the youngest offenders when they are still the most malleable. Anyone who has ever worked with any type of offender/victim/client/patient realizes that people are the easiest to change when they are young. That being true, one would think that the easiest place to begin addressing crime would be with the young.

However, as a simple comparison will demonstrate, it is far from true that our resources are invested in children. According to the U.S. Department of Justice (1990), approximately $74 billion was spent on the criminal justice system while only $2.6 billion was spent on juveniles. In other words, only about 3½ percent of all spending was directed towards juveniles.

Every state spends far more on the adult system than on juveniles. In fact, the juvenile area seems to be the one place where we skimp on prison funds. If there is an area where lavish spending is justified, it is here. By making the effort here we might stem the tide of a steady supply of adult criminals at a later date.

At this point I feel it necessary to address the hard-liners who feel that strong punitive measures are the appropriate actions to take against juvenile offenders. It is true that the need for retribution seems to be ingrained in humans. It is also true that there is a line of thinking that suggests adult crimes deserve adult time. I would respond that specifically in the case of juveniles time spent in adult prisons merely compounds the future ills of society. By forcing individuals to grow up in prison, we increase the future danger to us all. We seem to forget that someone who receives even a long sentence (20+ years) will get out. Even if a person does twenty years, those who were sentenced as juveniles will leave prison in their thirties. Is this really the desired result, an angry, damaged, prison-weary ex-con who feels justified in attacking society? Was that ounce of retribution or pound of flesh worth it? While some primitive need for retribution may have been satisfied, the end result is that a life has been wasted and as a society we are all worse off.

Juveniles, as I have argued, are different from adults. The possibility of change and rehabilitation is much greater and, as a result, worth a better effort than we are currently making. Juvenile law is already set up in such a way as to promote this. Contrary to popular belief, the juvenile system is not set up to punish but to rehabilitate. In most states juveniles are not officially found guilty. Rather, they are found "a child in need of supervision" or some other euphemism. The rules of evidence are also generally more lax and "proof" as determined in adult courts is usually not necessary for an adjudication as a juvenile delinquent.

This being the case, the purpose of the juvenile system is rehabilitation. Some courts have even interpreted this to mean that juveniles have a right to treatment (DeMonia, 1994). Of course, having the right to treatment and receiving it are two different things. As can be noted from comparisons of spending between the juvenile and adult systems, there can be no real treatment going on. Even with the enormous amounts of money spent in the adult system, there is little pretense of treatment (Clements, 1999), so how can there possibly be any in the juvenile system? Most juvenile programs I have observed or participated in spend most of their money on bed space and living expenses. In order to provide any treatment there must be more than simply minimal services that barely comply with court orders.

Early intervention is the key to any work with children. By making the school a central organizing area for students in trouble, we can make inroads into behavior. Making treatment available at school can go a long way towards ensuring followup. Further, by presenting this as a nonthreatening service, parental concerns about governmental interference in their lives can be mitigated. In order to begin to address this problem it is necessary to put forth a few organizing principles. These are:

- Early identification and intervention is crucial
- Children should be kept in their family or community of origin
- Parental and family involvement is crucial
- Efforts should be made to keep *all* children in school
- School should be the focus for intervention efforts

Research has demonstrated that remaining in school is the single most crucial factor in preventing delinquency. In Minnesota, daytime crime dropped 68 percent when police began citing truant students (Patania, 1999). To keep children in school requires major changes in our thinking by making it harder, not easier, to deny students the right to an education. This simple change would have amazing effects on the rates of juvenile crime. It also necessitates a change in the way educators approach their jobs. It has been my experience that it is all too common for teachers and principals to want difficult and/or problem students out of school and actively encourage them to disenroll, drop out, home school, or any other option that gets them out of the school. This is not to say that there are not many excellent teachers who work well with children experiencing trouble, but we need more teachers and more varied and clever programs to ensure success of all students.

To do the above requires major changes in our thinking. School attendance is already mandatory and compulsory in most states. However, as anyone associated with schools is aware, there are certain students who the school would prefer not to be there. It is this very group that most needs to be in school. Truancy laws should be enforced and not by expelling students who are truant. This common solution to truancy is one of the most nonsensical ideas ever put forth. It is analogous to someone being caught shoplifting and the store making them take a whole cart of groceries before they leave. So to approach this logically, we need to realize the point of truancy laws is to keep children in schooling, not provide excuses for kicking them out.

The issue of children not wanting to be in school must be examined. Many progressive schools have adopted alternative programs for those who do not readily fit the standard educational approach. Some such alternatives involve shifting times certain students attend school, providing opportunities for more hands-on learning, and relaxing or changing codes of conduct. More of this must be done. Programs that cater towards increasing the retention of minority and at-risk students should be implemented. Those students who are placed on some type of disciplinary procedure or are truly disruptive must be afforded the opportunity for an education. By this I mean real alternatives to expulsion, not a program housed in a basement or trailer with minimal staff. It is not this group with which we need to be tight-fisted with funds. We can either pay now or pay later, and as we all know the price will just keep going up.

Finally, school must become the center of these efforts to intervene with children for a number of reasons. By utilizing the school, the possibility of parental involvement will be increased. Further, coordinating outside agencies through a centralized location such as the school enhances the possibility of followup and coordination of efforts. By having those who work directly with kids, such as social workers, probation officers, even psychologists, in the school environment, it is more likely that problems will be addressed proactively. This approach will not solve all of the problems associated with juvenile crime. Indeed, the most important step when attempting to intervene with adolescents is to be creative and flexible by providing a variety of options to incarceration (Mixdorf, 1989). However, it would be a start to addressing the problem to develop a coordinated and thoughtful approach that is grounded in child development and research rather than gut reactions to "get tough."

RESTORATION OF CHILDHOOD

The experience of being a child in America has changed dramatically over the last twenty years. Childhood used to be thought of as a carefree period where adults shielded children from the horrors of the world. Childhood was about having fun, playing outdoors and going to school. That is not the case anymore. In many cities people won't let their children play outside for fear they will get shot. The threats of AIDS, crack, and violence have made it necessary to inform children of the dangers of life in order to protect them. Gone is the innocence of childhood and the knowledge that our children are safe at school. Increasing emphasis on homework and moves to year-round schooling are removing the last vestiges of joy from being a child.

It would be hard to find someone who does not view the loss of childhood as bad. Yet, every day adults send the message to children to grow up and act like adults. Well, that is just what they are doing, with the result that adults now bemoan the crime committed by juveniles, lack of respect for adults, and loss of control over children. The school board president who wanted to humiliate children also stated, "if students want to be treated like adults they have to start acting like them." Here we see that many adults have bought into the fallacy of adolescence, which is "I look like an adult and talk like an adult, therefore, I am an adult and should be treated like an adult." As a society we owe our children more than this. Children are not adults, no matter how much they may protest to the contrary, and should not be treated like adults. Quallah X of the Nation of Islam put it well when he stated that "If a cat gives birth to kittens in an oven, it doesn't make them biscuits."

It is time for adults to reclaim the childhood of our children. Instead of relying on "quality time" and trying to be our children's friends, we need to become their parents, examples, and even heroes. The basketball player Charles Barkley once stated in a television commercial that he was not a role model, it is up to parents to be role models. He is right. Only by making efforts to guide children and teach them their inner value and worth will the tide be reversed. The tendency to treat children like adults is insidious.

An example of this is happening in the field of athletics. More and more, several sports are dominated by young performers. The sports of diving, gymnastics, and tennis as well as the entertainment industry are full of young people who participate as professionals, receive monetary compensation, and live in the public eye even though they are too young to legally work. This use of children as entertainers and sports figures leads to even greater acceptance of the idea that children are just small adults. The excuses used to allow the participation of these children is some far-fetched appeal to the need to allow free commerce and not infringe on their right to make a living. This is nothing more than turning logic on its head because of economic gain. It does not matter whether the child is making a million dollars a day or two cents, he or she is still being exploited. These children are being robbed of their childhood, all for the entertainment of adults. It is easy to see why children in these professions rarely feel exploited and "want" to participate in these activities. But children often want to do many things that are bad for them like eat candy all day. So the fact remains, it is up to the adults to set the standards for children.

Sports and entertainment are good places to reverse the trends of children being treated like adults. Child labor laws could be revised and enforced to prevent the exploitation of children. I think we can all manage without fourteen-year-old celebrities.

More is required than simply altering the sports participation of children. As adults we must begin to take seriously the notion that it really does take a village to raise a child. We must live this rather than merely repeating it. I'm sure that many people of a certain age group can recall a time when adults corrected children whether or not they were their parents. While there is likely a tendency for some to go overboard in this approach, the real message is that adults need to accept and create an active collective approach to our children. Children are the future and our shortsighted approach to them will ultimately prove harmful to all our descendants. Native Americans of many tribes have the philosophy that one's actions should be guided by the effects on the seventh generation to follow. Such a long-term approach is what is sorely needed, not a quick fix that sends children to adult prisons to create an illusion of safety.

This will not happen overnight. It is all too common in our rushed society to take time-saving approaches to problems. This will not work in dealing with our problems or our youth. Many like to blame television, video games, and the Internet for the perceived rise in violence. Here is a perfect place for adults to take control. Instead of attempting to rely on technological gimmicks and censorship like v-chips, NetNanny, and other such devices, parents need to take the provocative step of actually supervising their children. All the supposed technological censors in the world will not work. If you can turn on a censorship device, your child can turn it off. It has been estimated that normal, healthy teenagers spend only twenty minutes per weekend with their parents (Goldman, 1994). What is needed is for parents to talk to their children. If children are attracted to something that adults find horrendous they need to find out why, not be content to suppress the problem and think it will end. Unfortunately, the trend towards suppression is unmistakable. The ACLU reported that it was swamped with hundreds of calls following the Littleton shootings from students who had been suspended for such actions as wearing black clothing and carrying certain books (Graves, 1999).

Television and the media are often made the scapegoats in the discussion of violence in society. Solutions such as rating guides, censorship, and the like all share the common characteristic of getting the government to limit the possibilities for children's viewing. Leaving aside the fact that trampling on the freedom of speech sends children a poor message, it also fails to alter the lives of children. Rather than using television as the primary pacifier of youth, adults need to turn off the TV and spend time with their children.

A proactive step that can be taken in our society is one that we can learn from the past or from traditional societies. Namely, the introduction of rites of passage for our youth. As noted earlier, there exists a rather vague and extensive period in western culture where individuals exist with quasi-adult status. This undefined and often undiscussed period occurs during the time when adolescents and young adults are developing their sense of identity. In more traditional societies, individuals are instructed at this time on their roles as adults and usually engage in some type of ceremony or ritual to mark the transition. This serves a tremendous psychological function for adolescents and provides a sense of guidance and stability in these formative years. It is likely that our culture's lack of such rites is responsible for burgeoning movements that seek to provide similar experiences for adults.

On a sociological level one additional change must be made to seriously address any type of crime in this country: to seriously deal with the levels of poverty in this country. Mike Males, a sociologist and author of *The Scapegoat Generation* (1998), states that poverty is the single largest contributor to violence in our society. The growing disparity between the wealthy and the poor can only increase levels of crime. The Luxembourg Incomes Study (1995), in a study of worldwide poverty, found that the U.S. raises three to eight times as many children in poverty as any other western country. Social policy aimed at terminating individuals from welfare roles may ultimately have its greatest effect on children so that the weakest elements of society suffer the greatest. It seems that a comment widely attributed to B. F. Skinner that "society attacks early, when the individual is helpless" still applies today.

A final word on the treatment of children as adults. Recall the seven- and eight-year-olds who confessed to killing an eleven-year-old. Physical evidence later cleared them and proved conclusively that they could not have committed the crime. So why did they confess? If your answer is that they are children, then you have understood the basis of this chapter.

Chapter 8

INSANITY AND MENTAL HEALTH

If a man is in a minority of one, we lock him up.
—Oliver Wendell Holmes

The area of mental illness is one often overlooked in the field of crime. True, there are laws to protect those who are completely incapacitated by mental illness and unable to fully appreciate the nature of their acts. Yet, the criminal justice system rarely reflects upon the mental status of those in custody beyond the legal findings of competency or sanity. In short, a forced dichotomy is imposed in the system with individuals recognized as competent or incompetent, sane or insane. This either/or conceptualization bears little connection to reality and likely hinders efforts at rehabilitation or appropriate treatment.

By looking at mental health issues only as they pertain to trial and criminal culpability, one misses an essential element related to the commission of crime. This element is the mental health of defendants and inmates. Estimates vary widely concerning the extent of mental illness, ranging from 10 to 75 percent in one overview (Adler, 1985). The fact is that mental illness is ubiquitous throughout the system. By mental illness I am not referring to schizophrenia or other conditions that excuse or remove culpability but to a broad range of psychological problems that affect an individual's ability to function, cope with stress, and examine his or her own behavior. While these problems or disorders may not be exculpatory or even relate to the commission of criminal acts, they are directly related to the ability to alter one's behavior and indirectly contribute to patterns and lifestyles that tie one to a life of crime. By failing to examine how pathology relates to behavior, one relinquishes bona fide efforts at rehabilitation. As anyone with a background in mental health who has worked in the legal system can attest, pathology is deep-seated and commonplace within the walls of a prison.

To illustrate the rather odd position our current laws have put us in, let us look at the case of Jeffrey Dahmer. Here was a man who lured victims to his apartment, engaged in cannibalism, forced sexual assaults, and even attempts to zombify some of his victims. Yet, the court that evaluated him found that he met the legal standards to be considered competent and sane. Although he met the legal tests, is it conceivable that an individual engaging in these acts would be psychologically sound and free of pathology?

Colin Fergeson, the Long Island Subway gunman who shot and killed numerous people, was almost certainly suffering from paranoid schizophrenia and committed the crime in a fugue state. He so closely fits the diagnostic criteria for the disorder that he is close to a textbook case, and I would venture that almost every psychologist in the country would concur with this assessment. Fergeson likely had a fair chance at a not guilty by reason of insanity defense but because of the way the law is written he was allowed to defend himself and avoid the issue of sanity (New York Penal Code, Sections 220.15 and 330.20). It should be noted that he also fired two of the greatest legal minds in the country, the late William Kuntsler and his law partner Ronald Kuby, in order to represent himself. This action alone indicates poor judgment and those who saw any of the trial were likely amazed at the spectacle of a delusional man acting as an attorney.

The efforts by attorneys for Unabomber suspect Ted Kaczynski to utilize an insanity defense and the subsequent efforts by Kaczynski to prevent such a defense renewed interest in this aspect of the law. Kaczynski eventually pleaded guilty to avoid being portrayed as mentally ill. Further, even though he was diagnosed as a paranoid schizophrenic (Johnson, 1999), the guilty plea was accepted. As in other cases involving crimes with a political flavor (e.g., John Hinckley) and mass murderers or serial killers, public interest is aroused when the insanity defense becomes an issue in cases sensationalized by the media. As seems to be the case, the more sensational the crime or the more deranged the defendant, the more attention such cases get. As a result, the few cases witnessed by the general public tend to present a skewed view of the defense itself.

The examples herein illustrate the counterintuitive and often illogical circumstances that arise in our legal system as a result of laws designed to look at a very narrow range of legal questions and a legal system that utilizes false dichotomies to categorize people. As most reading this are likely neither lawyers nor psychologists, some background is necessary to clarify terms and to present some historical context for the current approach to the mentally ill. It will be shown that our current approach is detrimental to rehabilitation, deprives the mentally ill of civil rights, causes enormous problems for the staff in prisons, and is ultimately self-defeating.

TERMS AND DEFINITIONS

Competency

Competency is generally speaking an exceedingly low standard that has little bearing on the issues of guilt or sanity. To be competent one need only be able to understand the nature of the court proceedings (i.e., be able to identify the function of the judge, attorneys, and jury and to follow court proceedings), and be able to assist one's attorneys and to understand the possible consequences.

The problem with competency as a standard is that one can easily meet the standard to be considered competent and still be suffering from extreme mental illness. Many extremely paranoid individuals are infatuated with the court process and have the capacity to assist their attorney even to the point of demanding to be allowed to represent themselves. Although the capacity and even a willingness to assist may exist, their mental condition may preclude any meaningful and helpful assistance. Colin Fergeson, for example, was found competent (no doubt he met standards of New York State as outlined in the New York Penal Code, Section 730) and allowed to defend himself even though quite delusional. To demonstrate Mr. Fergeson's mental state I offer this quote from him: "The reason there are 93 charges is the year 1993." Fergeson made numerous other delusional statements throughout the trial (the trial occasionally replays on Court TV and makes for very interesting viewing). This peculiarity in the law concerning competence led to an evidently mentally ill man defending himself while the best attorneys in the country were prevented from assisting him. Mr. Fergeson's competency was never the predominant legal question in this case. His actions and mental condition at the time of the incident were. However, blind reliance on a ridiculously low standard of competence led to the issues of his actions and his sanity never being fully addressed.

Sanity

First and foremost it should be pointed out that "sanity" is a legal term. Neither sanity nor the corresponding term "insane" are now, or have they ever been, psychological or psychiatric diagnoses or terms. The definition of sanity in the legal sense has changed enormously over time and has undergone a constant process of reformulation.

Efforts to define insanity essentially revolve around the concept of mens rea or guilty mind. Intent is seen as important, as is the concept of deliberateness. The major problem with the issue of sanity is that a decision is made that can only be yes/no. To a psychologist, this does not match the reality of mental illness, which exists along a continuum of severity. By forcing a decision concerning sanity to be made in yes/no terms, one is essentially allowing for judges and juries to decide what is "crazy enough." This is one of the major reasons for the constantly shifting notion of sanity in the legal system.

HISTORY OF THE INSANITY DEFENSE

Throughout history there have been numerous conceptualizations of what it means to be "sane" or "insane." Prevailing social attitudes have greatly impacted the treatment of the insane and by extension the legal view of one's mental state. While society may shift its view back and forth along a continuum of what is acceptable treatment of the mentally ill, it has long been recognized that mental status can affect behavior.

In ancient times the effects of mental illness were recognized by such early healers as Hippocrates and Paracelsus (Paracelsus, 1993). Even the Bible refers to depression as exculpatory of criminal behavior (Psalms 102). In addition, individuals with mental retardation and children have also generally been free from prosecution due to recognition that they may not have the ability to recognize the criminal nature of actions (Szymanski and Crocker, 1985).

The beginnings of the insanity defense lie in the English courts with the trial of Daniel M'Naghten in 1843. In this case, the courts ruled that knowledge of the nature and wrongfulness of an act is required for the individual to be held culpable for his or her actions. In the United States, this interpretation was further strengthened by Oliver Wendell Holmes, who in 1881 brought the idea of intent into the process. For several decades there was little change in what legal precedents held, with M'Naghten being the general rule. In 1954, in the case of *Durham v. United States*, a new standard was put forth by the presiding Judge David Brazelton. This rule stated that "an accused is not criminally responsible if his unlawful act was the product of mental disease or defect." The Durham Rule, as it came to be known, became the focal point of much legal haggling over several terms such as "product" and "defect" to the point that it was largely abandoned. Brazelton later presided over another landmark case in this area, *United States v. Alexander and Murdock* (1972), where he established a twofold judgment that all crimes must involve both voluntary conduct (actus reus) and intent (mens rea) (Slovenko, 1985).

This debate has continued with courts still searching for an acceptable definition of insanity. The American Law Institute (ALI) put forth its own definition of sanity in its model penal code proposed in 1962. The standard here basically reiterates the preeminence of intent and voluntary conduct along with sufficient capacity to appreciate the quality of one's acts (ALI, 1962). Many courts utilize this as the standard, while others rely on various other means such as those criteria directly spelled out in various state laws or even the ancient M'Naghten rule. The Insanity Defense Reform Act (IDRA) of 1984 sought to severely limit the ability of defendants to utilize the defense. IDRA eliminated the actus reus component of the defense, shifted the burden of proof to the defense, and required complete proof of mental impairment, among other features (Clark, 1999). Various cases have grappled with the issue since (e.g., *U.S. v. Pohlot* [1987] and *U.S. v. Childress* [1995]). The final resolve is that there is no final resolve and courts continue with this struggle.

Despite the wealth of legal arguments and various court decisions related to the insanity defense, recent research has reached some very startling conclusions. In studies conducted by the American Psychological Association (APA, 1978), it was found that regardless of the wording of the statute or how it was explained in jury instruction, by and large, the actual statute did not matter. In essence, jurors do not really consider what the actual law is when making the decision. Rather, individuals rely on some internal guide as to whether the defendant is guilty or not. Whether or not the defendant meets the criteria of the insanity defense is not important to the majority of jurors. These findings suggest a somewhat precarious position in considering mental status in trials.

PUBLIC PERCEPTION OF THE INSANITY DEFENSE

The public perception of the insanity defense seems to be one that views the matter as a means of "getting out of it" or "evading responsibility." In no small part this is due to sensationalism and a lack of knowledge concerning the use of such a defense. Lawyers rarely want to attempt such a defense, as it is really no defense at all but rather a plea for alternative placement. What most people fail to understand is that to even attempt an insanity plea one must generally stipulate that the crime was committed but that the defendant could not do anything to prevent or control his or her actions. As one can easily imagine, few lawyers are eager to take an approach that begins with an admission of guilt. Further, research by the APA also found that successful utilization of the defense had no relation to whether the individual met the conditions spelled out in the legal code (APA, 1978).

The idea that those found to be insane get off free is ubiquitous but wrong. In many ways nothing could be further from the truth. One of the most illuminating experiences I have ever had concerning this matter was when I served as an intern in a psychiatric hospital that had an entire unit of individuals who had been found not guilty by reason of insanity. One day while looking at files I began to notice entrance dates into the facility for the various patients. A clear-cut pattern emerged of extensive hospitalization periods for patients who had committed offenses for which they would have served little, if any, time in prison had they been convicted and sentenced in the normal way. A particularly noteworthy example was of a man who had set a bag of feces afire on the step of the home of the judge who had granted his divorce. What was nothing more than a childish prank led to a period of incarceration that stretched over several years.

For those who may think the above was just one aberrant instance in the legal system, consider actual court rulings. In *Jones v. U.S.* (1983) the Supreme Court held that those found not guilty by reason of insanity could be held indefinitely under less rigorous standards of proof than for those civilly committed. Indeed, Jones had already served seven years in a psychiatric hospital by the time the case was heard by the Supreme Court. Had he been sent to prison, he would likely have been released in one year. When John Hinckley, Jr. was tried for attempting to assassinate Ronald Reagan there was an outcry over the fact that he might one day be released. This occurred although a successful first-time murderer will likely be released in around seven years. Some researchers trace the uproar over Hinckley as directly responsible for the Insanity Defense Reform Act (Hess and Weiner, 1999).

Most lay people are surprised to learn that those found not guilty because of their mental status serve any time at all. Those who are aware believe hospitals are places where everyone is waited on and life is easy. Those who hold such beliefs have obviously never visited a psychiatric hospital, especially one that contains mentally ill legal offenders. Psychiatric hospitals are generally distressing places that can be chaotic or even frightening. One patient, who had previously been incarcerated in two different state prisons and who was widely believed to have faked his mental illness to the courts, confided in me that he wished he had been sent to prison because he "would have been out by now" and that it was easier to deal with prison inmates than "a bunch of mentals (sic)."

When one attempts any type of incompetency, diminished capacity, or insanity defense a completely different set of legal rules comes into effect. Among these rules are that defendants generally have to admit to the crime and stipulate to all evidence, even that in dispute, and open their entire psychiatric history to the court proceedings. Further, the burden of proof in these cases becomes shifted to the defense as opposed to the prosecution (IDRA, 1994). These rules are poorly understood not only by the general public but also by the courts and its officers, including attorneys and judges. In the media and often even in the courts, there is confusion as to what these terms mean. This confusion can lead to dramatic miscarriages of justice. Public defenders often do not know how to proceed and judges may not even know what to do with those who are obviously insane. I have on several occasions testified concerning the mental status of offenders and had judges ask me to fill out the court papers in their chambers because they were unfamiliar with the procedure in such cases.

A concrete example of the factors involved in the decision process surrounding the insanity defense should further illustrate the complexities of determining mental status. One of the factors often used to evaluate whether a person can form the requisite intent (mens rea) is whether by his or her actions the individual attempted to cover up the crime or escape detection. The use of such a standard, while widely accepted, is problematic because it is entirely speculative. By fleeing a crime scene an individual is deemed to appreciate the nature of the act (i.e., knew it was wrong). Such tautological reasoning can be particularly damaging because it makes the assumption that those with severe mental illness will behave rationally!

Mentally ill individuals might flee the scene of a crime in which they had no part other than being present or even wandering by. This could be due to any number of factors ranging from fear to a response to delusions. On the other hand, to stay behind and make no effort to flee might support the contention that the person did not appreciate the nature and quality of the act, but it might also be used to support the idea in court that the person is a brazen, brutal killer who should receive maximum punishment.

In short, the use of the insanity defense, whether prosecutors fight it, judges allow it, or juries accept it hinges on very idiosyncratic legal fictions that vary widely from one jurisdiction to the other. Factors such as culture, region of the country, jury composition, and race of defendant can all influence the success of the strategy. At present such a defense is not only a risky trial strategy, but there is little acceptance of the idea that justice is served by such a defense. I would argue that the public perception of the insanity defense is guided more by misinformation and media sensationalism than by fact. It is likely that everyone would be better served if it were easier to utilize an insanity defense and the severely mentally ill were out of the general prison population.

The idea of making the insanity defense easier, not harder, and then segregating the mentally ill does not seriously address the root causes of crime nor does it deal with the majority of crimes committed. Despite the pervasive fear of the mentally ill in our society, research has demonstrated that the mentally ill are no more likely to attempt or commit violence than the general public (Link and Stueve, 1994; Monahan, 1984; Prins, 1996). In fact, it is more often the case that the harm caused by the chronically, severely mentally ill in an assault is less because they have difficulty sustaining the appropriate focus or mens rea.

Thus far we have examined the issue of mental illness from the perspective of the insanity defense and the mentally ill. Let us turn our attention now to the majority of cases, the so-called normal people. As noted, the use of the insanity defense is extremely rare with the vast majority of defendants considered sane by the courts. While the legal system has forced a false dichotomy on the question of sanity, in real life this is not the way people are. Clinical psychology and psychiatry base diagnoses on discrete categories, to be sure, but the concept of mental health/mental illness is far more complex and exists along a continuum. Where the line falls between mentally healthy and mentally ill is open to debate. A broad gray area exists between the two. An example is the recent legal effort to establish the "black rage" defense, which essentially states that, as a result of a lifetime of abuse and racism, one can become so seriously damaged that one cannot prevent oneself from acting upon violent impulses under certain circumstances. As a result of this irresistible impulse the person is not responsible for his or her actions. Variations on this defense can vary from "postal rage" to the "twinkie defense." The "twinkie defense" was utilized in the defense of Dan White, the San Francisco politician who killed then mayor Moscone and council member Harvey Milk. White's defense, in a nutshell, was that he had become mentally impaired as the result of eating too many twinkies and processed sugar. This defense, black rage, postal rage, and others, takes the position that individuals are not culpable for their actions if these actions are due to circumstances beyond their control.

Such a defense creates a slippery slope if accepted into standard jurisprudence. This scenario could conceivably be extended to cases where a member of the Crips shoots a member of the Bloods or a skinhead shoots a member of a minority group and argues that they had no choice because they became enraged at the sight of the other person. Such a conceptualization, while unsettling, does begin to address the roots of crime. To spell it out clearly—people commit crimes for reasons. These very reasons, no matter how far-fetched or discomforting, hold the key to effectively changing behavior through treatment. Only by embracing the somewhat odd and unsettling idea that reasons for crime are important and should be addressed will the criminal justice system be able to have any effect other than producing better criminals

Interestingly, the only group of people in the criminal justice system for whom treatment is preferred and the reasons for their behavior matter is the small percentage of individuals (less than 1 percent) not deemed responsible for their actions and who are actually found not guilty. Going one step further, there are thousands of individuals throughout the country who have never been charged with any crime for whom confinement on the basis of mental condition and coercive treatment is considered acceptable.

"CIVIL" COMMITMENT AND A FREE SOCIETY

A profound discrepancy has insidiously crept into the civil and criminal legal systems. This process, already codified by a differentiation into civil and criminal proceedings, seeks to split into groups those individuals whom society deems to be behaviorally inappropriate. Members of the first group, labeled "criminals," are segregated from society on the grounds that they are dangerous or have violated societal rules of conduct. This group is considered by society as deserving of punishment because of acts they committed. The "criminal" group is viewed as being legitimately detained and punished.

Members of the second group, labeled "psychotic" or some other pejorative term, are segregated from society (in the vast majority of states) on the grounds that they are dangerous to themselves or others, based on behavior that also violates societal norms of conduct. These individuals are then "treated" by society by depriving them of their freedom and confining them to psychiatric hospitals through civil proceedings. This group is viewed as being legitimately detained in order to be treated.

Avoiding matters of paternalism towards patients and the difficulty in predicting dangerousness (an iffy proposition at best), the inherent problem of the legal system begins to emerge. Another false dichotomy has been created where individuals are labeled as either "criminal" or "crazy" if their behavior violates the norms or society. In both groups, dangerousness or protection of others is used as the reason for deprivation of liberty. However, an honest assessment of these reasons suggests they are little more than pretenses with little relation to actions. Laing (1967) pointed out long ago that far greater numbers have been killed by individuals operating under the guise of societal sanction (as in wars and police actions) than by all the "criminals and crazies" combined. When viewed in this way, it becomes clear that the violation of societal norms is what really lies at the crux of efforts to deprive individuals of liberty and not any ability to determine dangerousness.

The utter absurdity of the distinction between the criminal justice and the civil commitment systems was made clear to me by the juxtaposition of two professional experiences. The first occurred while I was an intern in a large northwestern psychiatric hospital, where I routinely witnessed civil proceedings that deprived individuals of their liberty in order to treat them. In part, this practice stems from the medical community's assumption that psychological problems are medical problems subject to conventional allopathic treatment. At best this is a very tenuous assumption. Yet, because of the idea that mental illness is a medical problem, it is assumed to be okay, in fact good and benevolent, to treat this illness coercively and forcibly. Interestingly, it is only in the area of psychological problems, where there is little evidence supporting a medical genesis for all but a very few specific problems, that forcible medical treatment is acceptable. Many individuals have languished through severe medical emergencies that likely would have been treated beneficially through hospitalization. This generally does not occur for the simple reason that their behavior is not troublesome or strange to others.

The second formative experience on the issue of civil versus legal commitments occurred when I began working for the Department of Youth Services (DYS) in a southeastern state with few resources. Thirty to 40 percent of youth incarcerated within the system were found to have diagnosable psychological problems (Cook and Brewer, 1992). Some were committed for trivial offenses such as truancy and trespassing and clearly ended up with DYS because their communities could not figure out what to do with them and/or there were no services available for them. One youth was involuntarily committed to a state hospital but due to a of lack of space was sent to DYS for a traffic offense. The community was afraid of the individual and our agency was able to expedite placement in the state hospital. Clearly, an individual committed to a psychiatric hospital would not have the mens rea for a conviction of any criminal offense as the law currently stands.

In the civil system, society assumes an in loco parentis role and determines that the individual cannot make competent and reasonable decisions. Although it has been held that one may refuse treatment in civil commitments (e.g., *Harper v. Washington*), for all practical purposes this right is abrogated. Patients may be informed that they have the right to refuse treatment, but the message supplied with this de facto is "you will participate in treatment or you will stay here forever." Less than subtle coercion may be applied and if this fails, there is the "med override" where one psychiatrist gets another to agree that such coercive measures are "for the good of the patient." I am sure that many reading this will be horrified and that the psychiatric community will protest loudly that this is a rare event. Nonetheless, I have observed this in a variety of settings and institutions.

From this point of view, many, including this writer, find coercive treatment to be a violation of individual liberty that is accepted primarily because the mentally ill are a disenfranchised group that is irrationally feared by the public at large. Treatment is foisted on this group, especially those who are unable to make competent decisions. Society feels justified in demanding that this group receive treatment, especially if they don't want it. Consider the case of Shirley Allen, who refused to participate in a court-ordered evaluation in Roby, Illinois. Law enforcement officials encircled her home and began a five-week stand-off to force her from the premises. Police used tear gas, pepper spray, loud music, turned off water and electrical power, and even sent a police dog into her home in an effort to force her out (Burghart, 1997). The fact that Ms. Allen was able to endure such treatment and hold police at bay for five weeks suggests that she was in possession of many of her faculties.

The above examples concerning civil commitment point to the inescapable conclusion that this process is inherently paternalistic with little substantive rationale from a treatment perspective. Further, given the inordinate number of individuals in the prison system who are suffering from psychological problems, it appears that it would be far more honest to combine the two systems and address problem areas up front. In other words, we must honestly admit that in the case of civil commitments it is not the state of mind or any ability to predict dangerousness that is at the root of the confinement, but rather it is the behavior of the person.

Before proceeding, I feel that to responsibly make this case I must state emphatically that I am not advocating that we close psychiatric hospitals and put the patients in prison. Quite the opposite. I am advocating that the two systems be combined administratively to provide treatment with placement to be determined by needs, not abstract legal questions. By taking this approach, the removal of mentally ill inmates from prison and placement in mental health facilities could be made much easier. This would also have the effect of making delivery of treatment in the prison environment easier by removing individuals with major mental disorders.

Ironically, those who demand that the mentally ill be taken off the streets and treated tend to be the same group that thinks providing social services to prison inmates is coddling criminals and being "soft on crime." Where is the logic that anger or substance abuse does not need to be treated but that schizophrenia must be? Those pushing the agenda against the provision of treatment have a strong ally in the incarcerated population. My experience in working with this population is that most criminals have no desire to change. The last thing most felons want to do during their incarceration is to confront their weaknesses or address the issues that led to their incarceration. Putting in your time and getting back on the streets to continue your life is the key feature of the criminal experience.

Recidivism rates support the contention that merely warehousing people is not addressing the root causes of crime. The primary studies examining the issue of recidivism conducted by the federal government and the state of Minnesota have found rates between 60–70 using only the criteria of no arrests within three years of release (U.S. Department of Justice, 1988, and Office of the Legislative Auditor, State of Minnesota, 1997). Providing opportunities for treatment is the essential step needed to change the direction of the criminal justice system. But to provide treatment in a successful manner also involves allowing the right to refuse treatment. The rationale behind this approach is that it not only protects civil liberties but also has the feature of making personal accountability and individual responsibility prominent features of the treatment. Constantly reinforcing to those incarcerated the idea that their actions caused them to be where they are and their actions will get them released is key. This approach confronts the inability to accept responsibility and the tendencies to blame others and make excuses that is so common among prison inmates.

An approach like that detailed above would require some incentive beyond release. A type of levels system would be a necessary component of such an approach so that those who are progressing and showing positive change would be able earn privileges. These privileges would be the hook that keeps prisoners involved and also feeds the need for tangible reward that many have in order to work for positive goals. The structure of such a system will be further delineated in later chapters.

It is easily conceivable that such a change in the system could obviate the need for insanity defenses. As previously pointed out, severe difficulties exist in establishing with certainty the sanity of many individuals. If everyone in the system were allowed or required to receive treatment, there would be no need for there to be a priori findings of sanity or insanity. The trial would focus on issues of guilt or innocence. The nature and place of treatment would be left in the hands of those trained in the field, not to the whim of court proceedings, judges, and jurors. Such a system also has the benefit of allowing treatment for those not suffering from a major mental disorder and those who may become mentally ill while in prison.

If such a system were in place, spectacles such as the Colin Fergeson trial would likely not have occurred and an individual like Ted Kaczynski would not have had to plead guilty to avoid an insanity defense by his lawyers. Making treatment and placement decisions independent of guilt determinations would lead to far better informed decisions and would eliminate the legal maneuvering that accompanies many trials where sanity is an issue.

There is one group of offenders who could be far more adequately addressed under the proposed system than is presently the case. Sex offenders, who notoriously lie about their actions and refuse to accept any responsibility, are a significant burden on the legal system due to the issues surrounding their treatment and any eventual release (Marshall, 1999). Few make any efforts to change while in prison and recent efforts to civilly commit them afterwards have led to enormous double jeopardy issues (e.g., Washington State). By making release predicated upon treatment and reports by mental health professionals one could adequately protect the public. It is likely that professionals would be more reluctant to release this group than prison officials and would be better qualified.

Individuals such as the late Jeffrey Dahmer, Charles Manson, John Wayne Gacy, and others could be studied under this system and possibly do some good for society. Individuals such as those listed here are realistically never going to be released and have no incentive to participate in treatment with this as a goal. The granting of minor privileges within the prison could, however, serve as incentive for their participation in evaluations and research.

In sum, society must become honest with itself about why we confine people and what the goals are behind confinement and deprivation of liberty. Until there is some recognition that only by providing treatment to individuals within the legal system will we be able to alter behavior and change people, we will continue to have ever-growing numbers within our prison system. Approaches grounded only in retribution, punishment and segregation from society are ultimately to the detriment of us all.

Chapter 9

COERCIVE TREATMENT, CIVIL LIBERTIES, AND CHANGE

> We are all inclined to judge ourselves by our ideals; others by their actions.
>
> —Harold Nicholson

Shortly after the end of World War II, Stanley Milgram (1963, 1974) conducted a series of experiments at Yale University that demonstrated the extreme degree to which individuals are susceptible to the demands of authority figures. In these experiments subjects were led to believe they were administering painful and even potentially lethal shocks to others. Only a few subjects refused to comply with the experimenter's demands and most acted without question. These studies on obedience to authority pointed out that everyday, average people would engage in atrocious behavior with little provocation.

Reports of brainwashing techniques being developed by the Soviet bloc during the cold war, coupled with LSD experiments conducted by the CIA, led to a heightened awareness that psychological techniques could be utilized for less than noble purposes. Recognition of the powerful influence a psychologist or psychiatrist can have on a person in their care has caused something of a backlash against the profession.

The provision of treatment against the will of any individual raises the specter of totalitarianism and mind control. Because of the very real possibilities of misuse of psychological methods to control or manipulate people, great care must be used to preserve the rights of the individual in any type of intervention. As a result of these concerns, the standard of care developed by both the American Psychological Association and the American Medical Association advocate that treatment be strictly voluntary.

Despite these proclamations of voluntary treatment and informed consent, most, if not all states, have statues that allow for involuntary treatment and confinement of individuals. Most of these statutes are couched in terms that imply the treatment is being provided "in the best interests" of the person being treated. In essence, society assumes an in loco parentis role and determines what type of treatment should be provided. Numerous legal precedents (e.g., *Harper v. Washington*) have established the legal right of states to provide coercive treatment even when it may not be in the interests of the individual in question.

Thomas Szasz (1982, 1984, 1994), the noted "antipsychiatrist," has pointed out on several occasions that the idea of treatment as conducted in current practice is coercive. Szasz makes the argument that those on the fringes of society are often and consistently treated coercively. Medications are forced on patients, court-ordered evaluations are routinely conducted and many individuals are confined by the state against their will. All of these events occur daily in our society to people who have never been convicted of any crime and have no intention of violating the rights of others.

These actions, as alluded to in the preceding chapter, are done under the guise of "helping" the person regain the ability to function independently. Legal hearings and constant review are mandated in all states to protect individuals from unjust treatment. However, as Szasz, this author, and numerous others have noted, this is little more than a sham to provide societal control over those whose behavior is out of the mainstream. Again, it should be reiterated that these individuals have broken no laws, their behavior is just considered aberrant.

Civil commitment statutes, almost without exception, utilize some concept of danger to self or others as justification for this treatment. In reality, provoking fear in others because of erratic behavior is a far more honest presentation of the route by which people are committed to psychiatric facilities. Those who appear different or who do not conform to the norms of society are at great risk for confinement.

I recall an incident when I served as an intern at a psychiatric facility, when a naked, tattooed Asian man was brought to the hospital by police because he had been found on the streets of Seattle babbling incoherently. Shortly after arriving at the hospital the man was able to communicate through sign language that he needed clothes, food, and an interpreter. When the interpreter arrived, it was discovered that the man was a Buddhist monk who had been mugged, probably for his robe. The "babbling" noted by the police turned out to be the Khmer language. The individual was quickly released and transported home.

Incidents such as the above, which luckily turned out well, point to the real nature of commitments. Being unusual and not conforming to societal expectations are the primary reasons one gets brought to the attention of authorities. As noted, the official justification is entirely different. Dangerousness to oneself or society at large is the stated legalistic criterion. Whether such individuals should even be confined is an interesting legal conundrum, but beyond the scope of this text. Herein, the interest is primarily in what to do with those who are confined for reasons that truly relate to the violation of the rights of others and individuals who are a danger to society. In effect, what are the rules that should govern the provision of treatment to those convicted of criminal offenses?

COERCIVE TREATMENT AND REHABILITATION

Judging from the rhetoric espoused by those who advocate a get-tough approach, the reason rehabilitation has fallen out of favor is that it is viewed as giving something to undeserving felons. Taken in this light, it is suspected that if social conservatives who oppose the rehabilitation approach were to see it as something that felons did not desire, they would become advocates for treatment. That is in fact the focus of the approach advocated here. Rehabilitation is, to the career criminal, an undesirable feature of the correctional system. Focusing on one's problems, insecurities, and pathology likely is viewed as punishment. To truly punish many of those considered criminals, society would have to provide a plethora of treatment options.

When it comes to treatment one notices a peculiar divide in the get-tough approach. Administrators and bureaucrats who rely heavily on draconian measures and refuse to express any concern for inmates all of a sudden become champions of human rights when rehabilitation efforts are mentioned. I have heard countless prison officials reject any type of treatment or rehabilitation efforts as legally questionable and as possible violations of civil rights. This excuse falls flat to any observer of the prison system, where rights abuses are commonplace. Treatment tends to interfere with the orderly operation of the institution and several researchers have noted this as an impediment to effective treatment (Clements, 1999; Rice and Harris, 1997).

Were prison officials even vaguely concerned with the rights of prisoners or the possible legality of their actions, many current practices would be prohibited. Instead, most officials are dedicated to the deprivation and punishment of prisoners even when there is no reason for it. I recall once trying to get a juvenile system to change the type of restraints used to control violent, out-of-control individuals. The chief of security denied the request on the grounds that the current restraints were physically painful (the very reason I wanted to use another type) and that he felt anyone acting this way should suffer. Pleas concerning the fact that these were juveniles and that many so restrained had psychological problems fell on deaf ears.

Other rights abuses are common throughout the prison industry. Restraint boards, on which the person is strapped down and rendered immobile, are commonly used (ACLU, 1999). Stun belts, which can deliver tremendous electric shocks, have been placed on prisoners to control them even in court rooms where bailiffs are present ("Stinging debate over stun belt," 1998). Riot dogs and tazer weapons are common in the arsenal of prison security (Wong, 1997). Overcrowding that violates established human rights guidelines is common throughout the entire system, with most facilities operating well over capacity as a natural state of affairs (FBOP, 1999).

But the preservation of rights is not high on the list of priorities for prison administrators. Rationales given to prevent treatment opportunities are nothing but excuses. Treatment is rejected out of hand simply because it is not viewed as punitive. In a somewhat unusual twist on treatment, several courts have held it to be a right that must be protected and as a result, provided (e.g., *A.W. et al. v. Phyfer*). Such rulings provide both the legal and, rational justification for the provision of these services. Unfortunately, having a right and it actually being acted upon are often two different things. On a personal note, while working at an agency under court order to provide treatment to those in its custody, I noticed a disturbing trend to do little to support treatment efforts. Publicly and on paper, the agency trumpeted that treatment was provided to everyone in its custody. At the level of actually supporting this in day-to-day operations, however, little was done. Inadequate numbers of treatment staff, enormous case loads, and paperwork requirements prevented anyone from adequately providing services. At one point, I personally had a case load of over 300 individuals. Only through ongoing court intervention including citing several administrators for contempt of court did the situation begin to improve.

The above example illustrates the difficulties in providing effective treatment and rehabilitation. Those with the power to make treatment a part of the prison routine, in effect prison administrators, must see this as valuable and in line with the goals of the prison. Given the mindset that prevails in the justice system, this seems to be achievable only if such efforts are viewed as punitive. However, for treatment to be effective, civil liberties must be preserved and made prominent in the rehabilitative efforts of the prison environment. The essential problem emerges of a way to provide treatment and ensure civil liberties. A new model of corrections is sorely needed that shifts the focus from the current punitive orientation to one driven by reform and rehabilitation. In many ways, dedicating all efforts to rehabilitation makes far more sense than dedicating them to punishment. Perhaps the realization that treatment is not desired by most inmates is one avenue to make this shift more palatable for those in policy-making positions.

PROTECTION OF CIVIL LIBERTIES

The abuse of civil liberties and human rights by prison officials only serves to further alienate convicted felons from the larger society. Prisoners, no matter their circumstance, rarely expect kind treatment from those who incarcerate them. In fact, poor treatment by captors is expected and serves to further strengthen the "us versus them" mentality that is so common within the walls of penal institutions. Being able to conceptualize his keepers as evil allows the felon to engage in a bit of cognitive distortion that prevents the evaluation of his own actions as wrong and any subsequent feelings of remorse. Further, those who work in the environment come to be seen as representative of society. When those representatives act in a manner that is abusive, society is likewise viewed in that way.

The fact that those who work in correctional environments are seen as societal representatives was driven home to me by a member of the Disciples street gang who referred to me as "the Man." Being the psychologist at the institution, I had never thought of myself as particularly aligned with the other staff or law enforcement in any manner whatsoever. My response to this comment was a rather incredulous "I'm not 'the Man.' " The quick response from the gang member was, "Whether you like it or not, just by being here, you are 'the Man.' " This was a disconcerting realization for me but served to point out the manner in which prison staff are viewed by inmates.

Due to the special relationship that exists for prison staff as representatives of society at large, the onus is on those personnel to behave in a manner that is beyond even the appearance of impropriety. Unfortunately, this is rarely the case in today's criminal justice system. Systematic abuses of rights and deprivation of prisoners are easily rationalized as necessary to maintain order or as perfectly acceptable because of who these abuses are committed upon. The use of guard dogs, physical force and mental abuse is justified as necessary.

I have observed countless staff members, under several different circumstances, state to inmates and me that "you lose your rights when you get locked up." While it is true that one loses certain legal rights while incarcerated, one does not lose the right to be treated as a human being. As evidence, the eighth amendment specifically prohibits " . . . cruel and unusual punishment. . . ." In addition, the fourth, fifth, sixth, and seventh amendments specifically address the rights of the accused and those in legal proceedings. Clearly, it is not the intent of our legal system to deprive the incarcerated of any rights other than those specifically outlined, namely, the right to be free. The point that seems to have been lost in our current discussions of criminal justice and the philosophy of incarceration is that deprivation of freedom is one of the most severe forms of punishment that anyone can experience. It is the desire to remain free that is most likely to shape behavior. Extreme forms of punishment only engender resistance and prove self-defeating in the long run.

Beyond legalistic or even human rights arguments for the protection of civil liberties lies the argument of effectiveness. In order for treatment to be effective, the person undergoing the treatment must be a willing and active participant. Who can expect anyone to be a willing participant in treatment if the very individuals assisting them are viewed as corrupt and illegitimate? I am not advocating that prisoners be pampered and catered to. What I do advocate is the establishment of a set of circumstances that provides an opportunity for an environment conducive to personal growth and change to exist and develop. Expecting anyone living under miserable conditions, where there is a constant fight for survival, to willingly go along with those incarcerating him is unrealistic.

In order for a therapeutic environment to develop, protection of civil liberties must occur. Not just lip service, but bona fide, committed efforts must be taken to ensure that human rights and dignity are preserved. Prisoners must be protected and safe from assaults and abuse from both inmates and staff. Hollow, shallow commitments to the ideals of human rights that are enacted only to satisfy minimal legal requirements will be seen for what they are and will fail to have the desired effect.

Providing for the development of a therapeutic environment will not be easy. It will require a real change in thinking from the approach currently weighted heavily in favor of punishment and borderline abuse to one grounded in rehabilitation and the encouragement of prosocial values. These values will require a day-to-day commitment on the part of prison staff, who will have to become models of prosocial behavior and stop reliance on force as the means of social control.

As stated, a radical shift must be made from punishment to rehabilitation, from deprivation of rights to fierce protection of those same rights. Staff members need to be encouraged to view themselves as treatment and rehabilitation assistants rather than as guards and security personnel. The very nature of serving as a guard or security in a prison has been demonstrated to have vast psychological consequences. A rather convincing demonstration of this occurred when Zimbardo and colleagues (Zimbardo, 1970; Haney, Banks, and Zimbardo, 1973) designed a mock prison setup and discovered that merely being assigned to the role of prison guard led to psychologically sound individuals (subjects were prescreened prior to the experiment) engaging in abusive and aggressive behavior. In this experiment, volunteer subjects were randomly assigned to either the role of prisoners or guards. Subjects quickly assumed their roles with extreme vigor. Those assigned to be guards in the experiment became abusive and engaged in behavior well outside of that expected, including hitting prisoners and denying food and even requests to use the restroom. This effect was so pronounced that the experiment had to be terminated well before the established conclusion date. This finding is one of the more shocking in all of the criminal justice and psychological literature. It seems to demonstrate that the expectancy individuals carry with them into a situation is far more relevant to their actions than one might suppose. When individuals participating in a simulated activity can act so far removed from their typical actions, what is to be expected of those with a more authoritarian bent who might reasonably expect violence in their daily occupational endeavors?

The only hope of countering this tendency towards violence in prisons is to begin with prison personnel. It is unreasonable to expect prisoners to initiate this change. By placing the burden on staff to create a better environment and rewarding them for doing so, the shift necessary to establish a therapeutic environment begins. Additionally, staff will need to become more professional and better trained. Encouraging prison personnel to view themselves as treatment staff and rehabilitation experts as opposed to guards and staff might begin to address some of the expectancy effects noted in the Zimbardo studies. Rather than squandering resources on construction and capital outlays, money should be directed towards the recruitment and hiring of professionals to provide treatment and training to inmates. Additionally, all prison personnel that work directly with prisoners must receive training that encourages them to view themselves as part of the solution to a social problem rather than a stopgap holding back a tide of violence.

INDETERMINATE SENTENCING

Preserving the civil liberties and human rights of incarcerated felons is a difficult but attainable goal. Thus far the focus of this need has been on the right to be treated humanely and for the efforts of the criminal justice system to be more about rehabilitation and punishment. Treatment, remediation, education, and training are also needed. The established legal right to treatment has been noted. However, in order for the current system to be effective, another right must be guaranteed. This is the right to refuse treatment. While this may initially seem counterintuitive, the right to refuse treatment actually aids the treatment process.

The process whereby participation in rehabilitation efforts is voluntary and under the control of the inmate confronts one of the great problems encountered in the psychological makeup of many criminals, specifically, the refusal to accept responsibility for oneself or one's actions. By allowing the inmate the right to refuse treatment or any other rehabilitative efforts his life circumstances are then under his control. To use a sports metaphor, "the ball is in his court."

Merely changing this aspect of the system will not solve the problem. If an individual can refuse treatment and is serving a determinate sentence such as a mandatory minimum, there is little incentive to participate. Most prisoners would likely choose the sit-and-do-nothing option if there is no incentive. In effect, the status quo remains. It is ironic that the option most likely to be chosen by prisoners is exactly the one that the get-tough approach prefers. As noted, change is difficult and confronting the very life circumstances that lead to criminal activity is not a desirable activity. But unless this occurs, there will be little possibility of change. When working with adolescents who have been adjudicated delinquent, I have noted that most individuals are rarely motivated to participate in any type of treatment or rehabilitative efforts at the beginning. There is usually some type of self-serving concern that can be summarized as "what's in it for me?" Typical penal answers to this question are "nothing."

Therein lies the rub. Given the current state of mandatory minimums and other determinate sentencing formats, there is little reason for a convicted felon to engage in any rehabilitative efforts. When behavior has little influence over treatment or release, it is unrealistic to expect that much positive change will occur. In fact, even attempting such efforts in a determinate sentencing model is likely to make life more difficult for the inmate. This is because such behavior may violate the "con's code," making survival more difficult behind bars. Conversely, under a situation of indeterminate sentencing, actions and behavior do matter and directly influence the behavior of inmates. Those who choose to work towards rehabilitation efforts are able to justify the behavior as related to release. In some ways, indeterminate sentences provide an excuse for the felon to act in a prosocial manner that does not endanger him with the rest of the inmates.

The biggest complaint from the "get tough" and victims' rights camps over this proposal is that it allows people to get out. The reality is that people get out anyway unless they are doing life without parole. The measure of success in any prison experiment is not how long people are incarcerated but how the person changes and whether illegal actions continue. By getting inmates to buy into treatment and work towards release, a win-win situation is created. The inmate wins by getting released and society wins by changing criminal behavior. A factor rarely considered by those who advocate determinate sentences is that once your time is up, you are released whether any change has occurred or not. Under indeterminate guidelines, only those who have demonstrated an ability to address problematic life areas and actually engage in rehabilitative efforts are released. Many individuals who get released under determinate sentencing would remain in prison for much longer under indeterminate guidelines. In this way, those who are truly the worst of the worst remain incarcerated.

In many ways this "voluntary" participation in rehabilitation is not voluntary at all. Many inmates will likely refuse to participate at first and will sit in their cells becoming more and more angry at the system and society. This is no different than the current state of affairs. However, as others are released and privileges are granted to those who participate, it will slowly begin to occur to the individual that unless he begins to participate and actively work on certain areas, he will remain incarcerated for a very long time if not forever. An approach that forces the incarcerated individual to make decisions regarding his own situation begins to confront the idea that life is being "done" to the inmate. He must assume responsibility for his own actions and take charge of his life in order to get released. This action alone would be a tremendous step for most incarcerated individuals and would benefit society in the long run.

In some ways I am not completely comfortable with the coercive nature of the proposed effort. However, taking steps to ensure that inmates have a right to refuse services and providing incentives somewhat mitigates the coercion. Further, as has been pointed out, the process of civil commitments involves precisely this same sort of coercion and manipulation. As a mental health professional I am uncomfortable with the degree of coercion that exists in the treatment of those who have committed no crimes. But if there is a place for at least some type of mild coercion (even if it is through incentives to participate), it would seem to be in the criminal justice system. Those convicted of violent crimes actually satisfy one of the standard requirements for civil commitment, which is danger to self or others. Further, the conceptualization of antisocial personality disorder as a psychological problem as outlined in the DSM-IV indicates that imposing a mental health framework on the criminal justice system is not entirely out of line. Using this idea as a starting point for a framework that views rehabilitation as the goal of any incarceration and punishment efforts is a beginning to a redirection of the criminal justice system..

The current trend towards punishment and the rejection of rehabilitation is grounded in illogical thinking concerning the nature of change. The focus on increasingly harsh sentences and draconian measures plays into the us versus them mentality that exists among a vast percentage of the prison population, particularly those who are diagnosable as antisocial. As has been noted previously, creating an antagonistic system that attempts to force a person to do something against his or her will is almost guaranteed to create resistance (Brehm, 1972). Present approaches used with a predominantly antisocial population only serve to further encourage this reaction, leading to greater alienation and continued criminal activity.

Rehabilitation efforts are not particularly welcomed by prison inmates. But providing the opportunity for this to occur and connecting it to release and other privileges is one means by which the criminal justice system can begin to address the factors that lead to crime and incarceration. Rather than encouraging prison to be a battleground between inmates, staff, and the legal system, a reformulation directed towards rehabilitation and therapeutic treatment would be far more logical and beneficial.

Chapter 10

THE NEW GULAG: THE FAILURE OF PRISON ARCHITECTURE

Stone walls do not a prison make.

—Proverb

The phenomenon of prison construction is likely one of the more misguided aspects of the entire criminal justice system. At present there is an explosion of construction in practically every state and jurisdiction in order to provide more cells and bed space. With more people incarcerated per capita than in any other country on earth, it seems apparent that this rate of growth should be completely unsustainable and as a result unjustifiable (Maver, 1994; Reinarman and Levine, 1998). Unless the criminal justice system is deliberately attempting to produce more felons, increasing prison capacity is nonsensical and can only be driven by the money flowing into the system.

Were the criminal justice system remotely successful, we would see a decreasing need for prison and jail space. Instead, new facilities are being constructed at breakneck speed in an effort to handle the incoming numbers. Unless there is some unspoken plan to round up even more members of the general public, perhaps efforts would be better directed towards the prevention of future crimes than the incarceration of future criminals. The construction of new prisons is nothing more than a surrender to the idea that the system is completely ineffective and exists only for warehousing.

The failure to make any efforts at rehabilitation is the primary reason we continue to have high recidivism rates and an abundant supply of repeat violent offenders. As previously noted, most studies on recidivism have found very high rates of return to prison even when using a short (three-year) time frame. The Department of Justice (*Recidivism of Prisoners Released in 1983*, 1988) found an approximately two-thirds recidivism rate among federal prisoners while state studies have found nearly identical rates (Office of the Legislative Auditor, State of Minnesota, 1997). Thus far, the failure to provide treatment and rehabilitative efforts has been identified as the primary culprit in the continuing cycle of crime. Beyond the lack of intervention and treatment efforts, there is another major problem that works to prevent possible change within an incarcerated population. This problem is prison architecture.

It has long been recognized in psychology that the environment is a major factor in behavior. The field of ergonomics points to the need for the environment to facilitate the goals of an institution. Even feng shui, an Asian decorating approach, recognizes this at a very basic level. Almost all large institutions recognize the effect the environment can have and attempt to construct facilities in such a manner as to further the goals of the organization. Factories, for example, tend to emphasize function in construction and are usually specifically built to meet the goals of production. As a result, adequate lighting, proper space, even safety facilities are incorporated into the design. Recognizing that the comfort level of the workers will affect production, efforts are made to address these human issues. As another example of large institutions, hospitals dedicate large areas of space to the treatment of patients, order the facility around the provision of medical care, and divide the hospital into different units according to need and function. Colleges and universities, having a somewhat different mission, seek a more aesthetic approach. Yet, emphasis is placed on structures that aid the primary mission of the institution by providing classroom space, library facilities, proper lighting, and even areas for relaxation and study. Prisons notoriously neglect these features in organization and construction. When it comes to prisons, principles related to the societal goals of prison are ignored.

Prisons operate on a completely different principle. The needs of the institution are put before the mission of the prison (rehabilitation) and the lives of those who exist within its confines. In theory, prison is a place for people to reflect upon their actions, see the error of their ways, and transform into productive citizens. In practice, prisons seem to be constructed around the idea of preventing escape (a statistically rare possibility) and containing outbreaks of violence. An analogous situation might be a hospital built to meet the needs of the billing department and to deliver bodies quickly to the morgue to the exclusion of providing medical care. This is what prison architecture does. Instead of providing rehabilitation or even punishment (and I think a good argument can be made that prison is not even very good at that, just at providing an inhumane environment), the prison serves as a warehouse that is dedicated to keeping everyone inside to the exclusion of all other purposes.

Prisons are supposed to be places where people learn to live in society, yet the standard architectural scheme bears little resemblance to anything one would see in the outside world. Gray concrete walls, harsh, stark lighting, and overcrowded conditions are the norm in prisons. The very environment tends to be depressing and create resistance. Instead of inmates finding prison a place for contemplation, it is a place to be survived. Even those who might have an interest in changing are unlikely to find prison the place to do this due to the dehumanizing nature of the environment. Prisoners are moved within the walls of most facilities like cattle, identified by number, and counted like inanimate objects. All of these environmental factors impede adequate treatment and rehabilitation efforts.

Prison architecture generally seems to be poorly thought out at best and at worst seems to have been given no thought at all. This is unfortunate because simple changes in the building of correctional facilities could lead to the creation of a positive medium for change and could push individuals towards change. Simply by attempting to create a therapeutic environment, prison architecture would be drastically altered. By adhering to a few very simple concepts during construction one could achieve the following:

- Lower the costs of incarceration substantially
- Create an environment where positive change is encouraged
- Minimize prison violence
- Enhance control of dangerous prisoners
- Improve working conditions for prison employees

By adopting the measures outlined herein it is predicted that recidivism rates would decrease and prisons would cease only to be places where one hones criminal skills and becomes a better felon. Even if one rejects rehabilitation as a major component of prison, giving some thought to the prison environment could lead to positive effects on society by producing less damaged and more accountable ex-cons. By focusing only on security and escape issues, the prison and jails of this country are disregarding the good of society in the name of expediency and punishment.

The need to address the flaws in prison architecture as it relates to the change of inmates is an issue that has received little attention (Clements, 1999). Instead, the needs of the institution are made paramount with security and capacity as the primary features. Control of prisoners is also important but only from the point of view of preventing riots and making things run smoothly. Part of the problem lies with the fact that there are few guiding principles in prison construction that relate to the promotion of positive or prosocial values. Little thought is given to the long-range effects of the environment on the individual prisoner and ultimately upon society. Adherence to a few organizing concepts related to human behavior could alter this situation for the good of everyone. The following concepts, based on psychological principles and the nature of human change, will be used as the means to organize prison architecture:

1. Solitude is good for the soul.
2. Neither Charles Manson nor Harry Houdini is the typical prisoner.
3. Large numbers are more difficult to move, manage, observe, and control. As a result, emphasis should be placed on creating a small numbers approach.
4. Successful behavior change is marked by an ability to demonstrate new behavior in a wide variety of circumstances. In order to achieve this goal, prison architecture must resemble that seen in the outside world.
5. Overcrowding is counterproductive, ultimately leading to violence and poor management of the prison population.
6. Living at survival level is defeating.
7. People solve problems not buildings.

The current approach to prison construction lines up very poorly with these principles. To begin, prisons are almost always massive institutions containing hundreds if not thousands of inmates in large monolithic cell blocks. If one looks at the numbers in most state and federal prisons (see Table 10.1), one notices a trend to house more than 1500 inmates in each prison. Does anyone really believe that putting 1500 violent felons together is going to lead to a positive outcome? Most correctional facilities in which I have worked or visited have the feel of a place barely holding back the tide of violence while prison employees are greatly concerned for their own safety. Additionally, because of spending on facilities and security measures, most systems skimp on employees. This leads to scenarios that provide one guard for hundreds of inmates.

It is ironic that the emphasis on security and building new prisons to deal with increased capacity leads to a scarcity of staff. An approach that emphasizes more employees, especially treatment personnel, might obviate the need for the other two. Yet, as systems, prisons generally treat their employees little better than inmates. Due to staff shortages, prison personnel routinely work overtime, operate in stressful and chaotic conditions, and are subject to abuse as a part of the job. This creates a dangerous work environment and forces prison staff to operate under a siege mentality as well as to buy into the "us versus them" mentality that is common among inmates. In a very real sense the prison environment becomes a battleground where employees can never win. This in turn leads to high stress levels, increased absenteeism, and high job turnover. An effect of prison reform that even the most ardent supporter of the "get tough" approach would support is the idea that prison employees, who are on the front lines in addressing criminal behavior, should have a decent work environment.

Table 10.1
Average Population and Capacity of Selected Penal Institutions

Facility	Design Capacity	Average Population
Atlanta USP (Federal), GA	1,429	2,146
Attica Correctional Facility, NY	**	2,100
Butner FCI (Federal), NC	992	1,228
Folsom State Prison, CA	2,064	3,828
Fort Dix FCI (Federal), NJ	3,331	3,600
Joliet Correctional Center, IL	761	1,200
Leavenworth USP (Federal), KS	1,197	1,856
Salinas Valley State Prison, CA (Soledad)	2,224	3,694
San Quentin State Prison, CA	3,283	5,694
Sing Sing Correctional Facility	**	2,200
Averages	1,812.9	2,647.8

**Design capacity figures not available.

Sources: California Department of Corrections (1999); Federal Bureau of Prisons (1999); Illinois Department of Corrections; and New York State Archives and Records Administration (1999).

What few seem to realize is that one cannot have miserable conditions for inmates without that transferring to the working conditions of prison personnel. The following principles serve the dual purpose of improving the conditions of workers while creating an environment for effective rehabilitation.

Solitude Is Good for the Soul

This is a somewhat obvious statement that initially may seem to have little to do with prison reform. But let us look at the realities of prison. One of the harshest difficulties for many inmates is living with their cellmate(s). Being forced to live in a small cell with another individual can hinder efforts to change. In many prisons, cells designed for one person are routinely filled with three to four inmates. At the former maximum-security prison, Alcatraz, three prisoners routinely lived in a 6½' × 4' cell. The Geneva convention set the minimum space per person during incarceration at 29 square feet. This is less than the area of a 6 × 5 room, which is smaller than a small bathroom. With most U.S. prisons operating with populations at 30 to 50 percent over capacity (California Department of Corrections, 1999; Federal Bureau of Prisons, Weekly Population Report, 1999), there is little possibility that most are in compliance with this standard.

Contemplation of one's actions is one of the time-honored rationales for incarceration from any viewpoint, liberal or conservative. The idea that prisoners have plenty of time to think about what they have done and will be forced to see the error of their ways is not entirely unjustified and may be therapeutic. In some ways the efforts to lengthen prison sentences pay a modicum of tribute to this idea. Unfortunately, the structure of most current prisons prevents the possibility of any serious contemplation.

Most nights or "lights out" in prison are filled with the sound of inmates. Ted Kaczynski, the Unabomber, had to be relocated at one point due to the noises in the jail affecting his mental state (Johnson, 1999). The constant noise, the fear of other inmates, constant movement, security counts, and numerous other factors prevent any serious contemplation from occurring. To put this in a perspective that most readers can relate to, think about time in your college dorm. Did the presence of a roommate or two help or hinder your ability to study? Now imagine that your roommates were violent, insane, or just plain bad. Add in the complication that you are locked in at a certain time and cannot leave. How likely does it now seem that prison encourages contemplation as a means of change?

By putting forth the proposition that solitude is good for the soul, I am not advocating mandatory solitary confinement. Just the opposite. Complete isolation can have vast psychological consequences and has been held by many courts to be abusive. An incident that occurred while I was a graduate student working part-time at a diagnostic facility for juveniles demonstrates the effects of extreme isolation. When I arrived at work one Tuesday I discovered that a student had stabbed a staff member with a pencil on Friday afternoon and as a result had been put in "time-out," the juvenile version of isolation, for the entire period (a clear violation of policy). When I visited this individual in the cell, he had psychologically decompensated to the point that he was actively hallucinating and required immediate intervention. Just getting him released, even at that point, required assistance from my supervisor and a great deal of tension between the diagnostic and administrative staff. This story, unfortunately, is probably not unique nor extreme, but demonstrates the callous nature with which prisoners are routinely treated. As the goal is to facilitate change, not cause mental damage, isolation as currently practiced in correctional facilities needs to be abolished. The concept of solitary confinement, where prisoners are routinely stripped and confined to a cell with no furnishings, is abusive at a very basic level, doing far more harm than good.

Shifting to single-person occupancy cells would reduce if not obviate the need for solitary and disciplinary placements. In addition it would save vast amounts of money in prison construction as the isolation areas are by far the most expensive to construct and maintain. With single-occupancy cells, an individual's own room could serve double duty in times when someone requires isolation. The difference between single-occupancy cells and solitary is that in one case it is your living area while in the other it is a punishment area.

The design of cells need not be deluxe or plush. The idea is not to create a luxurious environment, just one conducive to change. A stripped-down, small living space is adequate. Time spent in one's cell should confer an experience similar to monastic life as opposed to a sociology experiment on crowding. The advantages of single-occupancy cells are incalculable in this regard. Creating a "safety" refuge through the use of single-occupancy cells provides prisoners at least some time each day where more than survival is the dominant mode of life.

Single-occupancy cells also have several advantages for the process of rehabilitation. Foremost, prisoners would have a period every day for contemplation as there would be little to do after lights out. Second, the damage from other prisoners could be minimized if prisoners could retreat to their room during times of danger. This would likely necessitate the development of some interior locking mechanism that could be opened by staff but not other inmates. Third, those not participating in treatment or therapy activities would stay in their cells. This serves the double purpose of encouraging treatment and providing something therapeutic (contemplation) to those not in treatment or refusing treatment. With almost all current correctional facilities well over capacity, few prisons have single-occupancy cells for any inmates except for those on death row or being punished (*Correctional Populations in the United States, 1995*). As a result, only a small percentage of those currently incarcerated live in single-occupancy cells. One exception is the "super-maximum" facility in Colorado where all prisoners have single cells (Moore, 1998). Unfortunately, the reasons behind single cells in this case are punitive rather than rehabilitative.

Neither Charles Manson nor Harry Houdini Is the Typical Prisoner

Anyone who has ever visited a prison is generally awestruck by the security. Double fencing with razor wire and lethal voltage, guard towers, spotlights, 8 feet thick walls, and other such measures are the norm. In this type of construction there is the underlying premise that every incarcerated person is an escape artist who spends all day and all night trying to figure out ways to escape. The popular culture supports this notion with movies like *ConAir, Natural Born Killers, Papillion*, and so forth, all showing dramatic and daring escapes. Further, there is some promotion of the idea that when an individual escapes, he will immediately go on a killing rampage of apocalyptic proportions. The facts on prison escapes do not bear out these concerns.

Escape from prison is in a statistical sense exceedingly rare. According to the FBI, less than one half of one percent of prisoners escape (defined as getting outside the gates) and the majority of these are quickly apprehended

(*Uniform Crime Reports*, 1988). In an analysis of escapes conducted by he FBI in the mid-1980s, less than 800 inmates escaped nationwide from all federal, state, and local facilities combined in every year of the analysis (*Uniform Crime Reports*, 1988). Based on a prison population of around one million, these numbers indicate that the emphasis on escape is relatively overblown. An interesting feature of this analysis concerned the fact that just a few states accounted for the majority of all escapes. Florida consistently averaged between 25 and 30 percent of the total escapes nationwide and in 1986, Florida, Alabama, and Puerto Rico together accounted for over one half of the escapes nationwide (*Uniform Crime Reports*, 1988). An examination of the procedures used by these states would probably do more for security than all the security measures installed throughout the system.

Only a small percentage of prisoners even seriously contemplate escape for a variety of good reasons. Life on the run is difficult, stressful, and unpleasant. Most prison inmates are likely better aware than the general public of how difficult life on the run is. Contacting family or friends is the quickest way to get caught, so one is left with no support system. Those not aware of this are usually apprehended quickly. Many, if not most, escapes end when family or friends turn in escapees out of fear for themselves, fear of legal entanglement, or even simple reward.

Most felons associate with other individuals who are somewhat disreputable or may even be involved in illegal activities themselves. These individuals often will not help escapees out of fear of getting caught or attracting undue attention to themselves. Others simply turn in their past associates for reward. Typical prison escapes follow these two actual scenarios:

- In early 1999, three prisoners escaped from the New Mexico State Prison. By the end of the week all three had been apprehended. Two escapees were turned in by their drinking buddies for a reward. The third was turned in by his family.
- A juvenile escapes a facility one hundred miles from his home. By the time he arrives home two days later his probation officer is waiting for him in his living room.

Only those willing to avoid contact with others, establish new identities, and avoid contact with legal authorities are likely to remain free for very long. Avoiding contact with legal authorities is difficult for many felons due to the lifestyle they choose to live. Few escapees have wilderness survival skills and as a result avoiding contact with others is very difficult. The establishment of a new identity is beyond the ability of most people, even in our current technological age. Given the literacy level of most inmates, this is hardly even a consideration for them.

If escape is not a major problem, why the need for all the security measures? Certainly, there is the intimidation factor, but psychologically this just engenders resistance and may actually increase escape attempts. Remember the concept of reactance theory (Brehm, 1972). A juvenile facility where I once worked upgraded its security by installing an "escape-proof fence." The result was an increase in both attempts and short-lived successful escapes. Many who were incarcerated related that the fence was a challenge as well as a reminder of their incarceration. Thus, it served to make escape a more prominent thought throughout the day.

Surprisingly, the fence itself, which had only mesh at the top, no razor wire and no current, was fairly effective in that no one escaped by going over, under, or through it. Escapes instead centered around opportunistic times like medical visits, court hearings, and facility transfers. In most escapes these are the typical avenues. This is true in razor wire-rimmed, triple-fenced, lethal-voltage facilities as well. This assessment is based primarily on experience and discussion with other prison personnel since states are reluctant to disclose this type of information as a general rule. In reality, few people are good at any type of escape. Harry Houdini is not the typical prisoner, and most prisoners could not escape a pair of handcuffs much less a maximum-security prison. To illustrate the real level of inmate ability with security devices, I once challenged a group of individuals in group therapy to unlock my briefcase as several had bragged they were excellent at picking locks and "cracking safes." During the duration of the group (one hour), no one was able to open the briefcase. Despite the fact that each side of the case had only 1000 possible combinations and a careful, methodical approach would have opened it, no one in the group was able to open even one side of the case, much less both locks. Such fancy is the product of movies not real life.

The emphasis on maximum-security prisons where approximately 35 percent of all prisoners are incarcerated (*Correctional Populations in the United States, 1995,* 1997) is misguided. The vast majority of individuals incarcerated, while criminal, are not set on committing random acts of violence or killing members of the general public. As pointed out in Chapter 2, violent crimes usually occur between people who know each other (*Uniform Crime Reports,* 1998). Building prisons with the idea that everyone incarcerated is going to murder and maim if they escape, coupled with the idea that everyone is an escape artist, is just wasting money for the sake of image or the illusion of safety. However, it is the construction of prisons and the installation of security measures that expends vast amounts of funds allocated to the criminal justice system.

The illusion of safety, rather than actual safety, seems to be the preferred approach to security in our society. This effect can be clearly seen with the new reactionary approach to the mass shooting in the past few years. Increasingly, schools are installing security cameras, hiring guards and requiring students to wear identification badges. Similarly, workplaces have security systems, and workers attend seminars on violence in the workplace and carry identification cards.

At Columbine High School in Colorado, for example, the shootings in 1999 were met with the addition of fifteen new security cameras for the school and five new security guards. Keyless after-hours entry systems were installed and I.D.'s became a requirement for all students (MacNeil-Lehrer Report, August 16, 1999). Yet, at the time the shootings occurred the school already had security cameras and those who committed the shootings would have been given I.D. under the new system as they were enrolled students of the school. In other words, none of the new measures would have stopped the previous shootings.

In the suburban Georgia school shooting shortly after Columbine, there was a security guard present when the shooting happened. At the shootings that occurred in both the Atlanta office building and the Jewish Community Center in Los Angeles in the summer of 1999, the shooters just burst in and began firing. In the shootings in Jonesboro, Arkansas, the students did not even come on school grounds, instead firing from nearby woods.

The point is that shootings of mass numbers are essentially irrational acts committed by people who are unconcerned with the outcome or consequences of their actions. It is completely illogical to think that someone who is acting in a homicidal rage without concern for their own safety is going to be deterred by a few security cameras. Guards make little difference either, as the vast majority of these shootings end with the shooters taking their own lives. When this sort of approach is extended to prisons, the illogical nature becomes even more apparent. Lifers are completely unconcerned with breaking prison rules and cameras are easy to disarm, simply throwing a shirt or towel over the lens is enough to hide what is going on. Extra security, especially in the form of technological gimmicks, may actually lull prison guards into a false sense of security.

The simple fact of violent and irrational assaults is that whenever anyone decides to engage in such behavior, they usually carry it out without thought to the consequences. Given the poor judgment and notoriously impulsive behavior already discussed concerning prison inmates, it is unreasonable to think that technology and iron bars are going to stem the tide of violence. Addressing the causes of such behavior is the only way to enhance security and lower violence.

Large Numbers Are Difficult to Manage

College students often complain that at large schools they are faceless and treated like a number. Criminals, on the other hand, usually prefer large facilities for the very same reasons. Unfortunately, as earlier noted, that is precisely the trend in prison construction. Through building monstrous-sized facilities, enormous areas for hiding or causing violence are created. The extremely large numbers incarcerated in many prisons make it nearly impossible to keep track of all the inmates (see Table 10.1). Sheer numbers make it difficult to know who is who and where anyone is supposed to be at any given time. This inability of staff to track and familiarize themselves with inmates creates a very volatile and uncertain atmosphere, which works well for the inmates but poorly for the staff.

The effects of large numbers cannot be overestimated. Anyone who has ever worked in a prison is at some point struck by an awareness of how overwhelmingly the staff is outnumbered by the inmates. This fact serves to further strengthen the siege mentality of prison personnel. One of the most chilling comments ever made to me in a work environment related to this topic when a worker stated, "If they (the inmates) ever realize how easy they could take us, we're all dead." In a coordinated effort, prisoners could easily take over most facilities. This realization likely lies at the heart of prison construction and extreme security measures. Most facilities appear designed to minimize danger in riots and to rapidly shut down the prison in the event of widespread disorder.

The above points to a core problem in the entire criminal justice system. All efforts are geared towards stopping trouble once it is out of control. Few proactive measures are taken. As any fireman can tell you, it is easier to prevent a fire than to put one out. By the same token, designing prisons to prevent violence is far more logical than building them to contain it. Size is the key, not expensive security measures.

At present the pod concept is making great strides in newer, modern prisons. This is a great advance as it serves to keep prisoners in smaller, more defined areas. However, even these are usually too large and merely involve an attempt to split the prison into more manageable units. In some sense this is a nod to the idea that large numbers are difficult to manage, but overcrowding persists, and the lack of real funding for anything but security and bed space still leaves massive monolithic prisons in tact albeit divided into smaller administrative areas. While this approach may assist in the management of inmates, it does little to transfer behavior out of the environment.

Successful Change Is Marked by Transfer of Behavior

In psychology the key feature of success in any plan to change behavior is that it transfer from the training environment to the world at large. The idea is that unless the behavior is generalizable across conditions, no real change has occurred. In order to successfully transfer this behavior, the training environment should parallel to every degree possible the conditions of the environment in which we want the behavior to occur.

In prison the internal reality in no way matches that of the external world. It is a closed society unto itself. Those behaviors acquired to survive in prison are poorly suited to life on the outside. Any treatment or rehabilitation that currently goes on in prison takes place in an environment so far removed from real life that most prisoners make no connection to it once they are released. Some prisoners will make the changes needed to satisfy parole boards or make life easier on themselves while inside, but the transfer of this to activity outside of prison is negligible due to the discrepancy between the conditions. In psychological terms, the training environment does not match the test environment. Of course, since little treatment or rehabilitation has been going on, even less connection is made at present.

To prevent this lack of transfer, we must move towards a system that produces crossover effects. To do so, the inside environment of prisons must change. No matter what prison one chooses to examine, stark, concrete buildings and monochromatic color schemes are the standard. The look is unlike anything one is likely to encounter anywhere else. Dreariness and gloom seem to drip from the walls. This is not conducive to the development of positive behaviors, much less their transfer. All it is conducive to is alienation, depression, and similar counterproductive feelings.

Prisons need to be designed in such a way that they look like buildings one might encounter on the outside. A variety of building styles, color schemes, and even landscaping would aid development of a therapeutic learning environment. Inmates must be encouraged to develop skills that will serve them in the world outside the prison walls. In effect, prisons should encourage a sense of community and cooperation with others. This is a tall order, especially given the population. But without this effort there can be no realistic expectation of lasting change. Further, to address the problem of crime successfully, it makes sense to utilize state-of-the-art knowledge concerning the way in which people change. The current emphasis on punishment, to the exclusion of all other approaches, takes away from any efforts to counter antisocial behavior and even seems to imply a state sanction for ruthlessness for those with power.

Efforts to encourage crossover effects must not just stop at the color of the paint on the walls. Creating an environment as similar to the outside world as possible should be the goal. Misplaced regulations to contain violence illustrate one of the means through which prisons come to have little resemblance to the rest of the world. In most prisons anything that can be used as a weapon is banned. This appears to make sense until one realizes that almost anything can be used as a weapon. In prisons this notion is played out by restrictions on all sorts of normal everyday objects like pencils (great for stabbing), glass objects of any kind, tools, silverware, and so on. As a result, most prisons ban so many objects that they have an indefinable quality of peculiarity that is difficult to pin down. Much of this peculiarity is related to the lack of common objects such as those mentioned above.

Despite these efforts, prisoners still find ways to arm themselves and commit violence. I recall pool balls placed in socks used to commit assault, shoe strings used to choke, and light bulbs broken to cut someone. The fact of the matter is, if one is clever enough, almost anything can be converted into a weapon. Guns have been fashioned from toilet paper rolls and rubber bands among other things. Thus, removal of common objects does not really work, it only provides an illusion of safety. Further, such actions work against the transfer of behavior by making the environment so bizarre. To truly aid transfer of behavior, inmates must live in a world that resembles the outside. Such a plan also provides the opportunity to realistically sample the behavior of inmates while incarcerated. In essence, if we really want to be able to determine who is suitable for release, behavior on the inside is a means to examine who has really changed. At present, inmates are artificially prevented from engaging in many types of normal behavior, making it exceedingly difficult to determine who is rehabilitated and who is merely trying to survive the bizarre and violent world of prisons. In sum, the solution is not to remove all objects. The solution is to provide adequate supervision and staff in sufficient numbers to prevent violence from occurring.

Overcrowding Is Counterproductive

When individuals are forced to live in overcrowded environments the social order is altered by the conditions alone. In an experiment on overcrowding, rats were placed in compartments that duplicated the population density of a crowded urban area. Soon, some rats formed gangs that terrorized the weak, while powerful, high-status rats took over and controlled large areas. Social conditions generally deteriorated into fights over dominance and territory (Calhoun, 1962, 1971). These studies show only the tip of the iceberg when it comes to the effects of overcrowding on people. Some studies have found that high-density conditions impair the ability to learn (Goeckner, Greenough, and Maier, 1974) while others have shown crowding within correctional facilities to lead to increased rates of suicide, psychological and disciplinary problems, and even death (Cox, Paulus, and McCain, 1984). Yet, prisons are consistently overcrowded. According to the Bureau of Prisons (BOP), their ninety-four facilities have an average capacity of 946, yet random checks through November 1999 revealed the average number held in these facilities to be between 1214 and 1410 (Federal BOP, Weekly Population Report, 1999). That is a range of 30 to 50 percent over capacity. Further, these numbers would be even worse were it not for several small, specialized facilities holding small numbers as well as the 15,000+ inmates held in private prisons. Sadly, the federal system is closer to actual capacity than many state prisons and local jails. Not surprisingly, the overcrowded nature of prisons results in exactly the type of behavior seen experimentally with rats. Individuals become little more than subjects in a giant human experiment where social power and dominance become the focus of everyday life. Such overcrowding works against all stated purposes of the criminal justice system in that it serves to force people, just by the overcrowding and the ensuing conditions, to live at survival level. Ironically, the only individuals able to live at more than survival in the present prison system are the most ruthless and violent who are able to effectively subjugate their fellow inmates. The message given to inmates under such overcrowded conditions is not that prosocial behavior and values matter, but that those who are willing and able to brutalize others manage best. Surely, we can find a means to teach the incarcerated population of this country a value system that does not encourage antisocial behavior as the means to a better life.

Living at Survival Level Is Defeating

Maslow's hierarchy as presented in the first chapter of this book demonstrates the manner in which life at survival level is counterproductive. In short, only when one has lower-level needs of safety, food, and basic needs met can one even begin to attempt any higher-order functioning. Prison, as presently conceived, forces individuals to live at the level of survival. Most time in prison is occupied with efforts not to be subjugated or otherwise reduced to a level less than human. This prevents any realistic change from occurring. When one is consumed by efforts to meet even basic drives, therapeutic efforts have little impact. A drastic alteration of the makeup of prison must occur before there can be any realistic efforts at improving those incarcerated for various crimes.

Regardless of one's orientation concerning the purposes of prisons, be it punishment or rehabilitation, it seems obvious that for society as a whole to improve, the prison environment must shape people for the better. At present, the overemphasis prisoners must place on survival issues prevents this from occurring. Creating an environment where individuals have the opportunity to address the deep-seated issues that lead to crime will be difficult considering the starting point. To effectively address the long-range consequences of crime upon society, we must build up those incarcerated rather than tear them down even further.

People Solve Problems Not Buildings

Our current emphasis on the construction of new, more secure prisons to address the crime issue is sorely misguided. Building new prisons only addresses the issue of overcrowding and increased demand for capacity. There seems to be no real idea that this approach will reduce crime or even improve society. Rather, it appears only to be a stopgap measure. The whole emphasis on building new facilities seems to suggest that everyone believes the trend will continue towards greater and greater numbers of incarcerated people.

The use of different crime-fighting techniques, the use of RICO laws, the limitation of appeals, are all geared towards increasing the rate and length of incarceration. As a society, we seem to have made a decision to deal reactively rather than proactively with crime. If the trend were reversed and a goal was made to lower the crime rate by addressing the behavior of criminals, there would be no need for obsessive and excessive building programs.

The primary means to accomplish a lower crime rate is not through reactionary measures designed to incarcerate people only briefly. Rather, the real way to stop crime is to change criminals. A singular reliance on incarceration will not accomplish this task. People must change, and a clear means to bring about change is to shift to the approach from incarceration to treatment. Only by laborious face-to-face interactions and the installation of massive numbers of treatment personnel will criminals be held accountable for their actions. Instead of building new facilities to warehouse inmates, addressing the deficits of those already incarcerated presents an approach whose time has come. Hiring a vast network of treatment professionals to provide intervention services and adequate staff to supervise inmates and control violence with an emphasis on responsibility and accountability for inmates is strongly recommended. It is hard enough for mental health workers to change people; buildings never have. Not until there is some realization that change will only occur by focusing on the criminals and what truly motivates criminal behavior will we be able to make any real progress. Expecting incarceration alone to change people is highly unrealistic.

Chapter 11

GET SMART ON CRIME, PART II

If people are good only because they fear punishment, and hope for reward, then we are a sorry lot indeed.

—Albert Einstein

The thrust of criticism directed at the criminal justice system throughout
this text has centered on the manner in which the purposes of the system
are subverted by a lack of attention to psychological principles regarding
the nature of human change. Ever-increasing rates of incarceration are the
direct result of the current emphasis on punishment at the expense of rehabilitation. This politically popular approach is a doomed philosophy that
can only create an ever-increasing supply of more violent and sophisticated
criminals. A new approach that emphasizes the lowering of the crime rate
and a decrease in incarceration rates through the adoption of a coordinated
and scientifically based approach is long overdue.

Overreliance on punishment, coupled with the need to address increasing prison populations through new construction, has led to the exclusion
of rehabilitation efforts in the correctional system. There is a noticeable lack
of focus in the day-to-day operation of the existing system. Ideas of decreasing the crime rate and changing the behavior of those who commit
crime are absent in popular discussion of crime in America. Crime has become a topic marked by sensationalism and reactionary approaches designed to elicit voter support. In the meantime, the purposes of the system
seem to have been forgotten. Instead of utilizing state-of-the-art knowl-

edge and research concerning the rehabilitation of individuals, our emphasis is a one-dimensional orientation towards punishment. Even in terms of punishment, we pay precious little attention to the features that contribute to its effectiveness. Given this state of affairs, it is necessary to review the historical purposes of the criminal justice system prior to making any remarks regarding the goals of incarceration.

PURPOSES OF THE CRIMINAL JUSTICE SYSTEM

The purposes of the criminal justice system have become so twisted over the last couple of centuries that punishment is now seen as the point of the system. Historically, punishment has been seen as a means to an end. According to *Compton's Interactive Enclyclopedia* (1994), four justifications for incarceration are generally recognized: revenge, deterrence, expiation (making up for the crime committed), and rehabilitation. In our own system, punishment has come to exist as an end for its own sake. Of the four justifications, only revenge seems to have any place at the present time. Our incarceration rate seems to indicate that deterrence is not working and that rehabilitation has nearly become taboo. Expiation is rarely even mentioned in modern prison systems.

In the past, the justice system's emphasis was usually a reflection of the cultural values of the community. No matter what the rationale, the focus was mostly on the outcome or effects of the punishment. Thought was given to what methods would most effectively meet the needs of the society. In sum, the purposes were seen as moving towards the protection of society, the lowering of the long-term crime rate, and the development and improvement of a more civil society.

In effect, the historical goals of the criminal justice system were more about effectiveness and the end result than about the means to that end. At present, our society has become more focused on the means as an end rather than the means to achieve that end. In the discipline of philosophy, focus on the means usually implies an ethical orientation. However, in the area of criminal justice this has been turned upside down with the emphasis on means being almost antithetical to ethical considerations. The political climate has become such that "get tough" approaches are the rage and the long-term consequences are of little concern. Little discussion focuses on whether getting tough is effective. In some ways the punishment orientation is like a runaway train. It seems to conclude that if a little punishment doesn't work, more is needed. In a deep psychological sense, the current emphasis on punishment advocates torture as the final endpoint because that is what increasingly severe punishment will eventually become. Unfortunately, such shortsighted approaches are destined to create even more problems in the long run.

The emphasis on punishment, retribution, and societal segregation to the exclusion of all other concerns is producing a large number of angry, damaged, and well-trained criminals who will explode upon society in the near future. Further, since so many individuals currently incarcerated were sentenced as juveniles to long terms in adult prisons, they will be released at ages when they are still physically capable and energetic enough to inflict a great deal of damage on society. The institutionalization process and the inculcation of prison survival skills will further render these individuals incapable of successfully integrating into society. Such problems will only prove to be detrimental to us all. The effects that present levels of incarceration will have upon an entire generation of African-Americans who have been disproportionately imprisoned will not be known for decades. Further, the blatant racism that has led to these rates of imprisonment, through such actions as "driving while black" and disparate incarceration rates for minorities caught with drugs (presented in earlier chapters), can only deepen the wounds within society.

The trends noted above are ubiquitous and likely irreversible at this juncture. Only by starting over and reorganizing the entire system will there be hope for a positive outlook. Fortunately, there are some bright spots in the criminal justice system that point the way towards a more effective and positive means of addressing crime in our nation. At present, few of these efforts are widespread. Currently only a hodgepodge of programs exist in widely distributed jurisdictions that have little overall impact because of an extremely fractionated and piecemeal approach. But these programs can serve as a starting point without us having to reinvent the wheel completely. A cohesive, consistent, and coordinated approach is needed to address the crime and violence in our society. Programs that attempt to address long-range problems can serve as a beginning for a new, comprehensive approach.

Discussion of these efforts will bring to light several commonalities of effective intervention. Many of these address the historical reasons behind the criminal justice system and do not rely exclusively on the use of punishment to accomplish their goals. Instead, effectiveness and a concern for the betterment of society are primary in the formulation of these efforts. The factors that are common to these approaches can be summarized as follows:

- Prevention and early intervention work best
- Alternatives to incarceration serve the interests of everyone
- Effective solutions focus on the problem
- Principles of punishment are appropriately utilized

PREVENTION AND EARLY INTERVENTION WORK BEST

As any competent psychologist can attest, behavior is easiest to change before it becomes completely ingrained. It is much easier to change the behavior of a four-year-old than of a forty-year-old. By extension, it is easier to change the course for a young first-time offender than a multiple felon who has served several prison terms. Money spent on those at the entry level will pay for itself in savings down the road. At present, our system functions just the opposite way. Multiple felons confined to maximum security cost the most to serve while those just entering the system receive little of the resource pie.

The case has even be made (e.g., Donziger, *The Real War on Crime* [1996] and Males, *The Scapegoat Generation* [1998]), that the enormous sums being spent on the "end-of-the-roaders" are being done at the expense of society by taking resources from the very young. As noted in an earlier chapter on juvenile crime, few of our resources are put into addressing the needs of children. The average inmate costs approximately $25,000 per year while few states allocate even one quarter of that to each child per year for educational purposes (see school expenditures in Chapter 2). Even when correctional costs alone are the sole criteria, far less is spent per person on juveniles than on adults in the correctional system. Logic would suggest that children should be more costly as they have many special needs. Why then is this not reflected in the daily operations?

In many ways the approach to children in our society is to ignore problems and hope they will go away. Little attention is paid to children until they do something that alarms the adult world. The school shootings that occurred in the late 1990s served the purpose of directing some attention on youth. Unfortunately, most of the attention boiled down to political grandstanding that focused on minutiae and irrelevancies. Republican congressional leaders called for studies of "youth culture," President Clinton advocated requiring identification for R-rated movies, and more laws requiring expulsion were initiated. Tightening security, closing campuses and monitoring children with surveillance devices are the commonly proposed solutions. Advocating putting more resources directly into children through educational spending and the provision of more services are rare ideas.

Subsequent to the school shootings, a flurry of activity in the passage of laws and "get tough" rhetoric occurred. Finger pointing and the assignment of blame were prominent features of the discussions. In light of findings that demonstrate repeatedly that focusing on children prevents later problems with adults, these discussions were particularly disheartening. Education has long been known to be the primary protector against many risk factors associated with criminal activity. Unfortunately, all the efforts on increased security measures, school uniforms, and other shortsighted solutions serve only to siphon funds from already stretched educational budgets.

The outlook is bleak, but all is not without hope. There are some programs dedicated to prevention and early intervention. Head Start, for example, has been shown to be remarkably effective in assisting children to attain appropriate educational development. Further, many states and localities are developing programs such as Child Find Programs to identify children at very young ages who will require specialized services. The development of nationwide programs across age groups to identify those in need of services is a necessary and promising step.

Scattered programs exist throughout the nation that attempt to address one component or another of the societal problems that lead to criminal activity. The relative paucity of these programs combined with a poor funding structure hampers their effectiveness, generally speaking. However, these programs can serve as the blueprint for the direction of a coordinated and systematic effort to address social ills. The presentation of several of these efforts will provide some insight into the appropriate course for systemwide planning.

An example of a program that seeks to address the roots of crime by focusing on adolescence is the Edwin Gould Academy in New York City. This program is a residential facility that accepts the most troubled and damaged children and seeks to provide intervention services in areas like substance abuse, anger management, and poor life skills (Thompson, 1999). This program, rather than focusing on punitive measures, seeks to build children up and assist them in a positive transition into adulthood. Open less than a decade, this program has already been recognized by such organizations as the Ford Foundation and Harvard University (Thompson, 1999). An implicit awareness in this program is that a punishment orientation drives away those who most need the services. Focusing instead on the development of skills creates a positive environment that can truly address substantive problems.

The New Horizons School in Capitola, California, is another program that seeks to reverse the tide of desperation in children's lives. A private, nonprofit program that provides educational services to homeless street children, New Horizons attempts to reach the children who "fall through the cracks" (Maitre, 1998). Operating out of space it rents from a church, the program gets no federal or state funds. The school seeks to address areas other than simple educational needs, including emotional needs. Addressing needs rather than punishing children because of their parents makes this a unique program (Maitre, 1998). Providing education to street children is a difficult task and far removed from the dominant approach, which usually seeks to remove such children from school.

Bilingual education programs, much maligned in this country, have also proven effective in assisting immigrant children in receiving an education. Such efforts can have far-reaching consequences by bringing people into the mainstream of society and furthering their economic opportunity. Ironically, several states, notably California, have attempted to ban bilingual education and other states have passed "English as official language" statutes that attempt to prevent bilingual education. These approaches can only be seen as backwards thinking grounded in bigotry, racism, and xenophobia. In other countries people demand that their children receive instruction in a second language and view this as a sign of a well-educated person. It is only in the U.S. that people not only refuse to learn a second language but actively work to prevent others from receiving a well-rounded education. Being fiscally responsible is one thing, making children suffer because of their parents is poor policy with little eye to the future.

Ignoring efforts to thwart positive programs, as politics invariably influence all programs, several recent efforts fit in well with the proposed overhaul of the criminal justice system. Positive steps in the provision of early services include a type of program slowly emerging in many states that attempts to link services and provide a comprehensive solution to social problems. Similar programs in a number of states include the FACT (Families, Agencies, Communities, Together) program in North Carolina, Multi-Needs Child Services in Alabama, FLAG (Families Learning and Growing), and WRAP services (which relate primarily to juveniles entering the system). What all of these programs have in common is an attempt to intervene with families in total and to coordinate a vast array of services. The awareness that behavior does not occur in a vacuum and efforts to focus on family systems are major positive steps.

The FACT program provides a good example of this approach. Beginning out of a limited-time grant, FACT attempts to establish a coordinated system of care for children and adolescents with severe emotional disturbances. The program seeks to empower the family by making them the focus of all efforts. Treatment is tied to the development of strengths in the family and sees the agencies involved in the process as secondary. This is a radical reformulation from that formerly seen in the human services field with a deficit focus that places the family as subservient to the agencies providing intervention. Using a strength-based approach that places emphasis on empowering the family mitigates the typical adversarial nature of such efforts. A unique component of this program is that parents actually become employees under the establishment of a "parent-in-residence" program, where parents already in the program serve to assist others beginning involvement.

Extension of similar concepts to all youth throughout the school years and efforts to make the school the center of the community and service delivery would prove valuable in the prevention of later criminal activity. Several researchers have demonstrated that those who are at risk for committing crimes and engaging in violent behavior are readily identifiable as youth (Magnusson, Klinteberg, and Stattin, 1992; McCord, 1994; McCord and Ensminger, 1997). As such, identification of at-risk youth is another crucial step in the prevention of later problems (Lyman, 1996). Beyond identification, the coordination of services, such as a day treatment service (a program that provides on-site, highly specialized mental health services) to mentally ill students, probation services to legal offenders, and the like, are necessary to alter successfully the violence and trouble that plague our society and filter down to our schools. Discussion of culture and the passage of new laws are not the answer. People solve problems, not laws. Only through the provision of labor-intensive, viable intervention services will there be any likelihood of effectively addressing the future of our children.

ALTERNATIVES TO INCARCERATION SERVE THE INTERESTS OF EVERYONE

Beyond efforts to intervene and provide services proactively, there is rising awareness that incarceration will not solve all of our problems (Sarasohn, 1992). More progressive jurisdictions and some less progressive ones, driven by space considerations, are attempting to address first-time and petty offenders through means other than incarceration. Unlike the previous section discussing specific programs that are beginning to address multifaceted issues, the programs described in this section are generally more widespread and have somewhat larger goals. Many of these efforts have grown out of logistical maneuvers to deal with the burgeoning inmate population. As such, many are a product of necessity. Nonetheless, several of these approaches have underpinnings that make for good policy and seek to address the causes of crime.

Pretrial diversion programs scattered throughout the country, usually incorporating some type of deferred judgment, are one alternative that is popular. Deferred judgment withholds sentencing or a verdict until the offender has had an opportunity to address the issues that relate to the crime. The typical setup for these programs is that after arrest but before trial and sentencing the individual undergoes an evaluation and receives a list of actions necessary to avoid a conviction. If such actions are successful, the charges are usually dismissed and the person has no legal record. This approach recognizes that anyone can make a mistake and that a criminal record and sentence can be damaging. For many people, the initial shock of legal entanglement is enough to jolt them into a new mindset. Imprisonment at this stage may force people down a path that can only end in further criminal activities.

Pretrial diversion only allows a person to avoid a criminal record if he satisfies the conditions set forth by the court and has no further legal involvement. This approach is grounded in the idea of turning people around before they become habitual and serious offenders. The goal of creating better citizens and a better society is a priority and takes prominence over punishment. These programs actually address crime, save resources, and serve society. In sum, the goal is to prevent further crime, not to make sure that everyone suffers as much as possible for every wrongdoing.

Community service and restitution can be valuable features of pretrial diversions. However, they can also be incorporated into convictions and sentences. In some jurisdictions, primarily for political reasons, pretrial diversion and deferred judgment are likely unacceptable as "too soft" on crime. But in the case of first-time and petty offenders, where a criminal conviction may be warranted but jail time is not, some type of sanction may be appropriate. Community service, whereby the individual performs some action that benefits the community, serves both the purpose of punishment and can instill a sense of community connection and pride if handled properly. The difficult part relates to the proper selection of activities for community service. Far too often community service becomes an exercise in picking up trash or some other menial and meaningless work that makes little impact on the person so sentenced.

Restitution is an ancient and time-honored means of correction. Making things right as a means of addressing the criminal activity is the guiding principle here. Often this involves some type of monetary remuneration or compensation, especially in cases of theft, burglary, and vandalism. This process can be very punishing to felons in that they are forced to provide service or money in such a way that they are reminded of and confronted with their criminal acts. Further, restitution forces individuals to assume responsibility for their acts, a noted difficulty in most criminal cases.

Restitution, it should be noted, does not have to be in the form of monetary compensation. Having individuals perform labor or other services for their victims might be particularly effective in driving home the nature of the violation of others' rights. In many Native American cultures (e.g., Lakota and Navajo) restitution and the idea of making things right (i.e., restoring harmony) is viewed as far more important than punishment. In Asian cultures as well, harmony is seen as a prominent social value instead of retribution.

Alternative approaches to punishment, rehabilitation, and correction allow for the punishment to fit the crime and likely go a long way towards addressing the issues that lead to criminal behavior. Substance abuse and mental health issues are ubiquitous in the justice system. Yet treatment of these problems is noticeably lacking. In the area of substance abuse, treatment efforts are minimal. According to the Justice Department, there are only 6000 substance abuse treatment slots available annually even though their own figures show that at least 60 percent of the over 125,000 inmates have substance abuse problems (Federal Bureau of Prisons, "Quick Facts," 1999). At a bare minimum, this works out to over 70,000 who need treatment. This disparity between treatment availability and need occurs despite the presentation of treatment as extremely effective (Federal Bureau of Prisons, Office of Public Affairs, 1998). It would seem that in the massive prison budget increases there should be funds to expand programs that address the basic causes of criminal activity. Programs addressing core problems that contribute to crime should be able to lower the rates of incarceration, and hence costs to the system, as well as changing life patterns.

EFFECTIVE SOLUTIONS FOCUS ON THE PROBLEM

Drug courts, whereby individuals charged with drug offenses are sentenced to rehabilitation in lieu of prison, may provide an increasingly important means of addressing the effects of drugs on society. Further, many crimes, burglary in particular, are motivated by drug habits and as such are particularly suited to alternative means of intervention. Several states, Florida is noteworthy in this respect, have instituted similar programs to address the large volume of drug-related offenses. In these specialized courts, several procedures are in place that are similar to those of deferred judgment. The emphasis is on treatment of the addiction or substance abuse pattern instead of punishment. Successful completion leads to an expungement of the record instead of serving as a gateway into the criminal justice system.

In order for these programs to be effective, the growing trend towards punishment must be reversed. As treatment professionals can attest, substance abuse treatment and counseling tend to have a high failure rate and often require several efforts in order to "stick." Ingrained habits are often very difficult to break and the current HMO-influenced trend of twenty-eight-day treatment programs (magically the same length most insurance policies cover) may not be sufficient. In order to accommodate these factors and to further the goals of breaking habits, it may be necessary to allow numerous trips to rehab and increase the standard treatment time.

Those heavily into punishment might object that this is letting people off the hook and not holding them accountable. This suggestion is grounded in misunderstanding of the nature of substance abuse. Most substance abusers, especially those whose habits are so ingrained that they must resort to crime to support them, are generally disinterested in treatment. Being sentenced to a rehab facility is likely to prove far more punishing than a similar stay in prison where drugs are easily acquired. To those who might question the availability of drugs in prison, data related to executions in Texas should serve to illustrate the point. Since 1985, the state has had difficulty with the executions of at least six prisoners due to collapsed veins resulting from drug use. If those on death row have such access to intravenous drugs, what is likely for the rest of the inmate population who have greater freedom? A former federal inmate once described to this writer the process by which he would have two pounds of marijuana brought to him in the prison simply by making a phone call. Believing that imprisonment will keep a person away from drugs is naïve and unrealistic.

Farming drug offenders out to treatment facilities might prove very beneficial. By placing those sentenced to rehab in facilities where others are attending voluntarily would likely further the process of change. Effective programs often involve a component in which the patients/clients confront each other concerning use and attendant personality features. Mixing with the general population may aid in treatment. The other approach is to set up facilities dedicated to drug offenders who are court referred. Either of these approaches might work and both present positive and negative aspects. In the long run there is likely a place for both of these approaches. Comparison of the two might even provide valuable information on the treatment of substance abuse disorders.

Mental health issues are also prominent among persons involved in the criminal justice system. As noted in an earlier chapter, I am not referring to full-blown psychoses or other such conditions that might require hospitalization or might provide exculpation of the charges. Rather, I am talking about the presence of anger-related problems, poor coping skills, and so on, that are apparent in many involved in the system. First offenders, especially in the case of minor assaults, barroom brawls, and the like, could well benefit from counseling and anger management training. At present the response to such crimes is incarceration. Interestingly, the only area in which counseling has been adopted as a preferred mode of intervention is domestic violence. Many states mandate domestic violence counseling when parties that are in relationships become involved in domestic disputes. The provision of services to domestic violence offenders is important in that it can serve not only to maintain a family but to change the patterns of violence as well.

Victim-offender mediation is another tactic that may work particularly well in cases of conflict that have escalated. Because such disputes often occur between neighbors, relatives, couples, and so forth, this approach is unique in that it forces the offender to face his or her victim. The personification of the victim is something few have to deal with under the current system. However, this can have dramatic impact on the offender. The means that people use to psychologically distance themselves from their actions seem to contribute to the increasing violence in our society. Through the use of guns and other long-distance methods of committing crime, the actual effects on victims are lost.

Finally, among these concepts is a new approach called "restorative justice." Restorative justice is similar to restitution in that its core premise is the concept of making things right. Restitution and community service are two avenues commonly used in models of restorative justice. The basic tenet is that the harm done to the community and the victim must be addressed and that the offender must be part of these efforts (Quinn, 1998). In many ways a throwback to older models of justice, restorative justice is not a program per se, but a philosophical orientation that seeks to address the damage done to the individual or the community instead of relying on punishment by society in the name of the victim without addressing what happened to the victim.

All alternatives to incarceration seek to address the effects of crime while lowering the costs, both economic and social, of the criminal justice system. These methods seem to point to an awareness that punishment alone is not the answer to crime. The extreme incarceration rates of the past two decades with no coinciding drop in the crime rate are presented as evidence of the failure of the punishment orientation.

PRINCIPLES OF PUNISHMENT ARE APPROPRIATELY UTILIZED

A review of the literature as it regards punishment leads to only one conclusion about the criminal justice system: Those making policy must have been absent in their introductory psychology class the day punishment was discussed. It has long been established that in order for punishment to be effective, it must meet three criteria: punishment occur swiftly, moderately, and with some degree of certainty/consistency (Bower and Hilgard, 1981; Robert Dufort, personal communiqué, November 1985; Skinner, 1938, 1972). Our present system meets none of these conditions.

Interestingly, it is the condition that punishment be moderate that has been most ignored. Although neither swift nor certain can be used to describe our current system, those from both sides of the spectrum agree that it should be. But the emphasis on increasingly draconian and overly severe penalties subverts both of these. Due to the nature of penalties, those seriously involved in crime make every effort to delay their trials and sentences. The system, in an effort to handle numbers, sets schedules months in advance and constantly postpones and delays hearings. Rarely are the motives behind such legal maneuvers brought out in the open. Were individuals under the impression that they might receive reasonable punishment, we might be able to speed up the court process.

Let us look further at the idea of moderate punishment. In our rush to become more punitive, the goals of the system have been lost. Instead of trying to turn people from a life of crime, our current approach seems geared to drive individuals further to the fringes of society. We forget or overlook that excessive punishment engenders resistance and at a certain point becomes counterproductive. Excessive punishment does little to alter people's behavior but does a lot towards making them angry at and hate the agent who carries out the punishment. In the case of prisons, society at large administers the punishment. Is this really what we are trying to accomplish, making individuals hate society?

The U.S. is a tremendous hypocrite when it comes to the laws of other nations. We decry human rights abuses in other lands but seem to support institutional abuses in our own country by the police and other officials with little protest. For example, as much as we complain about the Chinese government's treatment of political prisoners and forced labor, there seem to be few demonstrations against the conditions in which people in U.S. prisons live. Have we developed some mindset that whatever we do is okay because we fancy ourselves champions of human rights? Events like the King, Diallo, or Louima incidents are rarely connected to state-tolerated terrorism, but where is the difference? This is especially true when the racism and violence present in our society are given any attention in this issue.

I recall in 1994, when a nineteen-year-old American by the name of Michael Fay was caught spray-painting graffiti in Singapore and sentenced to several lashes with a cane. There was an enormous uproar in this country over the inhumane nature of the sentence and the harshness of the legal system in Singapore (Elliott, 1994). Islamic justice was often discussed as barbaric and uncivilized. As a nation, we seem to ignore the conditions in our own legal system. Is it more humane to put people in a tiny cell for twenty-three hours a day, limit all outside contact, and sever ties with the family than to cane them? Is cutting off a hand more barbaric than subjecting someone to forced sodomy and gang rape? When examined in this light, many of the practices we abhor in other countries seem less drastic than they are usually presented.

In light of the above and in an effort to address the extreme incarceration rates, the appeal is made to alter some of the punishment techniques currently in use in this country. Punishment does have its place in the criminal justice system. But in order for it to be effective, we must alter our collective mindset with regard to punishment. Shorter sentences that could be served immediately would have a great effect. I am referring primarily to sentences for relatively low-level offenses such as petty theft, shoplifting, pandering, and the like. For many who commit these crimes, prison only makes their life such that crime becomes their only alternative. Long sentences create resistance. Shorter sentences of only a few days' length would likely have a greater psychological effect. It may seem difficult to fathom that a ten-day sentence might have a greater long-term effect than a ten-year sentence but consider what is likely to happen. In a ten-year sentence, filled with abuse and near-torturous conditions, the individual may lose hope and give up on any efforts to change. Further, the person may become so embittered that he is filled with rage towards society. Ten days, on the other hand, may convince the individual that a life of crime is not worth the hassle.

Our rejection of any approach not grounded in extreme, long-term suffering and punishment is nonsensical. Many approaches discarded in the past as cruel would now be considered too lenient. For example, discarded methods such as public stocks or even caning/whipping might serve a valuable place in the reformulation of a criminal justice system that focuses on the prevention of crime. These methods likely would serve us better and be far cheaper to administer than the current "lock them up and throw away the key" efforts. Seemingly harsh measures should not be discarded outright, but effectiveness should be the main criterion for any punishment instituted. At present satisfying bloodlust and some notion of extreme punishment as a measure of success guide the system. Pushing punishment to the limits of torture is not ethically justifiable nor is it good policy.

Using the principles herein would likely result in a substantial decrease in the correctional population and a drop in the crime rate. The outcome would not only be a safer society but would also create massive savings in terms of prison construction. Such savings could then be put into education and treatment programs that could further reduce the need for incarceration. On a positive note, support for the idea of early intervention and treatment has come from a very unlikely source. The International Association of Police Chiefs has recently become an advocate for just such policies ("Police: Pay now," 1999). Perhaps the voice of just such a group that few see as "soft on crime" can add weight to sway this debate. A consistent, coordinated and well-thought-out plan is necessary to address the effects of crime on our society. The "get tough" approach has been used for too long and has been a miserable failure. The strength of humans lies in our ability to use our brains, not brute force.

Chapter 12

CLASSIFICATION AND TREATMENT: EARNING RELEASE

It is not enough to be busy, so are the ants. The question is: What are we busy about?

—Henry David Thoreau

The overhaul of the criminal justice system presented thus far is directed towards early intervention and community-based treatment. No matter how effective this reformulation might be, the reality remains that some people will require incarceration. Some crimes, such as murder or pedophilia, likely require a sanction of prison. Certain individuals with whom previous efforts have failed may require some form of incarceration in order to address their problems.

Previous chapters have referred to the need to provide rehabilitation services to prisoners for the overall good of society. Violence and other antisocial behaviors have been conceptualized as not unlike other behaviors that can lead to civil commitment. These behaviors are considered unacceptable and dangerous both to the individual and the community at large. In this way, violence and criminal behavior are seen as not very different from actions ensuing as a result of mental illness.

When conceptualized in this manner, criminal behavior is seen as a symptom of a much larger problem. Szasz (1994) has presented the position that through the use of psychiatry, many people are treated coercively against their will because society sanctions it. As Szasz points out and as echoed herein, none of these persons have been convicted of anything. By extension, if individuals who are interfering with no one, have violated no laws, and do not wish to receive treatment have treatment forced upon them; is there any rational argument for *not* providing treatment to incarcerated felons? It seems that all of the rationales for forced treatment apply to those behind bars.

The reason why those incarcerated do not receive treatment is not that there is a movement to prevent coercive treatment, but because treatment itself is viewed as a benefit and is therefore withheld in the name of punishment. In effect, criminals are allowed to avoid any efforts to alter their behavior because of the shortsightedness of politicians and the mindless adherence to "get tough" policies.

In order to successfully address the various difficulties that bedevil those in the criminal justice system, a program must be developed that recognizes the individual and preserves his/her rights. Elements of the plan must both draw the individual into the plan (i.e., gain cooperation) and confront the actions that led to incarceration. In the current conceptualization, those that reach this point in the system are likely affected by multiple and fairly serious problems.

To address these various life problems and difficulties, an approach similar to that used in psychiatric and special education settings will be utilized. That is, a plan is developed for each individual by looking at both needs and strengths and then relating these to treatment goals. In this approach both long- and short-term goals seek to address major areas of weakness and build on areas of strength. These plans are variously referred to as treatment plans in psychiatric settings, service plans in social service agencies, and individualized education plans (IEPs) in education. The phrase individualized treatment plan (ITP) or treatment plan is used herein. While ITP will be used throughout the text, because of the author's preference, any term might be used. Individualized rehabilitation plan (IRP), for example, might be appropriate and serves to set the process apart from schools and hospitals.

Several factors are thought to be necessary to effectively utilize the treatment plan approach. These features, detailed following, include:

- multidimensional/treatment team concept
- continuous review
- incentives to participate
- release tied to successful completion
- individualized plans (no "canned" programs)

TREATMENT TEAM CONCEPT

The treatment team concept is one that is often utilized in psychiatric settings and stems from the idea that no one knows everything. Probable composition of treatment teams would likely include social workers, psychologists, education specialists, and other such personnel. The underlying assumption is that approaches to the same problem from different angles can lead to novel solutions and better coordinated treatment efforts. In the world of the incarcerated felon, treatment teams are also valuable in terms of developing a full and accurate picture of the individual in question.

As noted, many convicted felons are manipulative, deceitful, and antisocial. The practiced antisocial personality is able to successfully manage his image and the impression others have of him by reading the emotions and personalities of those with whom he has contact. Treatment teams are good ways to manage this tendency by having the individual meet with the entire team. It is easy for a person to manipulate or con one person, or even six people separately, but it is exceedingly difficult to do so with all six at the same time. Due to the fact that behaviors that are effective with one person may not be so with another and with increasing numbers it becomes exceedingly difficult to manage the entire facade. To bend an axiom from Abraham Lincoln, it is very difficult to deceive all of the people all at the same time.

The purpose of a treatment team, however, is not just to make it difficult for a manipulative felon to con prison staff. The primary purpose is to develop a program to meet these needs identified and to work with the individuals in addressing those needs. In order for this to work, a number of disciplines must be represented on the team. It is likely that specialized treatment facilities or different levels within the system might need to individually tailor their programs and thus their treatment teams. Presented herein is a rough outline of what could reasonably be expected with the "modal" prisoner at present.

At present, the average prisoner is uneducated, has few social skills or resources, is disconnected from both family and community, has few job skills, and displays aberrant behavior. There are also the commonalities produced by incarceration and the lifestyles that produced incarceration. These problems alone seem to suggest it would be reasonable to have a psychologist, a social worker, an education specialist, a vocational specialist, and other specialized personnel on the team to address issues such as substance abuse or other factors. Further, under the proposed system, there must be a primary counselor for each inmate who serves as case manager and treatment coordinator. Experience also suggests that it is a good idea to get those members of the staff who work most closely with the inmates involved. "Line" staff, as they are often called, are usually the least trained, poorest paid, and most endangered members of the prison staff. These persons are vital to the efficient running of any institution. They also spend by far the most time in direct contact with inmates. Placing these individuals on treatment teams serves the function of having a view of the inmate under "normal" circumstances and providing a less trained, but perhaps more honest view of the person. Such participation also serves to develop skills in staff through contact with professionals and also provides a more basic understanding of the total goals of the treatment approach.

A cautionary note at this point is that although the concept of treatment plans is borrowed in part from psychiatric hospitals, the focus should not be medical. Rather, the dominant feel of the institution would ideally be one that was a mix of an academic institution and a monastery. That is, inmates would have the experience of being active participants in a process designed to allow them the opportunity to acquire new skills while being in an environment compatible with self-study and contemplation. Medical focus or control over this process is thought to be misguided and opens the door to a variety of abuses, most prominent is that no one is ever released because of fears of malpractice suits.

As stated, the exact components of the team may vary. It is crucial that there be adequate staff to maintain this approach. Further, scheduled treatment team times must be adhered to as they are the lynchpin of the process. Slacking off or just going through the motions will sabotage this approach. Finally, administrative and bureaucratic control must be removed from treatment or rehabilitation decisions.

CONTINUOUS REVIEW

Under any program where people are expected to change, feedback is a vital component. Further, since the judgment of many incarcerated people is markedly impaired and there is a tendency to distort or misinterpret information, constant feedback is needed to prevent any number of problems. Regular feedback also serves the purpose of reminding the individual why he or she is incarcerated and what the parameters are for release.

Ideally, feedback would occur in the form of a regularly planned performance evaluation with the team. All members of the team would meet with the inmate and evaluate progress on short-term goals. Completed goals would be followed up by the development of other short-term goals that move the inmate closer to meeting various long-term goals established at the beginning of incarceration and tied to release. For example, an inmate who has the long-term goal of learning to effectively manage his anger would have a short-term goal of reducing angry outbursts or initiating conflict with others. When this short-term objective is accomplished, another level of anger management is introduced until the person has met the long-term goal. Inmates need to be actively involved in the development of the plan as this serves the psychological purpose of increasing acceptance and participation.

Logistically, inmates need to receive some type of number or grade that can objectively spell out for them how they are doing. Given the low levels of literacy and education common in most inmate populations, this procedure needs to be relatively straightforward and easy to comprehend. Subtleties are often lost in a forensic population and clarity is important to prevent misunderstanding and even manipulation. Assigning a specific number or grade serves the dual purpose of giving tangible feedback and allowing for the tracking of behavior.

The scheduling of feedback or review sessions should be done in a manner that it ensures maximum impact on inmates. In effect, a big deal should be made out of the evaluation. A way to achieve this is to set aside a specific time each week in the schedule of the institution where all that happens is evaluation and review. Approximately one fourth of all inmates should be reviewed each week by their team in order that everyone may receive a once monthly review. Thirty days is a reasonable time to allow for change efforts. Any longer and you risk losing cooperation, and if more frequent, treatment efforts are being forced. Those not up for evaluation remain in their cells for reflection during this time. To prevent this from becoming a session for staff to meet their needs through continuous disparagement of the inmate or the inmate from berating the staff, a time limit needs to be set for this evaluative period. One hour should be sufficient to allow feedback but not so lengthy as to be bog down the system.

I initiated such a treatment team approach at a juvenile facility with encouraging results. Those incarcerated were able to get some idea of how they were perceived by staff and if they were making progress towards release. Several institutional factors, such as understaffing, set release dates, and court orders to reduce numbers in the system, worked at cross-purposes with this approach. Nonetheless, the overall behavior of those incarcerated changed noticeably, primarily due to awareness that unacceptable behaviors would be challenged and that failure to progress would delay release. The "con's code" that prevents cooperation with the institution was also undermined because those in the facility could use release and treatment team review as an excuse to avoid various conflicts. An unintended consequence was that those who were most disruptive and antisocial were quickly identified, resulting in additional attention being focused on them.

Realistically, some inmates will progress faster than others through this system. Some will make little progress or resist treatment altogether. These factors only serve to make inmates aware of the control they have over their own fates. Seeing others progress and leave reinforces the message that it is up to the individual to change his or her own life. It further serves to encourage one to take responsibility for one's own actions. This can even have the effect of controlling behavior within the system as release is tied to action, not a predetermined sentence. It also allows for inmates to be confronted directly for unacceptable behavior by the people, their treatment team, who are most immediately in charge of their lives.

INCENTIVES TO PARTICIPATE

An unspoken feature of the treatment plan approach is that it makes failure to participate very uncomfortable. Those who decide to wait out their time and resist treatment are allowed to do so. However, they also must attend mandatory review with the treatment team on a regular basis. Here they are confronted with their lack of participation as well as reminded of the consequences of nonparticipation, which is no progress towards release. In this sense, the get-tough camp should love the feature of treatment teams that prevents release of those refusing to address their problems.

But allowing people to subsist in prison and not be released is not the goal of this approach. Instead, the goal is to encourage change through participation. One method by which that is done is progression through one's short- and long-term goals. An unfortunate reality of the treatment plan method is that individuals sometimes have a hard time motivating themselves to work for goals that are far off in the future. More tangible and immediate reinforcers are likely needed to ensure that the majority of inmates will freely participate. These reinforcers can be provided in terms of privileges that are granted through a levels system.

Levels systems are utilized in the field of mental health and institutional work to garner the cooperation of the population served. Individuals work towards the accumulation of points as tabulated on a card. The totals accumulated are then used to determine the level of privileges the person is entitled to. Infractions can lead to loss of level, but the idea is to get everyone to the highest level and maintain an orderly facility. In many ways the outcome produced by a well-developed levels system is directly in line with the demands of the institution in terms of producing a smooth-running facility. Yet I have witnessed a great deal of resistance from prison administrators to the use of incentives. The mindset seems to be that prisoners are being given something and therefore it is objectionable. This mindset is grounded in misunderstanding and misconceptions of incentive programs. Under this system no one is given anything, everything is earned. This is not just a semantic distinction. A very real and important part of the approach is that one must earn each level. Many inmates have a self-entitled outlook that is a major part of their pathology in coping with society at large. By instilling the idea that one earns a place in life, the attitude of entitlement is confronted.

The Nuts and Bolts of a Levels Program

The initial set up of a levels type program is crucial. In order for the program to be effective it must be tailored both to the institution and to the inmates who live under its guidelines. Incentives that occur at each level must mean something to the inmate and must also be able to influence behavior. In other words, if the inmates do not buy into the system, it is not going to work.

In a levels system some type of token economy or point system is utilized whereby individuals living under the system earn a token, which can be any type of object that can later be traded for various items or privileges. Many institutions use poker chips, play money, or some other tangible object. Point systems basically utilize the collection and tally of points on a sheet of paper (the point card), which individuals carry throughout the day. In order to encourage responsibility, it is up to the person who is receiving points to ensure that these are properly awarded.

Both of these approaches require safeguards to prevent inmates from manipulating the system, in particular cheating. It is unlikely that a token economy that provided an actual token would be suited to correctional facilities. One reason is that tangible objects small enough to be carried by inmates would be subject to theft and extortion among the prison population with the result that those not following the program would have the most incentives by engaging in antisocial behavior. Another reason to rule out the use of actual tokens is that they would quickly become the currency of the prison and this would alter the therapeutic goals. Logistically, tokens are too hard to keep up with and a constant supply would have to be repurchased. For this reason alone, another alternative would probably prove more beneficial. Use of a point tally or point sheet would be most useful and appropriate within a correctional setting in terms of conservation of resources and the furtherment of treatment objectives (see Figure 12.1).

In order to successfully use a point system, rather stringent control of whatever means is used to evaluate hourly and day-to-day effort is vital. Ways to prevent cheating on the cards or tally sheets should be given a great deal of thought in the planning stages. If not, the whole procedure will become a fiction manipulated by inmates. These assertions are based on experience, not conjecture. I recall once seeing my signature on a point card that I had never seen. The signature was so close that I could not tell the difference, but I had never seen the individual whose card my signature was on. Forgery and other such actions are fairly easy to commit under this system without safeguards. The use of a hole puncher to stamp out the appropriate block on the card is the best means I have seen to do this. The hole puncher becomes part of every prison staffer's complement of work tools and must be carried all the time. Staff initials are added to provide some means of checking up on those who might figure out ways to circumnavigate the hole-punch process.

Beyond changing or altering the point card, other types of cheating can occur. The most glaring is the "lost card." This is a scheme often used whereby when one has a bad day the card is reported as "lost" or "stolen."

Figure 12.1
Sample Point Card

NAME:
ID#:
LIVING UNIT:
CURRENT LEVEL:

TIME PERIOD	POINTS EARNED					STAFF INITIALS
6:00	1	2	3	4	5	
7:00	1	2	3	4	5	
8:00	1	2	3	4	5	
9:00	1	2	3	4	5	
10:00	1	2	3	4	5	
11:00	1	2	3	4	5	
NOON	1	2	3	4	5	
1:00	1	2	3	4	5	
2:00	1	2	3	4	5	
3:00	1	2	3	4	5	
4:00	1	2	3	4	5	
5:00	1	2	3	4	5	
6:00	1	2	3	4	5	
7:00	1	2	3	4	5	
8:00	1	2	3	4	5	
9:00	1	2	3	4	5	

TOTAL = _____

Perhaps the card really has been misplaced or stolen. However, to accept this as an excuse destroys all accountability. A method referred to as "total accountability" can work wonders in addressing this issue. Under this method one is totally responsible for whatever happens to oneself. If a card is lost, stolen, destroyed or whatever, it is the responsibility of the inmate. If a card is not turned in at the appropriate time, a zero is earned for the day.

Daily tallies are to be completed at the end of every day. This can be done by night shift personnel and serves to keep these staff occupied and alert during the night. Weekly totals accumulate and determine the overall level for the following week. By using a system that reassigns levels every week (or every two weeks), one ensures that inmates are constantly working to attain privileges and that no one is able to coast on the basis of past performance.

In the example, points are awarded each hour by the prison personnel who are in charge of that individual at the end of the time period. Individuals not participating in any activity and choosing to sit in their cells receive no points for that time period. This serves the purpose of encouraging participation in rehabilitation efforts and efforts made to address treatment goals. Note that every hour of the waking day is listed. The underlying premise is that inmates are to be kept busy and active every minute of the day if at all possible. There should be little idle time throughout the day.

The use of a five-point scale is for demonstration purposes only. According to scaling theory, the scale used in such a system makes no difference to the outcome (Thurstone, 1938). However, for simplicity and to ease understanding as most inmates are not expected to have good math skills, numbers should be small enough for the average inmate to work with under normal circumstances.

Levels System—An Example

In order for the concept of a levels system to positively affect the behavior of inmates, it is necessary that the privileges garnered through the point system be relevant and considered worth working towards. If not, it is unlikely that behavior will be shaped by incentives. Beyond the use of a levels system as a means to alter and control the negative behavior of inmates while incarcerated, it is possible to utilize the practice as a means to instill prosocial behavior and behavior that is adaptive outside the correctional facility. An example of this is through encouraging development and maintenance of the family unit on the outside. Again, it is important to keep in mind that the purpose of a point system and the levels that follow is to eliminate negative behavior and encourage positive behavior. The purpose is not to take away points through charging infractions, rather the goal is to give points and reward positive behavior.

For all point systems, the taking away of previously rewarded points is counterproductive. Focusing on negative behavior rewards it merely by the attention given. This is particularly true of those who are predisposed to negative and antisocial behavior. Along the way these individuals usually learn to revel in negative attention. Point and levels systems become ways to alter this reaction. Therefore, the deduction of points is to be avoided. This will only lead to reactance issues as discussed elsewhere in this text. Further, the deduction leaves the system open to abuse by staff members and creates an overly punitive mindset. In a psychological sense the best way to deal with negative behavior is to ignore it. This is difficult for many if not most individuals but is crucial unless one wishes to reinforce the very behavior one is trying to eliminate.

Particularly true in any behavioral attempt to change individuals is the old therapeutic adage that things don't get the way they are overnight and it is, therefore, unrealistic to expect them to change overnight. The changing of behavior is a slow, laborious process. Individuals must be held accountable, but there must also be a degree of reason involved that recognizes that most incarcerated people will have difficulty adhering to any type of system geared to change their behavior. As a result it is necessary to get the individual to buy into the process and view it as something that is to their advantage. Levels should be posted within the living unit and the current level should be indicated for each inmate, perhaps on the current point card. A sample of the privileges that might accompany each earned level follows:

Level 1: Few privileges. Receive only those things mandated by law. This level should be somewhat uncomfortable and should contrast starkly with privileges accorded to those at higher levels. Inmates functioning at this level are likely going out of their way to be uncooperative.

Level 2: Standard privileges. Examples of some privileges would be:

- all level 1 privileges
- phone time
- ability to direct own schedule
- ability to participate in group activities within living unit

Level 3: Increased privileges. Examples would be:

- all level 2 privileges
- increased phone time allowed.
- additional visitation
- work privileges are granted
- minor freedom of movement granted

Level 4: Highest level of privileges. Examples are:

- all level 3 privileges
- unlimited phone calls during free time
- daily or semi-daily visitation allowed
- increased pay for work
- increased freedom of movement
- conjugal visits

The number of levels presented, four, is by no means magic. As long as there are sufficient means to differentiate between levels, any number is acceptable. At a certain stage, one is likely to reach a point that makes the differentiation meaningless if there are too many levels. For general purposes four to six levels are likely sufficient.

The rewarding of privileges ideally should be based on the individual inmate. This is likely to be unfeasible given the constraints of prison life, so a generalized process has been presented. Please note that those entering the system do not start on the lowest level. The idea is to prevent complete discouragement upon arrival. Also note that privileges are earned, not given. Again, this is not just a semantic distinction but an integral part of the overall approach.

The list of privileges presented above is by no means exhaustive. Effort on the part of the treatment teams in a facility should lead to the development of many privileges that can be incorporated into the overall program. The idea is to create privileges that inmates value and want rather than something they get for just walking around. Note that many of the privileges presented herein such as phone time, visitation, and even conjugal visits relate to the maintenance of ties on the outside to family and friends. Conjugal visits alone would be a tremendous incentive to maintain appropriate behavior within the institution. In addition, conjugal visits could serve a function that would likely lessen the levels of violence within the institution.

RELEASE TIED TO SUCCESSFUL COMPLETION

Levels systems like that described above are primarily related to acceptable behavior in the prison environment on a day-to-day basis and the exchange of this for privileges. Maintaining a good level on the system is not related to release in any direct way. Indirectly, however, as one can accumulate points for participating in treatment and other rehabilitative activities, there will likely be a strong connection. A field test of this idea in a juvenile facility demonstrated a strong relationship between positive behavior as measured by a levels system and efforts to address problematic life areas. Despite this connection, actual release is entirely predicated upon the completion of treatment goals outlined in the ITP. The use of incentives and privileges in a levels system is intended to encourage participation. Levels should be conceptualized as a means of getting inmates to buy into the system, not an end unto itself.

An important fact that must be taken into consideration concerning the introduction of treatment plans and indeterminate sentencing is the reaction it will produce in inmates. Initially, there will likely be some grumbling and irritation. The subjective nature of this evaluation will cause some degree of stress through frustration. This can be therapeutic in the sense that the inmate must deal with ambiguity and develop new coping strategies.

Just such tolerance is necessary for successful reintegration into the workforce and life with others on the outside.

Therapeutic concerns aside, this proposed system seeks that release only occur after the inmate has addressed the very concerns established at the beginning of incarceration that led to his or her criminal acts. Evaluation of this progress by treatment professionals ensures that decisions are made on the basis of progress. Prison administrators often have pressure related to bed space, overcrowding, and financial concerns that can affect and alter their judgment concerning release. Placing these decisions in the hands of professionals creates some checks and balances to ensure that release does not occur just to satisfy the wheels of the bureaucracy.

INDIVIDUALIZED PLANS

An important facet of any individualized treatment plan (ITP) is that it be specifically tailored to each individual. A common approach to prisoners is to assume that they are all the same. That is, people are sentenced on the basis of their crime as if everyone committing the same crime is exactly alike. Common sense alone tells us that not everyone committing a crime is the same. Truly, it does matter if one is committing burglary to feed one's family or committing the same act to feed one's drug habit. In the first case the individual may need some job skills or social training while in the second he may need substance abuse treatment and reconnection to his family. Therefore, all rehabilitative efforts should be tied to the nature of the life problems and circumstances that are determined to play into criminal acts.

Conducting a thorough evaluation to determine needs and strengths is the first step in the development of a treatment plan. Initial assessment would evaluate the individual in a number of areas including psychological, social, educational, and vocational. These four areas are likely able to address most of the concerns that are usually present in incarcerated persons. Including a fifth category of "other" to address medical problems and any other factors would make sure nothing falls between the cracks.

Within each of these major areas, the establishment of both long- and short-term goals will identify the areas that each convict needs to address. Long-term goals are usually unattainable in the foreseeable future. Short-term goals serve as intermediate steps towards goals identified as long-term. The development of these goals, suffice it to say, should flow from the identified needs and strengths of the individual. In some areas an individual might have no concerns and therefore would not have to complete any tasks in this area. Most incarcerated people will have multiple areas of concern and will have to address most, if not all, of them. Many inmates will have multiple goals within an area. This assertion is made primarily based on experience and the baseline of most inmates. Psychologically fit, socially well-adjusted, graduate-school educated, and occupationally skilled individuals are not the typical prisoner.

The development of treatment plans is well known to most professionals in this field. They are the blueprint for successful intervention and provide guidelines for the progress and direction of all efforts. As this is not a treatise on how to conduct treatment, extensive detail on the development of goals is not presented in this context; instead readers are referred to the numerous manuals on the topic.

An important cautionary note is in order as it concerns the development of plans. Goals must be written specifically for the individual and not taken from some predetermined list of "canned" goals. This is nothing more than a cookie-cutter approach that falls back into the one-size-fits-all trap. Goals must flow from the evaluation. Involvement of the inmate in the development of the plan is also necessary. In this way, inmates begin to participate in rehabilitation efforts from the start. Completing the tasks outlined is their responsibility, and in order to progress prisoners must take charge of their own life.

SAFEGUARDS

Various safeguards will need to be put in place in order for the approach detailed in the preceding pages to work. Foremost, prisoners must have the right to refuse to participate in any type of activity. They will receive no points for these actions or inactions and no coercion will be applied to force participation. The rationale is that each individual is responsible for his or her own actions. In essence, one has the right to sit and do nothing, receive no privileges and make no progress towards release. This is a choice that inmates make of their own free will and as such they accept both the responsibility and the consequences for the decision. The treatment team will examine these actions at each monthly review.

It is not inconceivable that certain prisoners will actively refuse to participate in any type of rehabilitative effort no matter how much it might benefit them. To prevent the lifetime incarceration of minor and petty criminals who are just too stubborn to participate, some safeguards will need to be put into place. The establishment of a maximum determinant time should serve to address this concern. It is important that this time frame be such that those who do participate rarely reach this time, otherwise all functioning under the system would give up. However, establishing a time frame of maximum incarceration makes an effort to prevent severe human rights abuses related to unjustifiable terms of incarceration.

A safeguard necessary to counter the effects of authoritarian, punitive staff trying to meet their own power needs relates to the taking away of points in the point system. The deduction of points has no place in the system. In any point system, the goal is to make people work for the points. Deductions destroy motivation and defeat the larger goals of the system. This happens when individuals receive deductions that result in an inability to achieve any level. Once this occurs, there are no constraints on behavior, and we are back to the same uncontrolled state as presently exists.

My experience with deductions is that they tend to be arbitrary and capricious and more influenced by the internal needs of the person taking the points away than of the person from whom they are taken. For some reason, the giving up of punitive measures seems to be difficult for those involved in the correctional system. It is necessary to move beyond such an orientation. Focusing on what someone does wrong tends to perpetuate the cycle of negative behavior and does little to encourage prosocial actions. Keeping in mind that changing negative behavior patterns is the goal, there must be a shift in this attitude. Training in the purposes of a point and levels system is important. In the implementation of many of these ideas, I found great initial resistance among staff, but a few training periods to explain purposes and goals proved effective. Finally, the single most important factor to get staff to buy into the process is the message that all of these efforts will eventually make their work life easier and safer.

TRAINING INITIATIVES NEEDED

In order to staff the delineated program so that it can achieve success, it will be necessary for the criminal justice system to embark on a different approach to the recruitment and training of personnel. Rather than spending funds on guards, construction, and pointless security overkill, resources must be channeled into personnel. I am not advocating a gutting of prison budgets but rather a shift in the way funds are utilized. The creation of a professional criminal justice staff that involves personnel from multiple disciplines will be costly but is necessary if we are serious about reversing the tide of crime. The infusion of professional staff into the institutions would likely decrease some need for guards and security personnel by keeping prisoners busy throughout the day.

Greater numbers of treatment professionals will need to be trained in order to meet the objectives made necessary by this approach. At present, training in forensic areas is minimal for most psychologists and social workers, not to mention vocational and educational workers who typically receive almost no training in these areas. An example of the numbers needed can be seen by examining the actual number of psychologists working in the corrections field at present. Currently, an estimated 800 psychologists and 1200 master's level clinicians are working in the criminal justice system (Clements, 1999). This total of two thousand such personnel compares poorly to the close to two million inmates currently incarcerated. In effect, this is a ratio of 1000:1 of inmates to clinicians. Any hope of changing people must begin by recognizing this is insufficient. The establishment of programs to train corrections professionals makes better sense than relying on unskilled security personnel to maintain order and direct institutions. Further, criminal justice and criminology degrees should provide training for field work and not merely be avenues to train probation officers. The challenge is whether we can sufficiently train the numbers needed to make such an approach work.

Chapter 13

PREVENTION IS NOT A FOUR-LETTER WORD

> Let us put our minds together and see what life we can make for our children.
>
> —Sitting Bull

By the time people are incarcerated and forced to deal with their problems, these same problems have become ingrained and difficult to alter. The longer any problem, behavior, or attitude persists, the greater the difficulty in changing the behavior. As a good mechanic can attest, it is easier to take care of and maintain something than to fix it. By the same token, care and early intervention efforts with people prevent the need for constant remediation efforts in the future.

Unfortunately, taking care of people is remarkably lacking in today's society. There seems to be no shortage of funds to incarcerate our citizens or wage war on other countries' citizens. Even by the most conservative estimates (the U.S. government), approximately 20 percent of total government spending is for military purposes (Office of Management and Budget [OMB], 1998) and can range up to 50 percent depending on the source. Social spending, on the other hand, is hotly contested in the political halls. There seems to be little available to assist people or provide services of any kind other than necessities. Education, for example, receives less than 2 percent of total government outlays (OMB, 1998).

To illustrate that disparity in spending, contrast the availability of funds for different governmental programs and agencies. When the U.S. becomes involved in military conflict, cost is rarely a consideration. When the issue is raised, it is usually a red herring disguising a deeper political conflict. Whether the issue is war or police actions, NATO defense forces, "peace-keeping" activities, or any other military conflict, all spending is deemed to be necessary for the survival of our nation and its people. But when it comes to any type of social spending, questions of cost and affordability are inevitably raised.

The real question is not whether we can afford to spend on social issues. The real question is whether we can afford not to. Social problems rarely fix themselves and invariably worsen if not addressed. It becomes an issue of pay now or pay even more later, not a question of affordability.

A cynical viewpoint, but not without foundation, is that a decision has been made to pay later. We seem to operate under the idea that we should let someone else (i.e., our grandchildren) pay for our folly. Couched in terms of self-reliance and responsibility, the prevailing trend is towards a social agenda that places profits, free enterprise, and a low tax rate above the general well-being of the populace. Social spending, care for people, and the future of our children are being sacrificed in order to keep the economy running smoothly and increase short-term quarterly profits.

Efforts to eliminate welfare (Welfare Reform Act) for poor people, provide school choice (i.e., vouchers for the wealthy who send kids to private schools) and repeal capital gains and inheritance taxes while maintaining a regressive tax system (think sales tax) are among many tactics that indicate an ongoing, unspoken effort to transfer wealth from the poor to the rich. It is Robin Hood in reverse. The sham is that many of these ideas are couched in profamily and prochild terms. School "choice," for example, is presented as a way to gain access to better schools when in practice it is a subsidy program for those wealthy enough to afford private schools. Noam Chomsky has referred to this distortion as a "triumph of propaganda" as an "anti-child, anti-family agenda" being promoted for the benefit of the wealthy and multinational corporations (Chomsky, 1994). Look at the Welfare Reform Act for a demonstration of this truism. In an age of admonishing people to spend more time with their children, those formerly on welfare are now having to work two jobs to meet the demands of day-to-day life.

In reality, prochild, profamily language is, as Chomsky states, an attempt to manipulate people in the service of the wealthy. A glance at the corporate tax structure and the subsidies given to large corporations points to several interesting conclusions. While social welfare spending is being targeted for cuts, corporate welfare is at an all time high. According to the Cato Institute, corporations receive over $75 billion in direct subsidies each year (Moore and Stansel, 1995). Investigative reports by the *Boston Globe* compiling figures for subsidies, write-offs, tax-breaks and direct give-aways put the figure corporations receive each year at a much higher level, $150 billion (Sennott, 1996). Such give-aways of our national resources to for-profit businesses only serve to artificially stimulate the private business sector at the expense of the public social sector. As noted in the *Globe*, the level of corporate subsidies is greater than that combined for all of the direct primary assistance programs run by the government exclusive of social security and medical benefits (Sennott, 1996).

The actions discussed above do not necessarily indicate any deliberate or conspiratorial intent, but they speak of a very skewed set of priorities. Namely, economic considerations are preeminent with little attention being paid to the development of society. Profits have been placed before people. Mammon has become the ruler of America. The effects of this on society are difficult to estimate.

As the trend of decreased social spending took hold in the 1980s with the Reagan and Bush administrations, the numbers incarcerated rose dramatically (168 percent increase in the years 1980–1992 according to the Bureau of Justice [1998]). Interestingly, few government officials seem to make any connection between incarceration rates and the destruction of the social safety net. The notion that slashing social spending is to be fiscally conservative is more of a popular political fiction than anything based on reality. Any savings have been spent incarcerating more and more people. It seems that a realistic viewpoint on this issue recognizes that criminal justice spending and social spending are on different sides of the equation and that any savings in one area are costs in the other. Social policy alone is not the entire answer to the levels of crime in society but is a gauge of the nature of our attitudes. At present, an increasingly harsh approach is taken to citizens with incarceration as the preferred means of social control.

It seems unusual that a country founded on the basis of liberty and freedom would opt for incarceration as its primary means of controlling its citizens. This approach is likely reflective of the adversarial and aggressive nature that has become all too common in the United States. Incarceration does nothing to address our real problems, it just postpones the eventual clash by removing those elements most blatantly symptomatic of the schisms that exist in society. Examination of the issues that contribute to crime is one means by which to develop an approach that does not view incarceration as the only and final solution. The issues that affect the social climate and contribute to crime include poverty and the culture of materialism, misdirected social policy, ubiquitous substance abuse, the gun culture in which we exist, racism, intolerance, and police misconduct, among others. This list is not exhaustive, but it does serve to point out some of the more prominent problems on the social landscape.

POVERTY AND THE CULTURE OF MATERIALISM

Despite the fact that the economy of the U.S. is rolling along as the twenty-first century begins, this is not reflected in the day-to-day existence of most people. There is a growing disparity between the "haves" and the "have-nots" of the world. Increasing numbers live in poverty during these times of abundance. It is estimated that fewer than 400 of the world's wealthiest people control more wealth than the poorest 2.3 billion, according to the United Nations (1996). In the United States the wealthiest 3 percent have an average net worth of $1.7 million and control 46 percent of all financial resources (MacroMonitor, 1996) while 13.3 percent of the population lives below the poverty line of $16,558 for a family of four (U.S. Census Bureau, 1999).

How this inequitable distribution of wealth relates to crime is multifaceted. Poverty, while a major factor, is not the only piece of this puzzle. The overemphasis on material wealth in our society has elevated consumerism to a lifestyle, if not a quasi-religion. It is this need to consume and acquire possessions that fuels much of the crime in society. Even in the world of street gangs and cartels, the emphasis is on the money, not the drugs.

Money is what drives consumerism. The constant bombardment of sales pitches and advertising has greatly altered Western society. People receive the message that they "need" things to be happy or to be accepted. There is an unstated premise that external consumption can make up for what is lacking internally. The ultimate example of how Western society is manipulated and drawn in by advertising and the need to feel that one has it all is a recent ad campaign in New Zealand for a fictitious product called "Nothing." After billboards were placed for the product, people went to the trouble of calling the billboard company to find out how they could purchase the "needed" product (Cox, 1999).

It is unrealistic to think that the poor will be more immune to advertising campaigns than the wealthy. Being subjected to marketing at every turn and offered unsustainable lines of credit (at lending percentages that approach usury) only adds to the problems of consumerism. Those without money want the things they see advertised as much as those with money. Or as a gang member once stated to me, "I'm gonna get mine." The message is that in order to be acceptable in a materialistic culture, everyone must purchase, consume, and buy. The perpetuation of poverty in a society that values materialism and consumption is guaranteed to lead to increased levels of crime.

SOCIAL POLICY

Social policy is the logical avenue for addressing the effects of poverty upon our society. It has long been noted that the easiest way to become wealthy is through inheritance. Unfortunately, it is also the way in which most become poor. Social conservatives seem to operate under the assumption that the poor have brought poverty on themselves, as if people choose to live in poverty just to get social assistance. This is simply asinine. No one wants to be poor. Being poor is usually a difficult, miserable existence, which presents a unique set of challenges that can make life a struggle for survival.

Few wealthy people understand the challenges of living on a limited income. It is easy to tell people to live within their means but this is exceedingly difficult to do when one's means are not livable. Simple arithmetic demonstrates the challenges for a single mother living on an income of $10 per hour (nearly double the current minimum wage). Before taxes, this family has about $20,000 per year, which is well above the established poverty level. Consider minimal monthly living expenses of $400 for rent or mortgage, $200 for food, $150 for electricity, gas and water, $300 for social security and payroll taxes. The family is already down to less than $7500 for the rest of the year for all items like clothing, school supplies, automobile insurance, gasoline, emergencies, and all other costs.

In our example, the family can barely meet its needs for food and shelter. But then there are expenses like health care and savings for future educational costs. Is it at all likely that this family can afford any of these? In general, the working poor are forced to gamble on matters like health insurance and hoping nothing happens. Preventive care is usually out of the question.

Attacks on a proposed national health care system always involve complaints of socialized medicine and removal of choice. These are nothing but straw dogs set up to hide the real reasons for not establishing a national system, which are that the AMA and various HMOs have far better lobbies and contribute more to political campaigns than do poor, disenfranchised people. Public policy for the benefit of the wealthy and little in the way of services for the poor has become standard practice (Zepezauer and Zepezauer, 1992). Expecting services from one's government is not socialism. Failing to ensure the health of its citizens seems to go against the common sense of any nation that hopes to prosper. A recent article in the trade paper of the American Psychological Association called for recognition of the current HMO-guided approach to health care as a "failed policy" (Foxhall, 1999).

Education is another area where little is done with regard to social policy to confront crime. As noted, lack of education and the commitment of criminal acts go hand in hand. Yet, over the past twenty years or so, we have gradually reduced school funding by approximately the same amount that spending on prison construction has increased (Suro, 1997). The Justice Policy Institute indicates that the lack of priority for school funding will have deleterious long-term effects on society, including raising the cost of tuition for college students and making higher education more inaccessible for economically disadvantaged youth (Suro, 1997). Yet the trend is to make schools "accountable" and ensure that every dollar is well spent. It would be nice if education spending were allocated like prison spending, the worse the job is done, the more money comes in. If schools received additional funds because their students were behind, perhaps we could provide adequate education.

Providing adequate education does not appear to be a priority. The hottest issue in education today is providing vouchers for private school attendance (Bast, Harmer, and Dewey, 1997; Greene, Peterson, Jiangtou, Boeger, and Frazier, 1996; Moe, 1995; Toch, 1998). This concept serves to diminish public education by taking funds away from the poorest and giving them to the wealthiest. If voucher programs were providing people with real choice (the argument made for vouchers), then there would be a flood from the public schools. In most proposals, the amount of the voucher reimbursement is set at some figure well below most private school tuition. The result is that those who opt out of the public schools are given a figure like a $2500 tax break if they can afford the rest of the approximately $10,000 tuition. It does not require a high degree of mathematical knowledge to see that for the single mother described earlier, there still is no choice in the matter. What vouchers do in the long run is to gut the public school system of desperately needed funds in order to subsidize those wealthy enough to opt out of the system. The city of Milwaukee alone lost an estimated $30 million in revenue in one year after a voucher program was instituted in Wisconsin (People for the American Way, 1999). Schools improve with adequate funding and parental involvement, not by siphoning off funds and encouraging an exodus to private and religious schools.

Education and poverty are but two areas where properly directed social policy could have an effect that would drastically lower the levels of violence and crime in our society. Other programs related to prevention and early intervention would serve us well. Identification of at-risk youth and provision of services to these children could go a long way towards preventing delinquency and later adult criminal behavior.

Free availability of drug treatment programs and domestic violence counseling would serve society well. The question of funding is, as I have indicated, just a red herring. Money spent on any of these programs should be viewed as an investment in the future. As stated earlier, the question is not whether we can afford it, it is how can we afford not to. Proactive measures will save us money in the long run and reverse the tide of increased incarceration.

SUBSTANCE ABUSE AND CRIME

Estimates of the effects of substance abuse on crime vary depending on the source and the purposes of that source, but the essential outcome is the same, drugs have a tremendous effect upon us as a people. Ironically, our very approach to the problem of substance abuse seems to bring violence and criminal activities to the forefront. Dealing with drugs as a crime rather than as an emotional and physical problem causes a vast array of problems.

With the adoption of the eighteenth amendment in 1919, the U.S. embarked on a bold social experiment that lasted fourteen years and came to be known as Prohibition. The manufacture, distribution, and sale of alcohol was strictly forbidden and punished. Those who drank were treated as criminals and an entire government agency (Bureau of Alcohol, Tobacco and Firearms) arose to deal with the problems of bootleg whiskey. Prohibition also led to the organization of various criminal enterprises that became dedicated to the manufacture, distribution, and sale of alcohol. Vast networks of distribution developed and men like Al Capone became major crime figures and social icons. Eventually, the violence and other attendant problems led to the twenty-first amendment, which repealed Prohibition.

Today, the approach to substance abuse is much the same as that of the prohibition era. With the exception of alcohol and cigarettes, all other substances used by humans to alter consciousness have been made illegal. Individuals caught possessing, manufacturing, or distributing these substances are subjected to long periods of incarceration. These policies have led to the prisons and jails bursting at the seams with people convicted of drug-related offenses. According to the Federal Bureau of Prisons (FBOP), approximately 60 percent of those incarcerated at the present time are there for some type of drug offense (FBOP, Quick Facts, 1999). Throw in those convicted of burglary and other crimes related to obtaining money for drugs and the percentages are even higher.

The idea that anyone is going to be cured of a drug problem in prison is naïve. People rarely beat substance abuse habits in prison. Rather, many habits are exacerbated by the very nature of the low-quality, nearly toxic substances used in the prison environment to perpetuate drug use. Inhalant use becomes more prominent as it is nearly impossible to run an institution without cleaning supplies and industrial solvents. The concoction of alcohol in the form of sour mash or even moonshine is easily accomplished. Prisons are rife with drugs, many brought in by the prison staff and others. It should not be surprising that experienced criminals would be able to get illegal substances into prison. Further, given the desperate conditions of most prisons, it is unrealistic to think that inmates would not seek to engage in escapism. If someone can remain drug-free in prison, they truly have conquered their substance abuse and addictions. Knowledge of human nature suggests that it is far easier to develop a substance abuse habit during incarceration than to cure one.

Greater provision of substance abuse treatment programs before incarceration could go a long way towards lowering the rates and costs of the criminal justice system. There is a growing awareness that unless drug cases are handled alternatively, the entire system will collapse due to sheer volume. The development of drug courts that apply only to drug offenders is one solution that is beginning to have widespread appeal. The present system is unable to even begin to address the numbers in need of treatment with far less than 10 percent of those needing treatment having access to it, and this according to the governments own figures (Federal Bureau of Prisons, Office of Public Affairs, 1998; United States Department of Justice, 1997).

Beyond the implementation of alternative means to address the use of illegal drugs, a new approach is beginning to emerge. This approach is centered on the question of whether substance use and abuse is appropriately dealt with as a legal issue. As Prohibition taught us, the illegality of any substance leads to far-reaching consequences as concerns criminal activity and violence. Whenever any product has legal constraints placed upon its sale and use, the price immediately goes up and the profit potential increases. This is why drug dealers generally oppose legalization efforts, it robs them of their profit.

Legalization and decriminalization are beginning to be discussed by an array of politicians on both sides of the political spectrum. Kurt Schmoke, the liberal former mayor of Baltimore, and William F. Buckley, the ultraconservative pundit, have taken the lead on this. Others prominent in calling for discussion of this issue include Ethan Nadelman of the Lindesmith Center and the Republican governor of New Mexico, Gary Johnson. The difficulties in engaging in discussion of this issue have been made prominent by the reaction to Gov. Johnson, who caused a tremendous uproar in his own party by even advocating discussion of the issue. Residing in a neighboring state at the time Johnson first made his proposal, I was astounded by the attacks against him from within his own party. The nature of these attacks does not bode well for rational discourse on this subject.

Decriminalization, especially of marijuana, is the idea usually raised as the most reasonable starting point in this discussion. Decriminalization, while more palatable than legalization to many people, is a very unusual approach to the issue. It is like a civilian drug use version of "don't ask, don't tell." Decriminalization removes the criminal stigma from use but does not make the substance legal. Possession is not illegal, but manufacture and sale are not legal either. It is exceedingly difficult to think of any other example where this is the case. It seems that decriminalization is considered more palatable because society is not giving any type of approval of the use of drugs but is rather seeking to avoid dealing with the issue. When it comes to drug use, denial seems to be the fifty-first state.

Legalization, as opposed to decriminalization, accepts the right of individuals to do whatever they want to themselves. Legalization also has a feature that decriminalization does not: the ability to regulate and tax the substances in question. Under legalization, drugs can be regulated in such a way that they become more difficult for minors to obtain because they would have to show identification and adults would become reluctant to purchase for them. Adolescents with whom I have worked have routinely confided to me that it is much harder to procure alcohol and cigarettes than it is to obtain various illegal substances from marijuana to methamphetamines. Rarely considered, it is the very lure of the illegal that makes drugs more attractive to adolescents during the phase of rebellion. Zero tolerance strategies and the equivocation of all illegal drugs only add to the problem.

When all drugs are lumped together as one big bugaboo, a false message is given. There is a difference between occasionally smoking a joint and shooting heroin. To act as if these are the same is to make the message seem ludicrous and hence rejected out of hand. Rational and realistic discourse is needed on this issue. There is long-standing and pervasive recognition that societies that do not allow for social drinking tend to have higher rates of alcoholism (Rathus, 1999). Is it unreasonable to think that the same would apply to other substances? Ironically, the nature of the debate on drugs in the U.S. over the past thirty years has cut off valuable and promising research into substance abuse treatment. In the late 1960s, both here and abroad, a line of research investigated the use of hallucinogens such as LSD and mescaline in the treatment of alcoholism. The current political climate in the U.S. has made such research almost impossible. As a result, almost all such research occurs in Europe. In Africa, there is some anecdotal evidence that a substance called ibogaine has promise in the treatment of narcotic abuse. There is also some evidence, again anecdotal, that mescaline, used ceremonially by the Native American Church, has promise in the treatment of alcoholism. Due to the current political climate surrounding drugs, these avenues of research are cut off and unavailable for research.

Taxation and subsequent use of the money raised are strong justifications for legalization of the various drugs that are illegal at present. Consider the following: If only 4 percent of the U.S. population smokes marijuana (a gross underestimate of the actual numbers) at a rate equivalent to one pack of cigarettes per month (again, likely to be an underestimate) and a tax of 10 dollars per pack was instituted, over $1.2 billion dollars in revenue would be generated in one year! Actual numbers would make this amount far greater. Quite a bit of substance abuse treatment could be funded with a billion dollars. This could be real treatment of whatever length was needed, not the twenty-eight days allocated by HMOs. It may be counterintuitive, and certainly against the grain of moralists on the issue, but legalization of drugs would serve to decrease use through the provision of widely available rehab programs. Maybe the real hope is to show the medical industry how much money there is to be made from legalization.

Even many legalization proponents draw a line at marijuana. This is simply not consistent and is again driven by moralist thinking. Legalization of all substances allows for the development of a consistent and coordinated approach to our substance abuse problem. Drug abuse, like most problems, is rarely solved by being kept secret and in the dark. Only by addressing the issues head on can there be hope of resolution. Needle exchange programs, for example, where addicts can trade in used needles for clean ones, thus preventing the spread of HIV, can provide an avenue to get addicts into rehab services. When such programs are subject to legal harassment and political pressure, their effectiveness is diminished and junkies continue to use and continue to steal to finance such use.

To state that legalization is giving in to substance abuse is misdirected. Alcohol and opiates have been used for thousands of years. All societies seem to have some type of legalized drug. As soon as a new drug appears, large numbers try it just for the experience. Efforts to suppress and control drug use go against human nature. As a society we can either deal with this issue head on or we can continue to drive substance abuse underground, encouraging criminal involvement and illegal activity in the process.

AVAILABILITY OF HANDGUNS IN THE UNITED STATES

The United States is unique among the nations of the world in its dedication to guns and weapons. In Great Britain, despite years of IRA actions, even the police do not routinely carry guns. Many nations, such as those in Scandinavia, severely restrict or prohibit private gun ownership. So bizarre is our behavior to the rest of the world that in Japan we are dubbed the "Gun Society" (Preso, 1994).

But America is a unique nation in that guns are considered to be a sanctimonious right. The second amendment, which technically states the right to keep and bear arms, is the primary authority for private gun ownership. This would be a little easier to take if most Americans had any inkling of the historical reasons for the second amendment and were not supporters merely because they like to shoot things or have some psychosexual attachment to guns.

As one who strongly supports the Constitution and the Bill of Rights but sees the enormous societal costs, I have struggled with the issue of guns for several years. Having worked with gang members and various other criminals, I am greatly aware that many people who carry guns and use them to commit crimes have no philosophical commitment to the Constitution or the rights of others. On the other hand, the idea that one must understand one's rights or even be committed to them in order for them to apply is clearly ridiculous. From the vantage point of one who has observed this issue over time, most of the defense of the second amendment comes more out of paranoia over the government than any other feature.

This concern over government actions is, in my opinion, the reason why the second amendment was written in the first place. As stated in the Declaration of Independence " . . . whenever any Form of Government becomes destructive of these ends, it is the Right of the People to alter or to abolish it. ... " Given that the Declaration of Independence and the Constitution were largely influenced by a small group of people, Thomas Jefferson most prominent among them, it stands to reason that there is some connection between the two documents. If the real purpose of the second amendment is to ensure the right of the people to arm themselves for a revolution (or to establish an army), then possession of weapons is the real issue, not gun ownership. From this vantage point, I am sympathetic to the view that the right to keep and bear arms is grounded in the intent of the founding fathers and the Bill of Rights.

But protecting one's rights and taking up arms for political purposes is far removed from the day-to-day use and ownership of guns. Ironically, many criminals can state "I have a right to have a gun" without any real understanding of the legal basis for this claim. Although understanding one's rights may not have any legal bearing upon the validity of that right, the intention involved does seem to be of relevance.

Examination of the first amendment provides a framework for looking at the second amendment in the same light. The first amendment, which relates to free speech, is primarily related to political speech. In the course of exercising free speech one may not slander, libel, or otherwise defame another. Further, the injury to others is found to be the limiting feature of free speech. The example most frequently cited here is that free speech does not allow one the right to yell "Fire!" in a crowded theater. The rationale behind this decision is that the right to be alive supersedes the right to engage in physically endangering acts that have little to do with the intent of the first amendment. Intent in the second amendment can be seen as analogous to intent under the first amendment. The intent behind the act can be as important as the act itself.

Extending the argument concerning the physical endangerment of others to the second amendment suggests an interesting dichotomy concerning the possession and ownership of guns and weapons in our society. In effect, one has the right to keep and bear arms as long as one does not utilize them in the service of physically endangering others. This interpretation would allow for the possession of weapons by collectors, the use of guns for hunting and, I suppose, even the stockpiling of weapons for political reasons. What would be prohibited would be the use, procurement, and possession of guns for purely antagonistic purposes. In effect, use of guns for violent purposes is equivalent to yelling "Fire!" in a crowded theater.

Those following this argument thus far may wonder about the practical effects. It is obvious that such an interpretation would apply to those who use guns in the commission of crimes to prevent further gun ownership by them. But its effects could also be greater. One class of weapons that is particularly involved in the commitment of crimes and has little use under the legitimate purposes listed above is handguns. Handguns have little purpose other than the murder of human beings. As a general rule they are poorly suited for most hunting or military purposes. Yet, the effects of handguns are enormous.

According to a survey conducted by the Department of Justice in 1987, guns were the weapon of choice in nearly three-quarters of all murders committed by juveniles. Among adults the tendency is even greater. In terms of sheer numbers, the majority of murders are committed with handguns (U.S. Department of Justice, 1996). The simple fact is that guns are far more lethal than any other method used to kill people. Handgun use is so strongly implicated due to such commonsense facts as the idea that it is hard to sneak up on someone and take them by surprise carrying a shot gun or rifle. Indeed, a survey of murders published by the FBI and the Department of Justice indicates that the vast majority of murders are committed with handguns (*Uniform Crime Reports*, 1998). Simply by removing handguns from our general population, the effect on the level of violence in this country would be enormous. During discussions with gang members concerning the possession and use of handguns, one conclusion was startling: carrying a weapon makes one feel bold and empowered to the point that violence is almost inevitable. Carrying a gun makes one act in a manner that is unlike that of an unarmed individual. One takes chances, puts oneself into dangerous circumstance, and develops a false sense of security, all because the gun makes one feel safe.

This feeling is deceptive and false. Research has shown that those who own guns are 2.8 times more likely to be killed with a gun than those who do not (Preso, 1994). Further, the person most likely to be killed with a handgun is its owner. The false sense of security provided by guns is apparent in discussion with gun owners. An informal survey of coworkers within the criminal justice system revealed that many carried guns when off duty. Their rationale was that they were more aware of crime because of their jobs and felt a need to protect themselves. Yet, when I questioned them over whether they were prepared to shoot or kill someone, a surprising percentage (over 60 percent) stated something to the effect that they had no intention of using the gun, it was just to protect themselves and scare off attackers. I was stunned by this response. People who worked day after day with convicted felons and were seemingly aware of the nature of crime were thinking in a completely illogical manner.

Most criminals are far more comfortable with guns and violence than their victims. Pulling a gun on an armed criminal and being unable to use it is going to get one killed. This is the point that few seem to realize. Even individuals who work with criminals and are somewhat coarsened by the experience are not prepared to do what it takes when confronted by a violent individual. The reverse of this is that those who are willing to use the gun will, like Bernard Goetz, find an opportunity to do so.

Handguns, at least from this writer's point of view, have no legitimate purpose. As a society, addressing the wide availability of handguns is paramount to any efforts to reduce violence and aggression. Registration and background checks are a start. It is estimated that the background checks and registration required by the Brady Bill have already prevented thousands of convicted felons from obtaining guns. But as has been pointed out, most criminals could care less what the law is and obtain weapons through illegal means. As a result, strict registration is not enough.

Guns are already so prominent in the public domain that a need for innovative solutions is apparent. Gun purchase programs that attempt to get guns off the street by buying them or trading for them are one promising means to start. Related efforts such as the Boston Crime Project developed by David Kennedy of Harvard University that attempts to get guns off the street by tracking gun dealers also have great promise. Banning the production of new handguns would also be a major and decidedly contentious approach. Interestingly, a recent barrage of lawsuits against gun manufacturers is causing some level of economic inviability in their production. If the argument from gun makers is that their right to free commerce is being infringed upon, then I suppose narcotics manufacturers can make the same argument. Even the most ardent free market idealist is likely to reject that argument. There really is no legitimate reason for owning a semi-automatic machine pistol unless one believes one might have to kill many people at close quarters rapidly and without warning.

RACISM AND INTOLERANCE

Perhaps more than any other features, racism and intolerance alter the fabric of society in such a way as to add to the levels of violence and crime. The effects of racism not only in the criminal justice system but in the larger society as well directly contribute to the social ills of our country. Racism is ubiquitous and not well hidden. The posting of signs stating "whites only" or the presence of separate facilities are a distantly remembered part of history. Unfortunately, this does not mean that racism and intolerance no longer exist. The presence of groups such as the Aryan Nations, World Church of the Creator, and the Ku Klux Klan attest to this fact.

But racism in America does not stop with a few well-publicized white supremacists. It is the subtle, nearly undetectable intolerance of others woven into our society that diminishes us all. The case can be made that the reason our response to crime has shifted to punishment and a lack of rehabilitation and early intervention is the fact that most people associate crime with minorities. As long as crack was a primarily inner-city epidemic, there was little concern. But as soon as crack began to make its way to white suburbia, there was a rapid response to incarcerate dealers.

Minority youth being killed in the inner city reached near catastrophic levels in the late 1980s and early 1990s. At the time there was little concern about this other than protests that movies such as *Boyz N the Hood* (Singleton, 1991) were destroying our morals (interestingly, any viewing of this movie can only point to the conclusion that it is antiviolence in orientation). But when white kids in the suburbs and rural areas began shooting in schools, there was a great motivation in Congress to address the issue.

Likewise, the economic despair in the inner city has rarely been the focus of attention or remediative efforts. Banks and other lenders routinely refused to support economic investment into the inner city. Major retail chains would not open stores on grounds that it was unprofitable. The infusion of money and the development of economic projects from a few wealthy celebrities such as Magic Johnson with a chain of theaters has shown the fallacy of these arguments.

Driving while black, DWB, police stops have become routine in many areas of the country (ACLU, 1999). Many African-Americans feel completely alienated from the notion that police protection and societal inclusion are available to all (Galvin, 1999; McCall, 1994; Walker, Spohn, and DeLone, 1996). Even government figures support the disparity that exists, with minorities being twice as likely to live in poverty as the average population. Native Americans fare even worse, being three times as likely to be incarcerated (U.S. Census Bureau, 1999).

Such disenfranchisement of minorities from the spoils of such a rich country leads to feelings of alienation and frustration. The disparity in treatment is obvious to minorities who do not see how the dominant Anglo culture can fail to recognize this inherent mistreatment. The answer, of course, is that the dominant culture does not fail to recognize this, it attempts to deny it. Minorities and immigrants have become the scapegoats for our social ills. Placing blame is important in the American psyche, as it serves to absolve individuals of responsibility. Further, blaming the victim allows society at large to think little about the mistreatment and disparate social conditions by viewing the mistreated and disenfranchised as responsible for what they get.

Psychologically protecting themselves from negative self-evaluation, people have a tendency to turn a blind eye to their own faults. This must be overcome. Specifically, the onus to address racism is on white society. There has already been far too much of a burden placed on minority groups to assimilate and acculturate. English-only laws, banning t-shirts with Malcolm X on them in high schools, and other such actions only serve to perpetuate the current state of affairs. Our diversity makes us strong. Many efforts could be instituted to begin to address this issue. Community policing, with police reflecting the racial mix of the populations they serve, would be a good start. The promotion of programs such as Teaching Tolerance, a free program provided to schools at request by the Southern Poverty Law Center, is also needed. Such programs, which seek to address the causes of racism in young children, could greatly assist in the goal of producing a more civil society.

CONCLUSION

The goals of reducing crime and the development of a more safe and civil society are noble ones. Yet, the means we have chosen to accomplish this are less than noble and, moreover, highly ineffective. The psychological need of individuals and society to extract retribution and dole out punishment is counterproductive from many different angles. The lack of any coherent and consistent approach to crime has led to a confusing and at times contradictory amalgam of laws and responses from the criminal justice system. The effects this has upon society are far-reaching and can be seen in such ideas as the advocation of jury nullification. Jury nullification is a concept championed by Paul Butler, a prominent legal scholar and law professor, that urges juries to acquit even guilty defendants if they see the law as an impediment to justice. More than being a controversial issue in legal circles, this idea demonstrates the depth of disgust for our current system.

Emphasis on the development and implementation of a comprehensive and consistent approach to crime is primary in this text. Abandonment of time-worn efforts that have proven an abysmal failure is a must in our future efforts to combat crime. A reformulation of the criminal justice system in such a way that early intervention and prevention of incarceration are guiding principles would be one positive step in successfully addressing this issue. The criteria for a successful programmatic approach to the problem of crime in our society are that crime goes down and fewer and fewer people are in need of societal intervention as opposed to the current approach, which judges success by the length and despair of incarceration.

The ideas put forth in the final section with regard to treatment have been developed such that they may be adopted singularly or in total. Rehabilitation, greatly lacking in our system for decades, must reemerge as an important aspect of the criminal justice system. If not, we as a people will continue to pay the costs, both social and economic, for increasing levels of incarceration. The education of our children and grandchildren will suffer. Ultimately, it is future generations that will pay for misguided, poorly considered acts of retribution.

GLOSSARY

Actus reus: guilty action

beat cops: the police officers who patrol a specific area on foot, usually within an urban area. The territory in which the officers walk is referred to as "a beat."

blue wall of silence: term used to describe the manner in which the police fail to admit or identify wrongdoing by other police. The covering up of illegal actions by other police is viewed as not only appropriate within the culture of the police but as a positive and laudable activity.

capital punishment: the death penalty.

civil commitment: process by which those deemed to be a danger to themselves or others are committed to psychiatric facilities. Individuals forcibly retained under these laws have broken no laws nor are they charged with any type of wrongdoing.

cognitive dissonance: a cognitive or mental state created by a situation in which one is forced to accept two conditions that are the opposite of each other and act as if these two conditions are in some way compatible. This condition is not so much related to physical reality or action but more to psychological mindset.

community policing: a program designed to assign police to particular communities where they are able to get to know the residents and act as an integral part of the community rather than as police who arrive only when crime is committed. In some areas efforts are made to assign police to areas in which they live and to have the make-up of the force reflect the demographics of the neighborhood.

community service: an alternative to incarceration in which the individual convicted of a crime is sentenced to perform some sort of service that benefits the community at large. Provides a means of punishment without incarceration and lessens the jail population.

competent: a legal standard that relates to whether defendants can understand the charges against them, assist in their defense, and follow the court proceedings. In reality competence is a very low standard and is easily met except by those with severely impaired mental functioning. Has little to no bearing on the issue of sanity.

corporal punishment: the process of punishing through the infliction of physical pain such as whipping or hitting. In the United States such treatment currently is in disfavor and often held to be a violation of the eighth amendment. Generally not allowed for adult prisoners, but allowed for school children.

"cruel and unusual punishment": prohibited by the eighth amendment to the Constitution. A vague and somewhat difficult term to apply, it is often reflective of the social climate and cultural values of the time in which it is interpreted. For example, at present, capital punishment is allowable while corporal punishment is usually not.

determinate sentencing: process by which the penalty for various crimes is based on the charge. Individuals serve a predetermined length of time with no discretion allowed on the part of the judge.

diffusion of responsibility: tendency described by researchers Darley and Latane for individuals to assume less personal responsibility and consequently not act the greater the number of persons present in a given situation. Research was originally stimulated by the murder of Kitty Genovese in New York City where numerous people watched her be killed but failed to do anything to intervene or call for help.

DWB: "driving while black/brown." Refers to the noted tendency of police to stop motorists belonging to minority groups with great frequency.

generalizability: the effect of causing behavior learned in one environment to transfer or generalize to a different environment.

Geneva Convention: agreement signed in Geneva, Switzerland, relating to the treatment of prisoners by their captors.

guardian ad litem: refers to an individual who is appointed to act as representative for another individual in legal proceedings. Usually a decision has been made that the individual in question, either because of age or mental condition, is unable to act in his or her own best interests for legal purposes.

Hammurabi: king of the Amorite dynasty of Babylon, established the first written legal code approximately 4000 years ago. The Code of Hammurabi is the forerunner of all current legal systems.

in loco parentis: phrase that refers to either the state or an individual assuming responsibility for a person. Society assumes the function of deciding what is in an individual's, usually a juvenile or incompetent adult, best interests. As the name suggests, this responsibility is considered similar to that of a parent if present.

indeterminate sentencing: process by which the length of time served is flexible and based on a number of factors. Judges have great discretion under this approach and can consider the circumstances of the crime, past records, and other relevant information.

jury nullification: process through which the jury can acquit a defendant even if they believe him/her to be guilty. Basis for the action is that unjust laws should not be followed or enforced. Proponents argue that the intent of being judged by a jury of one's peers was to prevent the enforcement of unjust laws. Position associated most prominently with Professor of Law Paul Butler.

La Cosa Nostra: name for the Mafia.

legal fiction: a concept used in the law to describe something that is not true in reality but is treated as if it were true for the purposes of the law. An example of a legal fiction is granting corporations the right to be treated as individuals under certain circumstances even though they are clearly not individual people.

levels system: a behavioral management approach that grants privileges and rewards in increasing degrees based on the individual actions of the persons living under the system. In theory, a levels system seeks to encourage positive behavior by providing a payoff for appropriate behavior.

mandatory minimums: legal sentencing approach that requires sentences of a mandatory length for various crimes. Serves to remove judges' discretion and is geared towards increasing the time served for most offenses.

mens rea: guilty intent.

militias: organizations of individuals who generally view the government as illegitimate and have banded together for "protection." The mixture of anti-government, white separatists, and politically motivated individuals all under one camp makes these groups difficult to predict.

moot: legal term that means the issue no longer matters.

offender profile: system developed and adopted by many law enforcement agencies in the 1980s and 1990s to identify suspicious persons who "might" be engaged in illegal acts. Successful challenges by the ACLU led to this approach being deemed unconstitutional.

OG: acronym for "original gangster." Term used to signify a long-time gang member. Within the culture of street gangs is used as a sign of respect.

perpetrator: (1) phrase used by the police to denote someone who has committed a crime. (2) term used by gang members to refer to individuals who claim gang membership but who are not actually members of the gang.

plea bargains: deals worked out between the prosecutor and the defense that agrees to charge, plea and sentence. Plea agreements remove the need for trial by these arrangements.

prisoner's dilemma: originating in game theory, this is the name for a situation in which co-conspirator's are pitted against each other in an effort to get them to confess. It is in each prisoner's individual interest to confess before his co-conspirator does so. The one who confesses is usually given a deal that reduces time in prison or even leads to charges being dropped. Cooperation among prisoners is the best means of avoiding jail time or leads to minimum time but is also the most risky strategy. Essentially plays on the adage that "there is no honor among thieves."

private prisons: for-profit correctional facilities managed by corporations that serve to incarcerate and punish persons convicted by the court system. Have gained prominence and acceptance due to severe prison overcrowding and the privatization phenomenon of the 1980s.

pro bono: work performed for free.

prosecutor: the attorney who represents the state in criminal cases.

punishment: the process by which aversive treatment is applied to an individual usually because of wrongdoing.

reactance theory: theory set forth by J. W. Brehm, which states that individuals will react negatively to attempts to control their behavior or to treat them in a negative manner.

rehabilitation: process whereby individuals are made better or improved through the provision of services that seek to address the causes of illegal or negative behavior. Attempts to restore the person to a more productive and less disabled state of being.

resistance: the process whereby individuals seek to resist efforts to force them to engage in unpleasant or undesired behavior.

restitution: concept involving the payment of services or monetary compensation as a means of correcting one's wrongdoing.

restorative justice: broad-based approach towards addressing crime that is founded on the idea of making things right.

restraint board: device used to restrain unruly prisoners. When placed on the board, prisoners have all limbs restrained and usually the waist and sometimes the head. Placement can be face-up or face-down depending on design. Has been litigated as abusive.

RICO: acronym for Racketeer Influenced and Corrupt Organizations. These laws are statutes directed against racketeering and organized crime that basically lower the threshold of evidence for the prosecution of a variety of offenses. Originally developed to prosecute Mafia members, now are increasingly used against street gang members. Mere association is often used to demonstrate wrongdoing and garner convictions.

sanity: a highly subjective legal term that relates to the accused's state of mind at the time the offense was committed. Sanity generally relates to the ability to determine right from wrong, to be in control of one's impulses, and to appreciate the nature and quality of one's acts. Those found to be insane are not considered to be culpable for their actions.

stacking: series of hand movements that indicate one's rank within a particular gang.

supermax: nickname given to the highest level of secured prison. Intended to hold prisoners who are uncooperative and disruptive in standard maximum-security prisons. Exists primarily for federal prisoners.

testilying: police term for courtroom testimony that is deliberately distorted in order to make the defendant appear more guilty. This may range from shading the truth to complete fabrication. Term used in police departments throughout America.

"thin blue line": term used to describe the police as a boundary between crime and the public at large.

"three strikes": policy that advocates life imprisonment for anyone convicted of three felonies. Politically popular, it is another reflection of "get tough" policies aimed at removing convicted felons from society. At present is leading to a crisis of overcrowding and insufficient prison space.

triads: Asian crime organizations.

truth-in-sentencing: effort to require prisoners to serve the full time to which they are sentenced. Attempts to abolish "good time" and prevent early parole.

"wannabes": individuals who want to be perceived as gang members. Often will adopt the clothes and mannerisms of particular gangs. May hang around the fringes of gang life and even progress to full-fledged gang membership. Term is often used derisively by actual gang members to describe those trying to associate with the gang.

yakuza: name given to organized crime figures in Japan.

zero tolerance: policy whereby every infraction, no matter how minor or insignificant, is punished. Part of the larger "tough-on-crime" approach, zero tolerance is increasingly being advocated for a broader array of problems from shoplifting to the misbehavior of children in school.

BIBLIOGRAPHY

Adler, G. (1985). Correctional (prison) psychiatry. In H. I. Kaplan and B. J. Sadock (Eds.), *Comprehensive textbook of psychiatry/IV* (4th edition). Baltimore: Williams and Wilkins.

Adorno, T. W., Frenckel-Brunswick, E., Levinson, D. J., and Sanford, R. N. (1950). *The authoritarian personality.* New York: Harper & Row.

Africa2000 (1999). A multi-billion dollar prison building boom. [On-line]. Directory: http://www.africa2000.com/CNDX/prison10.htm

Alexander, P. (1999, November 17). Inmate labor saves Buncombe money: Prisoners enjoy freedom; county enjoys savings. *Asheville Citizen-Times,* pp. A1, A4.

Alleman, T. and Gido, R. L. (1998). *Turnstile justice: Issues in American correction,* 1/e. Toronto: Prentice-Hall.

Allport, G. W. (1954). *The nature of prejudice.* Reading, MA: Addison-Wesley.

Ambrosio, T. and Schiraldi, V. (1997). Trends in state spending, 1987–1995. *Executive summary report—February 1997.* Washington, DC: The Justice Policy Institute.

American Bar Association (1997). Report by division of media relations and public affairs on plea bargaining. [On-line]. Directory: http://www.abanet.org

American Bar Association, Section of Criminal Justice (1996). *The state of criminal justice.* Center for Media and Public Relations. Lanham, MD: Author.

American Civil Liberties Union (1999). Spotlight: "Driving while black or brown." Spring, 1999, Issue 4. New York: Author.

American Civil Liberties Union (1999). 1998 Litigation and advocacy highlights. *ACLU Newsletter.*

American Law Institute (1962). *Model penal code, Proposed official draft.* Philadelphia: Author.

American Psychiatric Association (1994). *Diagnostic and statistical manual of mental disorders* (4th edition). Washington, DC: Author.

American Psychological Association (1978). Report of the task force on the role of psychology in the criminal justice system. *American Psychologist, 33*, 1099–1113.

Bast, J. L., Harmer, D., and Dewey, D. (1997, March 12). Vouchers and educational freedom: A debate. *Cato Policy Analysis*, No. 269.

Bates, E. (1998, December 16–22). Shadow of a doubt: Is the state about to execute an innocent man? *Independent*, pp. 13–21.

Bell, B. (1998, July 11). Ignacio schools OK spanking. *The Durango Herald*, pp. A1, A8.

Bouza, A. V. (1990). *The police mystique: An insider's look at cops, crime and the criminal justice system*. New York: Plenum Press.

Bower, G. H. and Hilgard, E. R. (1981). *Theories of learning*. (5th edition). Englewood Cliffs, NJ: Prentice-Hall.

Brehm, J. W. (1972). *Responses to loss of freedom: A theory of psychological reactance*. Morristown, NJ: General Learning Press.

British Broadcasting Company (1999). Amnesty International says U.S. jails too many juveniles. [On-line]. BBC News Online Network. Directory: http://news.bbc.co.uk/hi/english/world/americas/newsid-216000/216492stm

Bruckheimer, J. (Producer) and West, S. (Director). (1997). *ConAir*. [Film]. Touchstone Pictures.

Burghart, T. (1997, October 31). Standoff involving Illinois woman ends peacefully. *Durango Herald*, p. 5A.

Burrell, C. (1999, May 17). Preliminary FBI figures show drop in crime. *Durango Herald*, p. 5A.

Butterfield, F. (1998, August 3). Crime data may be fudged: Police feel pressured to show decreases. *Denver Post*, p. 2A.

Calhoun, J. B. (1962). Population density and social pathology. *Scientific American, 206*, 139–148.

Calhoun, J. B. (1971). Space and strategies of life. In S. H. Esser (Ed.)., *Behavior and environment*. New York: Plenum Press.

California Department of Corrections (1999). California department of Corrections Website [On-line]. Directory: http://www.cdc.state.ca.us/facility/instfd.htm

California prison spending hurts schools and black students, report says. (1996, November 21). American Civil Liberties Union Freedom Network. [On-line]. Directory: http://www.aclu.org/news/

Carroll, G. (Producer) and Rosenburg, S. (Director). (1967). *Cool Hand Luke* [Film]. Warner Brothers.

Carter, R. (1999, March 13). *The death penalty and the right to counsel*. University of Maryland School of Law Invited Address. Baltimore: C-SPAN.

Cary, E. (1998, April 15). *Police violence: Causes and cures*. Brooklyn Law School Forum. BLS Subotnick Conference Center, 250 Joralemon St. Brooklyn, NY.

Cashing in on black prisoners. (1997, September 30). American Civil Liberties Union Freedom Network. [On-line]. Directory: http://www.aclu.org/news/w093097a.html

CBS News (1999, February 3). *CBS Evening News*. New York: Columbia Broadcasting System.

Chomsky, N. (1994, November1). Speech. C-SPAN.

Clark, C. R. (1999). Specific intent and diminished capacity. In A. K. Hess and I. Weiner (Eds.), *Handbook of forensic psychology*. New York: John Wiley and Sons.

Clements, C. B. (1999). Psychology, attitude shifts, and prison growth. *American Psychologist*, 54, 785–786.

Coen, E. (Producer) and Coen, J. (Director). (1987). *Raising Arizona*. [Film]. Circle Films, Inc.

Compton's Interactive Encyclopedia [Computer software]. (1995). Cambridge, MA: Compton's NewMedia, Inc.

Cook, J. R. and Brewer, T. (1992). *Reading scores and cognitive abilities among an incarcerated juvenile population*. Unpublished manuscript.

Corsini, R. (1945). Functions of the prison psychologist. *Journal of Consulting Psychology*, 9, 101–104.

Cox, V. C., Paulus, P. B., and McCain, G. (1984). Prison crowding research: The relevance of prison housing standards and a general approach regarding crowding phenomena. *American Psychologist*, 39, 1148–1160.

Cox, C. (1999, July-August). Nothing quite like it: A New Zealand billboard spoof works a little too well. *Utne Reader*, 94, 24.

Darley, J. M. and Latane, B. (1968). Bystander intervention in emergencies: Diffusion of responsibility. *Journal of Personality and Social Psychology*, 8, 377–383.

Death Penalty Information Center (1999). Executions of juvenile offenders. [On-line]. Death Penalty Information Center Homepage. Directory: http://www.essential.org/dpic/juvexec.html

DeMonia, R. (1994, June 30). Outside control asked for juvenile agency. *The Birmingham News*, p. D1.

Dollard, J., Doob, L. W., Miller, N. E., Mowrer, O. H., and Sears, R. R. (1939). *Frustration and aggression*. New Haven, Conn.: Yale University Press.

Donziger, S. R. (Ed.). (1996). *The real war on crime: the report of the National Criminal Justice Commission*. New York: HarperPerennial.

Dorfmann, R. (Producer) and Schaffner, F. J. (Director) (1973). *Papillon*. [Film]. Warner Brothers Studios.

Dudley, W. (Ed.). (1991). *Police brutality (current controversies)*. New York: Greenhaven Press.

Du Pont, P. (1997). A real no-brainer: As punishment goes up, crime goes down. [On-line]. Intellectual Capital. September 11, 1997. Directory: http://www.intellectualcapital.com/

Durkheim, E. (1924/1974). *Sociology and philosophy*. New York: Free Press.

Edna McConnell Clark Foundation (1993, April). *Americans behind bars*. New York: Author.

Elliott, M. (1994, April 18). The caning debate: Should America be more like Singapore? *Newsweek*, pp. 18–22.

Ellis, R. T. (1991). Perceptions, attitudes and beliefs in police recruits. *Canadian Police College Journal*, 15 (2), 95–117.

Erikson, E. H. (1963). *Childhood and society*. New York: Norton.

Fecteau, L. (1999, January 15). Problems at private jails worry governor. [On-line]. Oregon AFSCME Corrections Website. Directory: http://www. Oregon afscme. com/corrections/private/pril5/.html

Federal Bureau of Prisons (1999). Quick facts. [On-line]. Federal Bureau of Prisons Website. Directory: http://www.bop.gov/

Federal Bureau of Prisons, Office of Public Affairs (1998). New research reveals federal inmate drug treatment programs reduce recidivism and future drug use. Directory: http://www.conquesthouse.org/BOP1.htm

Federal Bureau of Prisons, Weekly Population Report (1999). [On-line]. Federal Bureau of Prisons Website. Directory: http://www.bop.gov/

Flanagan, T. J. and Maguire, K. (Eds.). (1990). *Sourcebook of criminal justice statistics, 1989.* U.S. Department of Justice, Bureau of Justice Statistics. Washington, DC: United States Government Printing Office.

Foxhall, K. (1999). Day of protest will target managed care. *APA Monitor,* 30, No. 10, p. 20.

Funk, T. M. (1997, July 7). Adult treatment fits "predators." *San Francisco Chronicle,* p. C1.

Galvin, K. (1999, March 14). President denounces misconduct of police. *Durango Herald,* p. 6A.

Gangster Disciples (date unknown). *Book of knowledge.* Likely origin, Chicago, IL.

Giuliani, R. (1994, January 2). Inaugural address. City Hall, New York City.

Giuliani, R. (1997, September, 29). New urban agenda. Kennedy School of Government.

Goeckner, D., Greenough, W., and Maier, S. (1974). Escape learning deficit after overcrowded rearing in rats: Tests of a helplessness hypothesis. *Bulletin of the Psychonomic Society,* 3, 54–57.

Goldman, A. (1994). *Aggression replacement training (ART).* Workshop presented at the Tennessee Correctional Academy, January 26–27. Tulahoma, Tennessee.

Graves, A. B. (1999, May 10). Students complain of rights violations: ACLU looks into shooting related restrictions. *Durango Herald,* pp. 1A, 8A.

Greene, J. P., Peterson, P. E., Jiangtou, D., Boeger, L., and Frazier, C. L. (1996, August 14). Paper presented to the Panel on the Political Analysis of Urban School Systems at the August-September 1996 meeting of the American Political Science Association. San Francisco, California.

Greene, R. L. (1980). *The MMPI: An interpretive manual.* Orlando, FL: Grune & Stratton.

Gun Free Schools Act of 1994 (1994). Public Law 89–10, 20 United States Code, Chapter 70, Section 8921.

Gynther, M. D., Altman, H., and Sletter, I. W. (1973). Replicated correlates of MMPI two-point code types: The Missouri actuarial system. *Journal of Clinical Psychology,* 29, 263–289.

Hamsher, J., Murphy, D., and Townsend, C. (Producers) and Stone, O. (Director). (1994). *Natural Born Killers.* [Film]. Warner Brothers.

Haney, C., Banks, C., and Zimbardo, P. G. (1973). Interpersonal dynamics in a simulated prison. *International Journal of Criminology and Penology,* 1, 69–97.

Haney, C. and Zimbardo, P. G. (1998). The past and future of U.S. prison policy: Twenty-five years after the Stanford prison experiment. *American Psychologist,* 53, No. 7, p. 714.

Harris, D. A. (1997). "Driving while black" and all other traffic offenses: the Supreme Court and pretextual traffic stops. *Journal of Criminal Law & Criminology*, 87, 544–582.

Hathaway, S. R. and McKinley, J. C. (1983). *Minnesota Multiphasic Personality Inventory manual*. New York: Psychological Corporation.

Herringer, W. (1999, March 14). Halting the machinery of death: Capital punishment is neither fair nor effective. *Durango Herald*, p. C1.

Hess, A. K. and Weiner, I. B. (Eds.). (1999). *The handbook of forensic psychology*. New York: John Wiley and Sons.

Hosenball, M. (1999). "It is not the act of a few bad apples": A lawsuit shines the spotlight on allegations of racial profiling by New Jersey State Troopers. *Newsweek*, 133, No. 20, pp. 34–35. May 17.

Huesmann, L. R., Lefkowitz, M. M. and Eron, L. D. (1978). Sum of MMPI scales F, 4, and 9 as a measure of aggression. *Journal of Consulting and Clinical Psychology*, 46, 1071–1078.

Hugo, V. (1862). *Les Misérables*. New York: Dodd, Mead and Company.

Illinois Department of Corrections (1999). Illinois Department of Corrections Website. [On-line]. Directory: http://www.idoc.state.il.us/institutions/adult/jol/

Insanity Defense Reform Act (1984). Public Law 98–473, 18 United States Code, Section 17.

Jacobs, J. (1994, August 12). Prisons: California's growth industry. *Long Beach Press Telegram*, p. B2.

Johnson, S. C. (1999). U.S. v. Kaczynski: Psychological evaluation of Theodore Kaczynski. Court-TV Online. [On-line] Directory: http://www.court-tv

Johnston, M. D. (1999, July 8). Parole curbs cram prisons: Lawmakers told fewer releases means beds needed. *Denver Post*, pp. 1A, 19A.

KOAT-TV (1998). *Target 7 report: Bernalillo county jail abandons "pay for stay" program*. Albuquerque, NM: KOAT-TV.

Laing, R. D. (1967). *The politics of experience*. New York: Pantheon Books.

Lamb, D. (1996, October). Main street finds gold in urban crime wave. *Los Angeles Times*, p. A1.

Lewis, D. O. (1985). Adult antisocial behavior and criminality. In H. I. Kaplan and B. J. Sadock (Eds.), *Comprehensive textbook of psychiatry/IV* (4th edition). Baltimore: Williams & Wilkins.

Life sentence upheld for food burglar. (1999, April 28). *Durango Herald*, p. 3C.

Link, B. G. and Stueve, A. (1994). Psychotic symptoms and the violent/illegal behavior of mental patients compared to community controls. In J. Monahan and H. J. Steadman (Eds.), *Violence and mental disorder*. Chicago: University of Chicago Press.

Los Angeles Times (1995, August 28). 1994 prison roles at an all time high. *Los Angeles Times*, p. A1.

Luxembourg Income Study (1995). [On-line]. LIS information server. Directory: http://lissy.ceps.lu/index.htm

Lyman, D. R. (1996). Early identification of chronic offenders: Who is the fledgling psychopath? *Psychological Bulletin*, 120(2), 209–234.

MacNeil-Lehrer Report (1999, August 16). *The MacNeil/Lehrer news hour*. New York and Washington, DC: Public Broadcasting Service.

MacroMonitor Marketing Report (1996, December). The wealthiest 3%: House-
    holds with financial assets of a half million or more. MacroMonitor, Vol.
    II., no. 14. [On-line]. Directory: http://future.sri.com/CFD/MRES/
    MRES.11-14.html

Magnusson, D., Klinteberg, F. B., and Stattin, H. (1992). Autonomic activity/reac-
    tivity, behavior and crime in a longitudinal perspective. In J. McCord
    (Ed.), *Facts, frameworks and forecasts: Advances in criminological theory, Vol.
    3* (pp. 287–318). New Brunswick: Transaction Press.

Maitre, M. (1998, August 12). A school for homeless youth. *The Monterey County
    Herald*, p. B3.

Males, M. (1998). *The scapegoat generation: America's war on adolescents*. Monroe,
    ME: Common Courage Press.

Maricopa County Sheriff's Office (1999). Maricopa County Sheriff's Office Website
    [On-line]. Directory: http://www.mcso.org/

Marshall, W. L. (1999). Diagnosing and treating sexual offenders. In A. K. Hess
    and I. B. Weiner (Eds.), *Handbook of forensic psychology*. New York: John
    Wiley and Sons.

Maslow, A. H. (1970). *Motivation and personality* (2nd edition). San Francisco:
    Harper & Row.

Mauer, M. (1994). *Americans behind bars: The international use of incarceration,
    1992–1993*. Washington, DC: The Sentencing Project.

McCall, N. (1994). *Makes me wanna holler: A young black man in America*. New York:
    Vintage Books.

McCord, J. (1994). Family socialization and antisocial behavior: Searching for
    causal relationships in longitudinal research. In E.G.M. Weitekamp and
    H. J. Kerner (Eds.), *Cross-national longitudinal research on human develop-
    ment and criminal behavior* (pp. 177–188). Dordrecht, The Netherlands:
    Kluwer.

McCord, J. and Ensminger, M. E. (1997). Multiple risks and comorbidity in Afri-
    can-American population. *Criminal Behaviour and Mental Health, 7*,
    229–352.

Meet the Press (1994, October 16). *Meet the press*. New York: National Broadcasting
    Corporation.

Megargee, E. I. (1966). Undercontrolled and overcontrolled personality types in
    extreme antisocial aggression. *Psychological Monographs*, 80 (No. 3).

Milgram, S. (1963). Behavioral study of obedience. *Journal of Abnormal and Social
    Psychology, 67*, 371–378.

Milgram, S. (1974). *Obedience to authority*. New York: Harper & Row.

Mixdorf, L. W. (1989). Juvenile justice: We need a variety of treatment, program-
    ming options. *Corrections Today*, pp. 120–123.

Moe, T. M. (Ed.). (1995). *Private vouchers*. Stanford, CA: Hoover Institution Press.

Monahan, J. (1984). The prediction of violence behavior: Toward a second genera-
    tion of theory and policy. *American Journal of Psychiatry, 141*, 10–15.

Moore, M. J. (Producer and director) (1998). *The legacy: Murder and media, politics
    and prison*. [Film]. Documentary.

Moore, S. and Stansel, D. (1995, May 12). Ending corporate welfare as we know it.
    Cato Institute Policy Analysis No. 225.

Moran, T. (Correspondent) (1999, March 9). ABC World News broadcast. New York: ABC News.

National Association of State Budget Offices (1995). *State expenditure report, 1994.* Washington, DC: Author.

National Association of State Budget Offices (1996). *State expenditure report, 1995.* Washington, DC: Author.

National Association of State Budget Offices (1997). *State expenditure report, 1996.* Washington, DC: Author

National Association of State Budget Offices (1998). *State expenditure report, 1997.* Washington, DC: Author.

National Association of State Budget Offices (1999). *State expenditure report, 1998.* Washington, DC: Author.

National Center for Juvenile Justice (1989). *Statutes analysis of the automated juvenile law archive*, September. Washington, DC: Author.

National Center for Juvenile Justice (1996). *Organization and administration of juvenile services: Probation, aftercare and state delinquent institutions*, January, 1997. Washington, DC: Author.

National Center for Juvenile Justice (1998). *Organization and administration of juvenile services: Probation, aftercare and state delinquent institutions*, January, 1999. Washington, DC: Author.

Nebraska, West Virginia pull youths from Colorado center (1998, April 5). *Durango Herald*, p. 3A.

New York State Archives and Records Administration (1999). Internet document. [On-line]. New York State Archives and Record Administration Website. Directory: http://www.sara.nysed.gov/holding/aids/correct/ descript. htm

New York State Consolidated Laws (1999). New York Penal Code: Mental Disease and Defect.

Nilus, S. A. (1919). *The protocols of the elders of Zion*. Translated by V. E. Marsden. Book widely believed to be a forgery and distributed, at present, almost entirely in unauthorized photocopy form.

Office of the Legislative Auditor, State of Minnesota (1997). Recidivism of adult felons. Directory: http://auditor.leg.state.mn.us/ped/1997/felon97. htm

Office of Management and Budget (1998). *Budget of the United States government: Fiscal year 1999.* Washington, DC: United States Government Printing Office.

Paracelsus. (1993). *The writings of Paracelsus.* Birmingham, AL: University of Alabama at Birmingham Press.

Patania, T. (1999). Combating truancy: What is the answer? [On-line] at YCC Legislative Preview. Directory: http://ppp.jax-inter.net/users/ycc/truant.htm

People for the American Way (1999, June). Newsletter. Washington, DC: Author.

Pettigrew, T. F. (1971). *Racially separate or together?* New York: McGraw-Hill.

Pierce, W. L. (1978). *The Turner diaries.* Hillsboro, WV: National Vanguard Books.

Police: Pay now to prevent crime later (1999, November 2). *Asheville Citizen-Times*, p. B5.

Preso, E. (Producer). (1994). *Gun Society.* [Film]. USC Film School.

Prins, H. (1996). Risk assessment and management in criminal justice and psychiatry. *Journal of Forensic Psychiatry*, 7 (1), 42–62.

Public satisfaction with local police varies by race. (1999, June 4). *Durango Herald*, p. 10A.

Quinn, T. (1998). Restorative justice: An interview with visiting fellow Thomas Quinn. *National Institute of Justice Journal*, 235, 10–16.

Radelet, M. L. (1999). Post-Furman botched executions. [On-line]. Death Penalty Information Center Website. Directory: http://www.essential.org/dpic/botched.html

Rathus, S. A. (1999). *Psychology in the new millennium* (7th edition). Fort Worth, TX: Harcourt Brace College Publishers.

Reinarman, C. and Levine, H. G. (1998, March 1). Casualties of war. *San Jose Mercury News*, p. C1.

Rice, M. E. and Harris, G. T. (1997). The treatment of adult defenders. In D. M. Stoff, J. Breiling, and J. D. Maser (Eds.), *Handbook of antisocial behavior* (pp. 425–435). New York: Wiley.

Roberts, B. (1999). Roberts: Race, ethnicity and the influence it has on stop and seizure. [On-line]. Directory: http://cs.sav.edu/~broberts/stops.htm

Rothwax, H. (1996). *Guilty: The collapse of criminal justice*. New York: Random House.

Sarasohn, D. (1992). Building more prisons won't solve our crime problem. *Birmingham News*, p. B1.

Schernberger, S. (Producer). (1999). *On the inside*. [Film]. Documentary.

Schlosser, E. (1998, December). The prison-industrial complex. *Atlantic Monthly*, 282, 51–77.

Schmalleger, F. (1997). *Criminal justice today* (4th edition). Upper Saddle River, NJ: Prentice Hall.

Senate OKs tighter drug penalties (1999, November 11). *Asheville Citizen-Times*, p. A2.

Sennott, C. M. (1996, July 7). The $150 billion "welfare" recipient: US corporations. *The Boston Globe*, p. 1A.

Sentencing Project. (1999). Did the growth of imprisonment during the 1980's work?: The NRA and the misuse of criminal justice statistics. [On-line]. The Sentencing Project Website. Directory: http://www.sentencingproject. org/

Sewell, J. D. (Ed.) (1999). *Controversial issues in policing*. Boston: Allyn and Bacon.

Shakespeare, W. (1969). *William Shakespeare: The complete works*. New York. Viking Press.

Sheppard, J. A. (1993). Productivity loss in performance groups. *Psychological Bulletin*, 113, 67–81.

Singleton, J. (Director and Writer) and Nicolaides, S. (Producer) (1991). *Boyz N the Hood*. [Film]. Columbia Pictures.

Skinner, B. F. (1938). *The behavior of organisms: An experimental analysis*. Englewood Cliffs, NJ: Prentice Hall.

Skinner, B. F. (1972). *Beyond freedom and dignity*. New York: Knopf.

Skolnick, J. H. (1994). *Justice without trial: Law enforcement in democratic society*. Upper Saddle River, NJ: Macmillan College Division of Prentice Hall.

Slovenko, R. S. (1985). Forensic psychiatry. In H. I. Kaplan and B. J. Sadock (Eds.), *Comprehensive Textbook of Psychiatry/IV* (4th edition). Baltimore: Williams & Wilkins.

Smith, P. (1993, Fall). Private prisons: Profits of crime. *Covert Action Quarterly*, 46, Washington, DC, 16–26.

Southern Poverty Law Center. (Winter, 1998). *Intelligence report: 474 hate groups blanket America* (Issue No. 89). Montgomery, AL: Author.

Southern Poverty Law Center. (Spring, 1998). *Intelligence report: Patriot games, common-law courts at the crossroads* (Issue, No. 90). Montgomery, AL: Author.

Southern Poverty Law Center. (Summer, 1998). *Intelligence report: Wrath of "angels"* (Issue No. 91). Montgomery, AL: Author.

State grapples with private prison problems (1999, April 15). *New York Times* News Service [On-line]. Oregon AFSCME Corrections Website. Directory: http://www.oregonafscme.com/corrections/private/pri170.html

Stewart, J. (Correspondent) (1998, July 23). Louisiana officials shut down private prison after allegations of abuse. CBS News broadcast. New York and Washington, DC: CBS News.

Stinging debate over stun belt: Security device characterized as an implement of torture. (1998, August 7). *San Francisco Chronicle*, p. A19, A21.

Streib, V. (1998). The juvenile death penalty today: Death sentences and executions for juvenile crime, January 1973–May 1998. [On-line]. Death Penalty Information Center Website. Directory: http//www.essential.org/dpic/juvexec.html

Suro, R. (1997, February 24). Institute urges changes in funding priorities. *Washington Post*, A12.

Susskind, R. (1994). Race, reasonable articulable suspicion, and seizure. *American Criminal Law Review*, 31, 327–349.

Szasz, T. S. (1982). The political use of psychiatry—The case of Dan White. *American Journal of Forensic Psychiatry*, 2, 1–11.

Szasz, T. S. (1984). *The therapeutic state: Psychiatry in the mirror of current events*. Buffalo, NY: Prometheus Books.

Szasz, T. S. (1994). *Cruel compassion: Psychiatric control of society's unwanted*. New York: John Wiley & Sons.

Szymanski, L. S. and Crocker, A. C. (1985). Mental retardation. In H. I. Kaplan and B. J. Sadock (Eds.), *Comprehensive textbook of psychiatry/IV* (4th edition). Baltimore: Williams and Wilkins.

Taugher, M. and Fecteau, L. (1999, April 8). Hobbs prison sizes up damage after inmate riot. [On-line]. Oregon AFSCME Corrections Website. Directory: http://www.oregonafscme.com/corrections/private/pri166.html

Thomas, C. W. and Bolinger, D. (1999). Private adult correctional facility census: A "real-time" statistical profile. [On-line]. Private Corrections Project Website. Directory: http://web.rim.ufl.edu/pcp/census/1999/

Thompson, C. W. (1998, July 28). Ohio, D. C., losing faith in privately run prison. *Washington Post*, p. C1.

Thompson, G. (1999, January 21). Special N.Y. school gives troubled youth a second chance. *Denver Post*, p. 18A.

Thurstone, L. L. (1938). Primary mental abilities. *Psychometric Monographs*, 1.

Toch, T. (1998, June 22). School vouchers get two breaks. *U.S. News and World Report*, 124, 24, 41.

Underwear thief gets life in prison. (1998, August 6). *Durango Herald*, p. 9A.

United Nations Congress on the Prevention of Crime and Treatment of Offenders (1995). Standard minimum rules for the treatment of prisoners, adopted 1955, August 30. United Nations DOC.A/CONF/611, annex I, E. S. C. res. 663C, 24 UN ESCOR Supp. (No. 1) at 11 UN DOC.E/3048 (1957), amended E. S. C. res. 2076, 62 UN ESCOR Supp. (No. 1) at 35, UN DOC. E/5988 (1977).

United Nations Development Programme (1996). *United Nations human development report*. [On-line]. United Nations Development Program: Human Development Report Website. Directory: http://www.undp.org/hdro/96.htm

United States Census Bureau (1999). Poverty thresholds: 1998. [On-line]. Internet available. Directory: http://www.census.gov/hhes/poverty/threshold/thresh98.htm

United States Department of Education. National Center for Educational Statistics (1994). *Digest of Educational Statistics, 1994*, NCES 98–015. Washington, DC: Author.

United States Department of Education. National Center for Educational Statistics (1996). *Digest of Educational Statistics, 1996*, NCES 98–015, by Thomas D. Snyder. Washington, DC: Author.

United States Department of Education. National Center for Educational Statistics (1997). *Digest of Educational Statistics, 1997*, NCES 98–015, by Thomas D. Snyder. Production Manager, Charlene M. Hoffman. Program Analyst, Claire M. Geddes. Washington, DC: Author.

United States Department of Justice, Bureau of Justice Statistics (1987). *Survey of youth in custody*, Special Report NCJ-113365, September, 1988. Washington, DC: Author.

United States Department of Justice, Bureau of Justice Statistics (1988). *Recidivism of Prisoners Released in 1983*, Special Report NCJ-116261, April, 1989. Washington, DC: Author.

United States Department of Justice, Bureau of Justice Statistics (1989). *Census of local jails, 1988*. Washington, DC: Author.

United States Department of Justice, Bureau of Justice Statistics (1994). *Census of local jails, 1993*. Washington, DC: Author.

United States Department of Justice, Bureau of Justice Statistics (1997). *Correctional populations in the United States, 1995*, NCJ–163916. Washington, DC: Author.

United States Department of Justice, Bureau of Justice Statistics (1998). *Census of local jails, 1997*. Washington, DC: Author.

United States Department of Justice,Federal Bureau of Investigation (1988). Crime in the United States, 1989. *Uniform crime reports*. Washington, DC: United States Government Printing Office.

United States Department of Justice, Federal Bureau of Investigation (1989). Crime in the United States, 1990. *Uniform crime reports*. Washington, DC: United States Government Printing Office.

United States Department of Justice, Federal Bureau of Investigation (1990). Crime in the United States, 1991. *Uniform crime reports*. Washington, DC: United States Government Printing Office.

United States Department of Justice, Federal Bureau of Investigation (1991). Crime in the United States, 1992. *Uniform crime reports*. Washington, DC: United States Government Printing Office.

United States Department of Justice, Federal Bureau of Investigation (1992). Crime in the United States, 1993. *Uniform crime reports*. Washington, DC: United States Government Printing Office.

United States Department of Justice, Federal Bureau of Investigation (1993). Crime in the United States, 1994. *Uniform crime reports*. Washington, DC: United States Government Printing Office.

United States Department of Justice, Federal Bureau of Investigation (1994). Crime in the United States, 1995. *Uniform crime reports*. Washington, DC: United States Government Printing Office.

United States Department of Justice, Federal Bureau of Investigation (1995). Crime in the United States, 1996. *Uniform crime reports*. Washington, DC: United States Government Printing Office.

United States Department of Justice, Federal Bureau of Investigation (1996). Crime in the United States, 1997. *Uniform crime reports*. Washington, DC: United States Government Printing Office.

United States Department of Justice, Federal Bureau of Investigation (1997). Crime in the United States, 1998. *Uniform crime reports*. Washington, DC: United States Government Printing Office.

United States Department of Justice, Federal Bureau of Investigation (1998). Crime in the United States 1999. *Uniform crime reports*. Washington, DC: United States Government Printing Office.

United States General Accounting Office (1990). *Death Penalty Sentencing: Research Indicates Pattern of Racial Disparities*. Washington, DC: Author.

Walker, S., Spohn, C., and DeLone, M. (1996). *The color of justice: Race, ethnicity and crime in America*. Belmont, CA: Wadsworth.

Weitzer, R. (1996). Racial discrimination in the criminal justice system: Findings and problems in the literature. *Journal of Criminal Justice*, 24, 309–322.

Wideman, J. E. (1995). Doing time, marking race. *The Nation*, 261(14), 503–506.

Wolfgang, M. E., Thornberry, T. P., and Figlio, R. M. (1987). *From boy to man, from delinquency to crime*. Chicago: University of Chicago Press.

Wong, J. (1997, November 23). Police dog use at center of controversy: Critics make claims of police brutality. *Durango Herald*, p. 7D.

Wood, D. B. (1998, July 21). Private prisons, public doubt. *Christian Science Monitor*, 1, 14.

Woodruff, J. (News Anchor) (1999, April 26). Cable News Network broadcast. Atlanta: Cable News Network.

Wright, J. W. (1998). Voter turn-out in presidential elections. *The New York Times Almanac*, p. 115.

Wright, J. W. (Ed.). (1998). *The New York Times Almanac*, New York: Penguin Books.

Wylie, M. S. (1998). Throwing away the key in an increasingly popular solution to juvenile crime. *Family Therapy Networker*, May/June, 25–37.

Zepezauer, M. and Zepezauer, N. (1992). *Take the rich off welfare*. New York: Odonian Press.

Zeskind, L. (1998). White nation: Basis of freemen's philosophy is racism. In *Intelligence report: Patriot games, common-law courts at the crossroads* (Issue No. 90, p. 20). Montgomery, AL: Southern Poverty Law Center.

Zimbardo, P. G. (1970). The human choice: Individuation, reason and order versus individuation, impulse and chaos. In W. J. Arnold and D. Levine (eds.), *Nebraska symposium on motivation, 1969* (pp. 237–307). Lincoln, NE: University of Nebraska Press.

INDEX

About the Author

JOHN RAYMOND COOK is Assistant Professor of Psychology at Mars Hill College in North Carolina. He has worked extensively throughout the criminal justice system.